Mystical Intimacy

Mystical Intimacy

Entering into a conscious relationship with
your spirit and human nature

———✵———

Linda L. Nardelli
And the Teachings of Masiandia

*May there be a place
in between that unites
us all.*

*Linda Nardelli
2017*

151 Howe Street, Victoria BC
Canada V8V 4K5

Thank you to Sheila Geraghty for permission to include
her poem at the end of Chapter 10. All other poems
written by the author except as otherwise noted. All
illustrations by the author. Photographs on the cover and
inside the book © copyright Vern Minard.

Mystical Intimacy
ISBN 978-1-927755-52-5 (paperback)
ISBN 978-1-927755-53-2 (ebook)

Cataloguing information available from
Library and Archives Canada.
Printed on acid-free paper.
Agio Publishing House is a
socially-responsible enterprise, measuring
success on a triple-bottom-line basis.

10 9 8 7 6 5 4 3 2 1

Information about Linda's inner-journey
counselling practice and transformational
healing workshop can be found at
www.lindanardelli.com

TABLE OF CONTENTS

Welcome

Be still and surrender
to the mystery you hear.
The great drumming of my heart,
wild like the forest –
welcomes you.

Un-tame your dance and
ease into your longing.
I am the child guiding
the offering and gratitude –
I welcome you.

Come into my embrace
and see forever and beyond.
I am the child that brings
hope and forgiveness –
I welcome you.

The Unfolding Mystery

*M*ystical *Intimacy* was born out of my communication with Masiandia, a group of seven spirits that have been part of my life since 1999. Their channelled messages and my own life-experience interweave within the pages of this book, providing a voice to the relationship between spiritual consciousness and human nature. For me, connecting with spirit is a way of life that welcomes mystical companionship and belonging. When a person's ego partners with spirit, he or she merges higher-consciousness with physical reality. By joining our soul-essence with our human focus and intent, we bring to life the mystery of our sacred purpose.

For most in our world community, we have long forgotten the co-creative dance of soul and form; we have neglected our spirit-consciousness, focusing primarily on the reasoning mind. This book is an invitation to remember your true essence, an invocation of the profound nourishment that comes when you unite with your soul.

In these pages, I collaborate with Masiandia, the collective of spirits that I channel, whose purpose is to help us remember who we are. They endeavour to help us know, beyond all limitations, conditions and fear, that *the true nature of our purpose is joy*. Our joy is a state of complete presence, celebrating the fullness of who we are, body and soul. It is a way of being that welcomes everything, doesn't reject any aspect of our humanity and thus encompasses a fluid, forgiving and surrendered relationship with the world and ourselves.

Spirit dwells within the divine beauty of Earth, in the hearts of strangers, in the day-to-day unfolding of our lives and especially in the moments when our greatest fears demand that we show up and be more than we thought possible.

Masiandia shares their support to help us re-connect with our essence, and their communication has the quality of reaching beyond the intellect, moving us into liberated perceptions of reality. I weave their message with personal narratives and stories of people who have touched my heart, to share the profundity of the spiritual journey and to support a deepening of readers' experience with spiritual guidance.

Renewed Vision

*C*hannelled messages have the power to draw us into an inner sanctuary of belonging, tethering us where we are, illuminating where we have been and offering us a renewed vision of ourselves. Amazing things happen when we let spirit guide us: we tap into a well of self-awareness and purpose, we discover a richness of creativity and reach beyond what we think we're capable of. We also assimilate spiritual understanding with more ease: spontaneously and effortlessly.

Often, we believe that there is so much work to do: that manifesting our true desires requires hard labour and reconstruction of the self. We forget that we are perfect in this moment – that who we are now leads to the next step. And that each step we take is not governed by our willpower, but by our willingness to follow guidance and find within our innate wisdom a way in which we can transform obstacles into allies.

When we acknowledge who we are, we have the ability to experience so much more than conditioned impressions of reality. We emerge as clear witnesses through eyes of curiosity and enthusiasm. And when this happens, the "hard" lessons in life become opportunities that expand our consciousness and enhance our sense of self-value. This allows us to experience life through liberating expressions, to explore, take risks and embrace our journey despite limitations. In this way, we become filled to overflowing with the beauty of our souls and can gift this abundance to the world.

Community Spirit

In the process of birthing *Mystical Intimacy*, a small community of friends coalesced to support me in studying the channelled messages. Their questions and insights helped me look at the channelled material from a different angle, and also inspired mutual exploration. In our book study circle, each of our inquiries, ideas, challenges and feelings strengthened a deeper understanding of Masiandia's teaching, while our intimate sharing encouraged mutual support and belief in one another. Sometimes what is a conditioned framework for one person simply doesn't exist for another; therefore, our shared discoveries fostered an opportunity for me to provide a more in-depth perspective on Masiandia's teachings.

This small group of friends compelled me to fulfil my calling in sharing Masiandia's teaching and my insights, as their spiritual inquiries served as a springboard from which I dove in deeper into exploring the teachings and my own storytelling. Sometimes I plunged in with confidence, inspired by the channelled messages, while at other times I was discouraged by the lessons that conflicted with my life. Still I persevered, to find within the pages of this book a voice of wisdom and truth, to share with the readers my knowledge and experience, faith and curiosity.

Writing is a joy, and it is also hard work, a reality I stumbled into when Masiandia asked me to join them on this project. Little did I realize that I would not only share their message, but also edit it to provide clear understanding in written form. They're message also carries energy, which does not always translate well into printed word. This led to developing a writing process akin to that of co-writing with a partner.

Through this partnership approach the spirits offered their message for each chapter, which I related to personally and with the reader in mind, as I made inquiries about psychological, spiritual and health related issues pertaining to the journey of mystical intimacy. With my questions and input, Masiandia would elaborate on a particular subject, and at times

I would disagree or insist on further details. Sometimes they would con-
cede and at other times leave me in utter silence, leading me to realize that
I was asking something of them that I needed to discover for myself. In the
process, I developed a creative weaving of their messages with my own
life-experience and understanding, for the purpose of lending guidance
and insight to the reader.

Within these pages, Masiandia's teachings interrelate with examples
of personal experiences and my clients' healing processes. My healing gift
has been a profound blessing, affording me connections with people that
are personal, real and heartfelt. I am honoured to share these connections
with you, with names changed for privacy except where permission was
given.

Energy-medicine

*I*t is also meaningful to note that Masiandia provides their gift of
communication not only through their message but also through energy. They interact with our physiology, our senses and with the underlying framework of our beliefs and thought patterns, to assist us in receiving
their communication and in growing our understanding.

In private and group channelling sessions, participants are often
aware of body sensations very similar to what is experienced in deep
meditation, such as feeling light-headed while their bodies become heavy
and expanded. One person described a sensation of spinning very fast.
With hypnotherapy, she relaxed into the feeling and was brought into a
deep trance to enhance her sense-perception and more easily absorb the
channelled message.

If you experience altered sensations whilst reading Masiandia's messages, take a moment to observe the feelings in your body and notice your
breathing. With trust and surrender, you can relax into the experience and
find yourself connecting more and more to your own inner-resonance.

Breathing-in any unfamiliar sensations followed by focusing on the out-breath is deeply comforting.

In the Words of Masiandia

Masiandia: *"We work with a channel who is aligned with our purpose to help people awaken to who they truly are. Linda, who we honour by her spirit name, Dofila, is committed to the healing path, and her longing to fulfil her karmic purpose drew us towards her. This connection brought into form the necessary life lessons she needed to learn to prepare herself for our partnership, for the work of channelled healing and for writing this book. We are truly blessed to be in partnership with her, and her willingness to evolve allows us to guide her to grow beyond her human conditioning, so that she can realize her true gifts. We have witnessed Dofila grow stronger and more flexible in relation to our teaching, and we have in turn been blessed by her in-depth commitment.*

"We interact in a co-creative relationship with Dofila to learn from her soul-expression, as she endeavours to surrender to her life's journey with love. We have chosen to work in this way, to share the responsibility of birthing the full essence of this book. The book is given to the reader from two joint perspectives – one in human form and the other in spirit.

"Our voice, our communication and our message is supported by Dofila's ability to challenge us, work with us, guide us and in turn surrender to our guidance, our healing and our love. She has asked us to change our writing approach regarding some passages that were too esoteric and unrelated to human experience, and we have challenged her to believe in herself and step beyond her constrained perceptions. Together we are divinely appointed to give you this beautiful gift – this book.

"It is important to know that spirit guardians communicate much more than information. We embrace you. We love you when you forget that you are worthy of love. We are here to love you; that is our gift, and you don't have to do

anything to deserve it. You don't have to do anything to prove yourselves. We are here to love equally your resistance, uncertainty and fear.

"Ultimately, we are here to establish a vibration of resonance to help you connect with your spirit and experience a more fulfilling relationship with your life. The vibration of resonance is a profound quality of belonging that moves you from within, that helps you embody your soul and live from a sacred code of honour, which is to travel within and without, to be both the container that houses your divinity and its expression. It is a journey of courage and deep repose, and the more that you journey inwards into the subconscious, into the realm of spirit, the unknown, you pass through the door that we hold open for you and thus share your essence with the world."

CHAPTER ONE

Healing into Consciousness

There is a place for us to meet
to know one another anew,
re-create whole and unharmed
and make beauty the scars.

The old finally at peace.

Will you meet me there?

Seeking Beauty and Wholeness

I've been drawn to the path of healing ever since I was a child. I sought beauty and wholeness; I wanted to make peace and for everyone to be okay. In fact, I did everything I could to make people feel better, but I did this at my expense; I became as small as I could to lessen the overwhelming situation my family was experiencing. But the more I disappeared, the more I suffered; the more I felt unloved and unwanted.

I could say that my parents were neglectful and taught me to disregard my needs, however it would be equally true to say that I chose to abandon myself to fit in and be as safe as possible in the turmoil of family life. Disappearing inside myself was my protection against feeling too much.

I was highly sensitive as a child and felt other people's suffering as though it was inside of me. My mother's pain became my own. My father's grief permeated my innocence with distrust and disappointment. My sister's anger bore into me like a thorn, and my grandparent's scorn was threatening. All their dreams and desires were haunting; I felt responsible for answering their prayers; I felt trapped. I took part in the same despair as the rest of my family. It was the common thread we all shared – the world of abandonment and wounding.

It's been my life long journey to let go of the hurt and reconnect with Source – a journey that I am privileged to share with others. I feel blessed to have stumbled upon the path of healing – the path that has led me into the arms of love and grace. There have been many times that I've resisted, but eventually surrendered because there is nothing more fulfilling than releasing the struggle. It feels enlivening and simultaneously peaceful.

Within the pages of this book, Masiandia teaches us how to open our senses so that we can surrender. They teach us how to be open by guiding us to feel more. To feel more means to witness feelings and allow them to evolve. Feelings are a channel, like a river bed, through which our soul flows and awakens us to who we truly are.

By discovering how to navigate through our feelings, we connect with the deeper well of wisdom that lies within, and enjoy a profound sense of belonging that is beyond family, beyond the mind and beyond our collective agreement of reality. We, in essence, enter a renewed relationship with our souls.

Masiandia: *"Awakening is simple, dear ones – it is who you are! It is not some arbitrary destination that you must be worthy enough to achieve. It has nothing to do with accomplishment, but rather it's about opening to the beauty and magnificence of your Divinity. You are so much more than humanity; you are body and soul, human and spirit interwoven. Awakening is falling in love with all of you and recognizing that all of you is sacred.*

"Your life with its many turbulences, the ups and the downs, the success and failures, is a perfect conduit for the emergence of Divinity, which is your wholeness and sense of interconnection with all that is.

"Your work on this planet is to fall in love with the Earth and all its inhabitants, which first begins by falling in love with yourself. It's so much easier than it seems. Begin by growing your curiosity in regards to your life experiences. Marvel at the complexity of feelings and sensations that you are constantly experiencing. Cherish everything! Let surrender play a larger role in between your thoughts. Suspend your judgements and remain willing to see, sense, hear, smell, and know so much more than you think you know."

Suspending the mind actually feels good, as it gives the mind the opportunity to rest. A restful mind is surrendered to the wisdom of our feelings. Our feelings, like our reactions and thoughts, serve as countless sources of information. But when we're busy controlling our experience, how can we possibly connect with this sea of information? Any form

.ontraction obstructs our sense perception, as well as our compassion .or others and ourselves.

You may have heard the phrase, 'What you resist, persists!' Conversely what you welcome dissolves. Our openness and willingness is the fertilizer for healing and growth. Tension, dis-ease, limited beliefs… transform into new expressions. That is the path of healing into consciousness – into the intimate connection between spirit and matter.

Towards Healing and Awakening

I don't know that we ever truly choose to heal or awaken. I think it's more accurate to say that healing and spiritual emergence chooses us. For me, childhood trauma threw me onto a life-path that I would have otherwise not found. I discovered a great love for healing and a profound affinity towards the spiritual.

Everyone who embarks on the path of healing will experience an initial push, a motivating nudge towards *awakening*. Perhaps it is a strong catalyst, such as an illness or accident, or it can be a deep yearning from within for spiritual fulfillment. My understanding of awakening, based on Masiandia's teaching, is that it is a relinquishing of the holding patterns that cause disharmony, and a reconnection with who we truly are. It is a return to our inner-resonance, to what feels authentic and enlivening.

Awakening is a joyous surrender that exists for a passing moment or may linger, and it may be sustained for long periods of time. But the instance that we reach for it, we become attached to it, which contracts the natural flow of our energy. Like a tight muscle that impedes the fluid structure of the spine, attachment to awakening intensifies our resistance.

But nothing can remain inert, for energy seeks to fulfill itself and ultimately flow freely without obstruction. The energy of our essence cannot be fettered, therefore subtle or powerful catalysts evoke the necessary release required for rebalancing and reunification with spirit.

The art to healing then is to *allow* – to say *yes* to everything that shows up, even resistance, because when resistance is welcomed we feel good. When we feel good, we no longer need to resist. When we feel safe and wanted, there is nothing to hold on to and nothing to prove. The art of healing then requires letting go of having to heal by embracing the present tense of being *healed*. It's all about *being* what we seek now, which means no longer trying to suppress the part of us that we judge as imperfect.

Invoking Your Dreams

*A*s Masiandia suggested earlier, awakening is not a set goal. Awakening is an ongoing spiritual practice and a way of life where every moment is an opportunity to explore life, not as a linear plan but rather as an invocation of our dreams.

Dreams are born out of conviction and willingness to evolve. They call for us to *surrender* to the process of becoming conscious, rather than endure the scrutiny of strategies and expectations. Dreams need to linger in the subconscious, in the deep treasure-trove of our yearning, before we grasp for the material outcome. To realize our dreams, we need to cultivate an intimate relationship with them, opening ourselves to the wellspring from which they arise.

When we hold our visions and simultaneously relinquish control of them, we are in essence positioning ourselves in a place of receptivity, which connects us with our spirit – a necessary step in the fulfilment of our dreams. To become responsive to our dreams, we must believe in what we long for and welcome the help of the unseen, which opens us to experiences we wouldn't have thought possible. By contrast, when we work overly hard towards our goals, we don't make room for surprises; we fill every space with expectation as if we're responsible for everything, when in fact our soul plays a much larger role here.

Being conscious of our soul strengthens our dreams, as it calls for us to relinquish aspects of ourselves that do not serve who we truly are. We are compelled to move beyond limiting conditioning, such as the belief that we're not smart or worthy enough to achieve our dreams, or that our longing is irreverent. Our soul-consciousness moves us towards discovering our true potential, which helps us make discerning choices and enhances our emotional and mental well-being. This awakening consciousness is a call from within that beckons us to surrender into *trust*, which supports us to witness life with an open mind and heart and curiosity.

Through this surrender, we come to recognize that all life experiences – despite the challenges we perceive as setbacks, losses and health issues – are an opportunity to heal, grow and return to wholeness. By remaining willing participants in life, we are awakened to greater levels of understanding and deep fulfilment. For me, it is curiosity borne of surrender that ignites my sense of wonder – my intuition as a healer and as an artist. It kindles my desire to free my essence and give fully of myself.

A Call to Spirit

*I*n my early twenties, it was my strong desire to free my essence that propelled me towards a spiritual journey through artistic expression. I believe that my art literally saved my life. The desire to paint forced me to believe in myself; it gave me a sense of purpose and life-direction. It was my initial forage into the healing journey that led to unearthing my buried feelings, and it also supported me in understanding my empathic sensitivity. Creating art served as a way to "see" myself. I couldn't conceal my psyche and still create beautiful paintings; I had no choice but to reveal myself to me, otherwise my art was lifeless and unfulfilling.

But what I saw in my art also disturbed me; it revealed a shadow aspect of myself I feared – a darkness in me that refused to go unseen. I drew children's faces with impressions of profound sorrow and hurt. One drawing showed a small girl holding a broken doll, her hand covering the doll's mouth. I sensed that as a child I had felt stifled in some way, held back – frightened.

My art served as a force of healing by illuminating my inner child. It showed me how sensitive I am and revealed a truer expression of my purpose, which I both wanted yet resisted. I had suppressed myself for so long; how could I begin to understand or welcome what I feared?

With the help of a supportive friend, I found the courage to enter into therapy where I faced my fears and childhood traumas. Gradually I unlocked myself; I came out of hiding and reconciled with my past. I also accepted that I had an inherent ability to see beyond people's behaviour, thus freeing my empathic sensitivity.

Oftentimes, people's outward expression conceals an underlying flurry of discordant energy, controlled feelings, beliefs and conditioning. As a child I was frightened by the incongruence between a person's outer expression and my sense of his/her subtler energy. In reaction I protected myself by holding back and separating myself, and as a result, I starved for connection.

Over time, I realized this empathy was a gift – and this revelation helped me feel calmer and less overwhelmed by the contradictions I experienced. I learned to *trust* my intuitive sense of what lay beneath people's communication and behaviour, which helped me refine an ability to see the hidden wisdom contained therein.

Though the subtle energies behind a person's expressions, physical symptoms and emotions hold the key to personal fulfilment, typically these energies remain closed, secreted away as people resist exploring the unconscious. But these energies will inevitably surge to the surface to be revealed and understood, drawing attention to what each of us needs for fulfilment. This need is natural; it is a call to spirit. Whether it is a prayer for abundance, health, joy, success, or a deep yearning to be met in ways that support our sense of value, our need is a call to the light of divinity. For me personally, in my early healing journey, it was a call I sent out in my darkest hours. I prayed, I journaled and sought for deeper meaning. I called in spirit and made it my friend.

―――――⚮―――――

The Initiation

*L*onging for wholeness opens us to love and ultimately to spirit. We are beckoned by an inherent need for connection, and it is this need that opened me to channelling. I remember longing for a closer partnership with spirit, frustrated with the subtlety of their guidance. I could feel spirit around me, but I didn't understand what messages they had for me, so I prayed for an expanded awareness of their guidance. I prayed to free my consciousness through my art, to witness my alliance with spirit evolve.

In answer to my prayer, my art brought me into communication with my subconscious – an inception into altered creative-states beyond critical thought. The subconscious is a storehouse of metaphysical senses and knowledge, accessible through trance-induced states. In my art, I learned to surrender my logical mind into hypnotic states, and allow the paintings to reveal a deeper awareness into my feelings and essence. But I didn't set out to be a "channeller." I just wanted to "feel" the spirits in a more direct way and know that I wasn't alone.

The first channelling experience took place quite unexpectedly in 1999. I was climbing the flight of stairs to my second-storey apartment when I felt the presence of someone behind me. I turned to see who was there, and though I could distinctly feel a presence, the stairway was empty. This was not unfamiliar to me, as I was often "visited" in my studio. But this time something was different: I felt a clear, strong urge to write. In fact, I could swear that the spirit was telling me to go get paper and a pen. The sensation was so intense that I hurried without hesitation to comply.

Yet when I began to write the spirit's message, the process was very slow: one word, pause, another word, pause, until the full sentence emerged. As the week progressed, however, my ability strengthened, and by the following week I couldn't write fast enough. The words came through me like water spilling onto paper – fluid, clear and concise, interconnected with my unconscious understanding of vocabulary. It was almost as though the spirit was searching through me for better leverage to communicate with me, constructing words and sentences from my own understanding while simultaneously expanding me.

Channelling was an exhilarating process that I greeted with trust and willingness, and which influenced my professional life within two weeks of my initial experience. At the time I was in the second year of my counselling practice and working as an integrative bodyworker with intuitive energy healing. When I felt the presence of Jessier in one of my sessions, I didn't hesitate to ask my client for permission to channel for her. I believe that my willingness came from my familiarity with subtle energy-work and because channelling felt so natural to me.

While my client lay comfortably on the massage table receiving the energy healing, Jessier wanted to communicate with her directly. It's difficult to explain how I knew this, except to say that I felt a nudge from him, another sense of urgency as with the first time he communicated with me through my journal writing. My client was receptive to the message, as it opened her to a deeper understanding of herself and a profound sense of being loved by Source.

I think she was more excited about the experience than I was. I was in a state of shock, completely amazed and equally intimidated. Once she had left, my hands trembled as I changed the sheets on the massage table. I couldn't believe what had just happened, and I was frightened about how this was going to change my life. I had an indwelling sense of what was to come – an expansion of my sense of self and my work as a healer. While I was delighted and uplifted at the prospect of this change, I was also uncomfortable with the unknown, which I had much to learn about, commencing with understanding why Jessier had chosen to work with me.

> Jessier: *"My dearest friend, I am so fortunate to be able to communicate with you. I have longed, as you have, to join together. Please do not be afraid. I am a passage for you, a guiding light towards your chosen path. I am truly your friend. You ask so many questions; please be still and relax your thoughts, let me guide you, let me show you the way.*
>
> *"First I want to tell you that we have known each other since forever; we have been reaching towards one another since your incarnation, and now you are opened to me, and for that I am overjoyed.*
>
> *"Your fear is understandable though truly not warranted, for you have already been initiated into channelling through your art, dear one, through your practice of 'getting out of the way' and letting the essence of a painting reveal itself. Through your art, your faith and trust was challenged and freed, allowing you to receive my presence without hesitating to understand what I was communicating.*
>
> *"We have much work to do, beginning with you allowing me to love you. In time I will communicate to many others through you, but only when you are ready. There is no pressure and no expectation. There is only the beautiful flow of our connection that is growing stronger with each day."*

It was exciting for me to make the link between Jessier's message and my art. When he acknowledged the similarity between channelling and "letting my art reveal itself," I was elated with wonderment as I realized that in pursuing my art, I had been answering my deep-seated prayer for spiritual communication.

One of my first experiences of connecting with spirit in my art was during a time when I was doing drawings of children, part of a series on capturing the soulful essence of portraits. It came to me one day that the portraits were not only aspects of my own childhood, but also expressions of children from other lifetimes. This idea was confirmed in a reading with an intuitive who, without seeing my art, asked if I did drawings of children. She acknowledged that some of the children were linked to my past lives, and others were spirits in the afterlife who were drawn to me for help.

I didn't know how to help them until I found myself working on a drawing of a little girl who stood beside an angry-looking adolescent boy. I had a sense that this drawing reflected a lost and abused child, but I didn't understand the significance of the boy. It so affected me that I couldn't even look at the drawing for a number of weeks; it faced the wall until a clairvoyant friend told me what had happened to the girl. She saw details of the girl's molestation by the boy and her subsequent death, which provoked in me a deep desire to help heal the spirit of the girl.

After my friend's message I found the strength to pull the drawing away from the wall, confront it and help transform the dark energy. Facing the picture, I was guided to draw a wolf over the face of the boy to help protect the girl. I later learned that in Native Spirituality, the wolf symbolizes the protector of children along their passage into the afterlife. As the painting progressed, it was strange and amazing to see that without reworking the girl's facial features, her expression became calmer and finally joyous. Until I completed the artwork, the girl was a constant presence in my home, and I even dreamed about her and felt her spirit at a healing circle I attended. She remains with me to this day a loving memory.

The Emergence of Masiandia

As time went on, the communication with Jessier continued to bathe me in an incredible aura of love and guidance, which was breathtakingly meaningful. It answered so many of my prayers. It helped me understand where I had come from and why I had chosen to be a part of my family and traumatic childhood experiences. It served to open me to a deeper sense of heartfelt connections and spiritual fulfilment.

After a while though, I began to have difficulty following what Jessier was telling me, and I grew more and more frustrated with what seemed like contradictions. Jessier's communication suggested concepts like, *"You are not bound by time or space, thus must challenge your initial thought patterns and continuum beliefs and cease marking your life-path with past expectations and fear. You are a free agent and will discover a life much less travelled, but more meaningful to you than anything else has been. Follow our direction; it is the spark of your own magical delivery into an Earth-reality that is evolving quickly."*

I didn't understand what this meant, as I was interpreting Jessier's words through a naïve mental framework. Jessier then asked me to not follow the guidance in the way one would follow a parent. He told me that he and the rest of the team were not an authority over me, but my partners. But how was I supposed to work with that? I was so confused by this point. After all, I just needed to figure out some seemingly straightforward directions regarding my work, health and relationship. And what did Jessier mean by "the rest of the team"?

> *Jessier: "Please do not be alarmed. You are undergoing profound transformation and initiation into an expanded state wherein you can welcome the entirety of our purpose – the group being which I am a part of. Masiandia is the name you will grow to be very familiar and intimate with, a group of*

spirits that belongs to your whole Entity. This is a magical interplay of karmic purpose which is here to partner with you, to help you live with greater levels of fulfilment and existential meaning."

At this point, about six months after I began channelling, I was in absolute turmoil between home and work issues and with trying to understand the channelled guidance. It was then that I met up with a close friend to help me decipher the messages. He sat quietly while I channelled for myself verbally for the first time, as the written form had become limiting. With his questions and input, I came to understand that Jessier was a spirit-member of a larger team, a group consisting of six spirits who Jessier referred to as Masiandia. Much later, a seventh member joined the team, adding her unique essence to the whole group-spirit.

But at the start of my relationship with Masiandia, I experienced difficulty: tension headaches, blurred vision, chest pains and confusion for about a week. By the time I met with my friend, I was a total mess. I understand now that for the first six months Jessier had been preparing me for the higher vibrational energy of the whole team. And while my first contact with Masiandia was daunting, it was equally exciting, and I quickly learned how to open myself "wider" to the higher vibrational energy streaming through me. I learned to strengthen my nervous system, to conduct and ground the high voltage of electrical current that Jessier's messages had initially carried through my body's circuitry, and to expand and encompass the whole of Masiandia.

Now, many years later, I am profoundly grateful to Masiandia for helping me grow my perception of reality. I have had to let go of so much that stood in the way of our work, yet never did their purpose override my own; our work together has always been both an extension of my prayers and a fulfilment of their purpose.

Co-Creative Dance

*T*he beauty of connecting with spirit is that it is a co-creative dance that merges with the input of our personality. Our human self is a magnetically charged energy-field whose prayers draw in the guidance of spirit, and spirit is compelled to answer our prayers.

I have come to realize that our need to connect with spirit-guardians is also mutual; their purpose is interwoven with our lives, and together we serve a greater whole. Our need for guidance welcomes their offering and enriches their evolution, and together we form a mirror reflection of purposeful intention, reconciling need with support.

This symbiosis between Earth-reality and Source-energy is a beckoning that calls us back to our spirit. Our part and our gift in this union with spirit is absolute receptivity, as we join in a consummate partnership and expand our sense-perceptions to encompass the larger framework of our relatedness.

From my experience, connecting with spirit is much like listening-in for the subtlety of my inner thoughts, the place within that speaks on behalf of my emotions, dreams and deep-felt experience. The guidance of spirit is an unfolding of my inner resources that want to be born through me. It is a creative doorway leading towards the opening of my heart.

I receive so much more from the channelled communication when I am willing to grow from it. In fact, it is impossible to fully comprehend the guidance of spirit without expanding our consciousness and embodying it. We grow our consciousness when we transform old scripts, when we let go of beliefs and attitudes that separate us from Source.

In order for spirit to nurture and answer our prayers, it is our responsibility to believe in our prayers and plant the first seed of faith. It is up to us to cultivate an intimate relationship with our longing, to deepen our receptivity and thus receive the generous support of our spirits. In this way, we create space for the guidance of spirit; we allow it to touch us like the sun that warms a blossoming flower.

But when we feel unworthy of its illumination, we deny and reject the guidance that is naturally there for us. With self-doubt, shame and the belief that we are alone, the light of divinity cannot reach us. Our capacity to receive guidance is determined by our willingness to surrender. By yielding to the ever-present support of spirit, we receive their help and raise the vibration of our human experience.

Masiandia: *"We respect your free will as you integrate spirit with human reality. The two together form an alliance that is similar to sperm fertilizing an egg, plants offering nourishing and medicinal properties to humankind or a mother's breast milk that sustains her growing infant. These are symbiotic relationships between supply and need, two distinct elements mutually benefiting the other. Similarly, there is a natural reciprocity between your spirit-guides and you. Just as light illuminates the dark, spirit-guides shine the light of love upon you, and you in turn provide us with your willingness to co-create.*

"Our co-creative partnership supports higher purpose, elevating human and soul consciousness and Earth's quantum vibration within the Universe. We do this together to serve the greater whole, to lessen suffering and awaken multidimensional awareness. This gives you the opportunity to raise the level of your magnetic frequency, which is your point of attraction, and which helps you manifest the life you long for by gaining a higher conscious awareness.

"With incarnation, you are here to see through the eyes of Divinity and recognize the beauty in all life, which replenishes the cells of your body. Your spirit-guides continuously love you, and since you are spirit in matter, it is your purpose and divine responsibility to shine the light of love upon yourself as well. Only in doing so can you recognize the quality of assurance that is being given to you at all times. Love is a gift; it is sweet freedom, which you fully receive when you remember who you are. You are interdependently connected to Source – you are one with God/ Goddess/ All That Is.

"However, when your mind is limited to familiar reality, it is unable to fathom greater possibilities; it becomes entangled in controlling life and fighting with the essence of who you really are. How can your spirit-guides help you discover your soul freedom through this limited perspective? It is not possible, because the human mind impedes the flow of spirit. Thus your guides can only help you as far as you will let them.

"We who are spirit cannot bypass your control, your ego-minds, and neither can you. All we can do is continue to love your present awareness to help you evolve, as must you. Love thy self!"

*I*n relationship with spirit-guides we must allow their guidance, in its exalted offering, to pull us upwards towards a greater sense of self and possibility. But the moment we mull over the teachings through the lens of the intellect, we impede the flow of expanded consciousness, activating our unconscious patterns and fears. It is the awakened heart that no longer blocks spirit, that receives the support of Divinity, which is able to lift off from the limitations of three-dimensional existence.

Human consciousness alone cannot lift the veil of our controlling natures or our pain and distrust; this requires higher energy, like the germinating seed in the soil that needs to be touched by the Sun. Human beings need to be touched by the unseen realm of ascended love to receive the guidance and support of spirit.

The help of spirit transcends the ordinary; it bypasses our judgment and resistance as it beckons us to open, blossom and take it in. We become like dried earth that lets in the moisture of fresh rain, rather than try to be the rain that replenishes us. We are not alone after all; higher consciousness is always here to fill us with beauty and meaning. We don't have to do it alone.

Our need for fulfillment creates an opening that draws in a stream of spiritual support. It is up to us to draw from this source, to allow it into our being and connect to the guidance. We are responsible for connecting with spirit. It is not up to spirit to connect with us; they simply exist in all time, as do their messages. As with the inhalation of oxygen, we are the ones who breathe it in more deeply or shorten our breath.

Stream of Spiritual Consciousness

Spiritual support is timeless and exists in partnership with our needs and soulful longing. It is a stream of consciousness that exists in the culmination of all time: past, present and future. It does not fit into our human linear-concept of past and future time; it exists in the present in a non-linear way. This means that a message given today has always existed. The reason that we are given a message at a particular time in our human-evolution is because we have tapped into that stream of higher-consciousness through our inquiries and with our desire to receive the guidance.

Masiandia: *"The purpose of spiritual support is divine love: to assist you in creating peace on Earth by helping you live peacefully within your own lives and in relation to all that you experience. In this way, your lives become purposeful, interactive forces that serve to expand all of humanity's consciousness on Earth.*

"Humanity's collective consciousness is a direct reflection of the expansion of individual-consciousness; therefore, as you expand personally, collective awareness also expands. The personal growth and soul evolution of each person on Earth determines mass-conscious evolution. This means that you impact all of humanity with your own beliefs and interactions with life. You do this in the present, as well as the past and future.

"We want you to understand that all timeframes coexist in the present. You are an adult, but you are also a child and an elder. You are still the child that you

were, and your childhood memories are still part of you. The future has memories too, and you know this through your longing for love. You already know your future heartbreaks, struggles, successes and happiness.

"*The future is not predestined, however; your beliefs, thoughts, emotions and desires in the present are creating diverse probabilities of life choices, and you are also creating myriads of diverging probabilities in parallel lifetimes. Therefore, you are more than one present, more than one future, and as we shall see in a moment, more than one past.*

"*In your past you are what you remember. But isn't it interesting how memories can change depending on how you experience your present. What you thought was so dark and shadowy in the past... one day you look back and see something shining there in the dark. It all changed, because what you do today can change your past.*

So you see, the child that you were is still alive and very real in the present. Your compassion and understanding in the present can go back in time and re-write the past, rewrite how it affected the very cells of your body and your soul's vibration and create the peaceful life you are praying for."

*W*hen I ponder this message about changing the past, I am re-minded of my friend Brian's encounter with his own past. In a meditative trance, he saw a young adolescent boy overshadowing his body, who he realized was himself from a time when he lived in Ontario. Simultaneously, the boy saw him and was frightened by the apparition of himself as a man. There was a moment's hesitation between the two of them, and then they merged.

When Brian told me this story, he remarked on how difficult a time it was in Ontario. As he looked back on that period of his life he saw it as a "war" where he had to face two fronts, one at home with his family's destructive behaviour and the other at school with bullying and being out of place. He only had energy to withstand one continued assault; he chose to guard against what he thought was the greater negativity and held his ground at home.

As an adult sitting in his reading room in an altered state, Brian remembered that at a point of profound desperation, the boy he once was had projected his pain into the future, hoping to find a future self who would show him that life was worth living. Through his extensive reading of spiritual books as a boy, he had come to believe in the potential to communicate through time. The immensity of his emotional charge was a profound need that superseded all limitations and caused an opening in time, connecting him with his future.

In that present moment in the reading room, Brian recalled that the boy of his past had reached into the future and simultaneously the man he now was had reached back in time. In that shared moment, the man gave the boy hope and the promise that life would get better, but that he had to hold on. Without preconceived notions or grasping for understanding, Brian let himself be brought into a meaningful interaction with his past. He let himself be taken into the internal dialogue of timelessness.

Multi-faceted Existence

*B*eing part of a greater wholeness connects us to the inner propulsion of life; it is the force that guides our spirits into consciousness. Masiandia asks us to expand our thoughts to consider the immeasurable quality of non-linear, multidimensional existence and look at our Universe as a direct reflection of our spirits. We are more than what we can comprehend. We are part of a unified system of energy that encompasses everything from the smallest particle to the whole of the cosmos.

Each of us is a meaningful element in the larger spectrum of existence. Each lifetime is the form, personality and expression of the embodiment of our soul. And the soul is a fragment of a larger host, the Oversoul, or what some spiritual philosophies refer to as Spirit, and which Masiandia calls the *Entity*.

Masiandia: *"The Entity is an enormous force of cosmic energy that is too comprehensive for physical embodiment, therefore, it is tapered down into souls to sustain physical incarnation. The soul, which is a facet of your Entity, then branches out into a multitude of lifetimes.*

"Your soul incarnates within your lifetime to support your Entity's purpose, which serves the whole of Divinity – the whole of the Universe that is oftentimes attributed to God, or the Creator. Why does the Creator need the Entity's support? Because the Entity is a fragment of the Creator – it is an individuated expression of God/ Goddess/ All-That-Is.

"You are part of a magnificent web of multidimensional existence that encompasses so much more than words can describe or explain. What we can say is that 'All That Is' exists because of you, because you are a part of it, just as the various parts of your biological system function together to support the whole body."

Our Entity is the overseer of a multitude of souls, and the soul fragments into myriad lifetimes, past, present and future. The Entity is like the body that hosts all the organs. Without the organs, the body would not exist. Similarly, without our soul, our Entity would not exist. Our soul is part of what I call a family of souls that comprises the whole of the Entity, and this family of souls provides the Entity with the necessary means to carry out its contribution to the Universe and the Earth. We can lend support and communicate with other souls within our soul-family, because we are all interconnected within our whole Entity.

For me personally, knowing that I am affiliated with my soul-family helps me remember that I am part of something bigger than I – that I am truly supported – and that my lifetime, my soul-expression, serves a larger purpose. To me I am an expression of my soul, which fills my body like a ray of light from the Sun that warms me and fills me with a deeper sense of meaning.

Masiandia: *"Your soul is the vital force in every cell of your body. It is the communication tool that you can utilize to better understand the perfection of your Entity, which is your expression of the whole of Divinity. This is precisely why you seek God; you seek to connect with who you are. You search for wholeness, that which belongs to a greater organism that is not separate or alone.*

"It is common to feel alone, hence you long for connection, yet many of you tend to separate yourselves from God by believing in death. When you believe in death, you resign yourself to living in the shadow of the fear of death, rather than live life fully. You disconnect from the Divine by adopting the misleading impression that your soul originated from a starting point, such as with the conception of an embryo. This misleading belief results in an attachment to time. It is important to not get caught up in time or linear details of time, and instead become a witness to life as a changing, fluid expression of your soul embodied in physical form.

"Your soul incarnates for the sole purpose of giving its higher vibration, its God-essence, to all life. And manifesting your purpose in physical form is all about belonging to a whole, to all that exists, because if your spirit-consciousness did not belong to all that exists, all that is would not exist.

"In truth, your soul had no beginning; it has always existed. All souls, or God for that matter, did not originate at any point in time. Divinity never began, it has always existed. You may ask, why does it exist? And we would ask you, why does the Sun exist? To give light to the world. Why does rain exist? To nourish the world. Why do you exist? To be what you are — life vitality.

"Consider life as an infinite circle with no beginning and no end, because a beginning could never have occurred without an ending. The tree could not be formed; its seed could not germinate without the decomposing of a dead tree, as it would not have the richness of the new soil to take shape in. So you see, new-life

is born out of the fertile matter of decay, and death is a continuation of life, woven together into a non-linear cycle.

"Reality is simply not as linear as it appears to be. But this does not make sense for the conscious mind that is rooted in the progression of time. We want to help you understand infinity, but how can we do this when your concept of time and existence is linear, indicating that you are born, you age and with age you die? But it is the body that dies, not the spirit, not your eternal self. And furthermore, it is your human perception of time that gives you the impression of death; to us there is no death; there is permanence of all time and all existence.

"There is no end. There is only continuous form. But how can we teach this to you within your linear concept? We cannot, because there is no beginning or end to our lesson; it is continuous. In your own divine time you will open yourselves to more expanded knowledge, and you will discover something that you do not know today but have always known in the eternity of your being."

We are our own oral history. A living memoir of time. Time is downloaded into our bodies. We contain it. Not only time past and time future, but time without end. We think of ourselves as close and finite, when we are multiple and infinite.

~ Jeanette Winterson, *in* The Powerbook

A Unified Whole

*I*t's exciting to think that all energy in the here and now coexists in a unified whole with all of our lifetimes. We are multiple and infinite; we are more than our human experience and more than our death. We are agents of life longing to remember our divine origins. As we remember, we step forth out of old restricting patterns into a new world; we embrace our sacredness and freely gift it to the world, for we have nothing to hide, nothing to withhold.

We are in essence generous beings, and when we remember this, we become a waterfall of abundance. We have so much more to offer of ourselves beyond the confines of our insecurities, shame and control. Our generosity is an act of gentleness towards all life that is most often overshadowed by fear of the future and reliving of the past. Who are we right now, but the colliding of past and future into the present? The present is infinite; it is the entrance to our innermost purpose, where we recognize our divinity and pass it on to the world.

With this divine recognition comes a deep desire to serve humanity, which is hindered by a lack of awareness of one another's needs. In addition, how can we be of service to each other if we do not know what we ourselves need? And how can we honour one another when we are defended against each other's inadequacies?

Masiandia asks us to welcome one another's life experiences, however different they may be, for our life experiences are parallel, a synergistic interplay of magnetic energy interconnected and whole. As a reflection of you, through my writing I am an expression of your longing. If in reading the pages of this book you become skeptical, you are a mirror of my self-doubt. When I am afraid, I feel your despair. When you are angry, you utter my frustration. When I struggle to understand Masiandia's guidance, my healing journey mirrors your own.

In the infinite circle of all life, our differences do not separate us; we are part of a greater existence where our dissimilarities form a tapestry of eternal divinity. Though we may not understand each other and inadvertently offend one another, may our differences reveal a unified language of forgiveness, acceptance and peace.

CHAPTER TWO

Journey into Trust

The arms that hold this
precious soul
in body so small and tender
wish to give you the world.

The world as I know it with joy
and the fear of falling.

I worry sometimes
that I'll make mistakes.
I do not wish to harm you,
or trace an invisible scar
of innocence lost.

For a child,
I'd like to paint a world
full of wonder.
But sometimes life
isn't like that.

The Healing Journey

*T*he healing journey is a return to our inner-self, to the heart of our soulful body-awareness. The journey takes us into and through the inner landscape of our thoughts and feelings – to release our limited concepts of reality. Here we are awakened to the in-depth wisdom latent within our desires and our innocence. Compelled by our inner-consciousness, the healing journey reveals the wisdom that lies within our inner-child's vulnerability – to connect us with the purpose of our soul, from which creativity is born. The healing journey is thus a way into creation, into restoring our sense of value.

For many of us, our innocence needs to be reborn into a new world of possibility and beauty, but we are frightened of entering the underworld of our feelings. We fear the unknown – the shadow side of our forgotten awareness. But this shadow side is equally liberating for it strengthens our partnership with soul; it connects us to our spirit's divine blessings in a way that no amount of rational understanding can provide for us.

Still, when I first approached this chapter, I hesitated, as Masiandia urged me to speak of my own childhood, of past recollections that I find painful to share. Initially, I proceeded with trepidation, cautiously writing the first draft as though I was composing a book report, deliberate and matter of fact, retelling my childhood from a safe distance. Over a year later after numerous drafts, my friend Brian recognized that I had not given voice to what I really needed to express. He helped me "let go" of trying to understand my inner-child, to let it speak the truth beyond my rational mind. I had been holding her back because I was uncomfortable with what she had to say. To free my inner voice, I sought Masiandia's guidance; I needed to know why they wanted me to write about my childhood.

Masiandia: *"We want you to write about your childhood to ignite the spirit of the child you once were – the child you still are. You are all of your ages, the child,* adolescent, young woman and elder. You are multi-faceted. The child-within is interconnected with your whole purposeful essence. All children are born with a strong link to their souls, until their innocence is stifled by the miasms of Earth-illusions, family conditioning and limiting beliefs.

"On the quest for spiritual enlightenment, many people aspire to be mature and in control, focusing on the intellect rather than their childlike instincts. They forget that the message of their spirit expresses itself through the innocence of childhood remembering. We are referring to the instinctual qualities of early childhood experiences, closely knit with spirit, before the intellect becomes sharpened with pain. Most children are born with psychic, intuitive power, able to 'feel' at an instinctive level all that is occurring around them. Your childhood remembering is significant for it reveals your spirit's innocence longing to grow in partnership with life, with integrity and truth, in a family heritage where truth was scarce.

"You might ask, 'but why is it important to reveal the innocence of spirit?' To support a truer vision of who you are – your beauty and the beauty of the reader. But over lifetimes, the essence of your souls has been overshadowed by trauma, and the innocence wounded. Through healing and re-establishing this innocence, your higher-vibrational being can fully manifest its purpose here on Earth. And by doing so, it reveals a larger scope of vision for all beings on Earth. We are asking you to free your past, to free the pasts of many others who are interwoven into the larger tapestry of all life. By freeing yourself, you give others permission to do the same. This is true for everyone; by healing yourself you help others heal because you give your essence to form.

"All physical form needs energy to thrive, and essence is fluid energy. In a state of balance, the physical body circulates this energy throughout the meridian system, providing the life-force needed for organ vitality and for the health of connective tissue. When you give your essence to form you raise the level of life-force in your body, and your physical field radiates a stronger life-pulse which naturally raises the energy in everyone around you.

"The way in which humanity gives soul-essence to form is by maintaining a *curiosity about life. This has far more benefits than all the energy practices you can do, such as chi-gong exercises. These exercises are only helpful when you cultivate a state of wonderment – when you see the world around you through the lens of interest, receptivity and openness. Otherwise, you shut out what you see around you, as well as your own essence. Curiosity is a way of life that welcomes all of your emotions and perceptions with acceptance and compassion. It is a way of exploring your life-experience with grace, surrender and willingness to evolve.*

"Throughout this book we will continuously affirm the importance of being curious and willing to witness all of your life experiences. It is paramount that humanity establishes and maintains an intimate relationship with all feelings without censorship, as this serves to establish a healing rapport with the whole body, mind and soul. Feelings are the fundamental energy centres within your body/mind experience, which open the inner door to your souls. Yet most people exert so much effort to avoid feeling that they inadvertently hinder their capacity for soulful awareness and connectivity.

"Feelings are feared because they threaten to redefine your sense of identity, which is the ego-self that through painful life-experience has been distorted into a persona of self-protection, not a servant of spiritual devotion. Most of you do not know how to connect to your feelings, or express them without blame or shame. Our intention here is to alleviate the stronghold which your fear has had on the natural cycles of your feeling states, feelings that hold the key to sensing, knowing and relating to your physical-reality and spiritual wisdom."

In the desire to free my emotions and my innocence and honour Masiandia's request, I have had to let go of the belief that it was wrong to examine the past. I grew up with my father telling me to not live in the past, that it no longer existed. While this spiritual philosophy can be helpful at times, it can be equally confusing and out of context with one's present-day experience. I've listened to inspirational speakers advocate living in the moment and avoiding thoughts of the past or the future, so that one can live a happy and more fulfilling life. Many people interpret this as evidence that one must be happy to be "spiritually enlightened," to the point that they control their negative feelings. There is a common belief that it is wrong to be upset, to be angry or react.

But in fact, feelings are an intrinsic part of life, as they help us evaluate our experiences; they define our boundaries and what we need. Attempting to suppress our thoughts of the past or future leads to censoring our emotions, which diminishes our sensitivity as well as our sense of contentment. Living in the present moment is not about avoidance but rather surrendering into the moment, which means embracing the past and also imagining the future through the lens of curiosity. The secret then to spiritual fulfilment, for health and deep joy, is not to carry the past or worry about the future, but to accept it in the present with conscious awareness, willing to observe all our thoughts and feelings without judgment.

This reminds me of an audio recording I heard of an empowerment seminar, which told a story of a participant introducing herself at a workshop as a survivor of child abuse. The motivational speaker at this event interpreted this to mean that the woman was attached to the past, attached to being a victim. Maybe this is true, but perhaps the participant was being brave in disclosing the reason she was attending the group. It is assumed that we must look away from our past to live in the present. People believe that if they deny the past and move beyond it, the abuse will go away. But it doesn't, it continues, it shows up in our present relationships, at home, at work and in our bodies.

I want to look at the past with appreciation for the gift that it holds and how it can unfold naturally in our present lives. Like the petals of a flower blossoming, there is so much more to gain as the past opens up for us. In this way, we deepen our acceptance of the past with grace and courage. Further, we honour any discomfort and pain in the past as valuable and worthy of our attention and become aware of its deeper wisdom. I have grown to understand that to awaken to the fullness of the present, it isn't enough to stop identifying with the past; we need to make peace with the past, shed light onto the areas of ourselves that we unconsciously believe are undeserving.

Masiandia: *"Our sweet Dofila (Linda), we are asking you to speak of the past to make way for the new: shed its faltering history to reveal an exalted presence. You, who have always known more, relinquish the masks of old and renew your journey – receive your wisdom. Be brave and take heart. Trust the voice of the child who is at times angry but also filled with love. You must allow the inner voice of the child you once were and still are to reveal the secret of your early childhood experiences, which is embedded in her ability to 'see' and 'know' so much more than you can as an adult.*

"As a child, you learned to look after your own emotional needs to protect yourself from disappointment and abandonment. Thus, during your early development you acquired a tendency to protect yourself from harm as a survival-response. Within all survival-responses is a paradox: the barriers that people erect to protect themselves later protect them from the very essence of their inner-wisdom, which longs to surrender into compassion and love.

"Throughout the healing journey, you must expand your consciousness to free yourself from conditioned responses and to encompass the higher vibration of who you truly are. Give yourself permission to feel more and intuitively connect with your inner-innocence, because this child-like aspect from your past is still deeply connected with your spirit and longs to be seen, loved and healed."

*I*n seeing and feeling more, I offer my supporting hand and lift up the exiled fragments of myself, which dispels my father's belief that I should leave the past alone. As I contemplate my childhood memories, my body feels heavy, and my breath is shallow. I'm letting go of the belief that I don't have permission to talk about it.

When the past speaks, I hear a story that I have been telling for a very long time. It's the story of being alone. I can try to convince myself that it isn't true, but the "feeling" remains because it is revealing something to me. It's not just an old script repeating itself. It's an old script repeating itself for a reason; it wants to be heard. In listening, I realize that there are aspects of myself that my inner-innocence has always known and yearns to awaken in me, including an emotional intelligence that is interconnected with my spirit and is highly intuitive.

My inner-self has longed to be freed from the need to shield itself from the misleading confusion of people's lies and oppressive rules, including the rules and conditioning I agreed to in my childhood. The layering of deceit and confusion many of us experience in our families sheaths itself around us as children, preventing us from remembering our karmic agreements, our spirit connection and the true purpose of our lives.

Masiandia: *"We endeavour to support those who have been neglected and over-shadowed by misconceptions to come to understand that it is highly necessary that they reacquaint themselves with their inner voice. Not the inner-child you may think she/he is supposed to be, but the child she/he is before all the illusions have settled in. Pay no mind to the agreements that you made as a child, just listen inwards to the voice of your innocence. Listen to his/her rage, hunger, pain, joy, silliness and desires, but mostly listen to his/her personal, intimate and receptive needs.*

"Under the heavy weight of obligations, moral conduct, limiting rules, denial and self-neglect, who are you? Who are you really? You are a joyful, emotional, empowered being who is innocent and interconnected with the grace of your spirit. Let your child reveal your amazing innocence. Let it be the doorway to your spiritual wisdom."

Out of the Shadows

*M*y inner-child was quite tentative when I first connected with her for the pages of this chapter, but in a trance-experience I discovered her innate awareness. Providing much-needed support, my friend Brian helped me to create a safe environment for her to come out of the shadows of her hiding place, to speak of the karmic bond between my mother and myself, a bond that was abandoned long before my mother's death. It has always been difficult telling people how my mother passed away, as it was not a natural death. She died in 1976, found strangled and beaten on the banks of the Esquimalt military base, on Vancouver Island in British Columbia. My family never learned who took her life.

Prior to her murder, she had tried ending her own life countless times, as she wrestled with insecurity and abuse from her childhood. During this time, she also neglected her children. She left my two sisters and me alone at home to fend for ourselves and would arrive late at night in a drunken stupor, often carried in by a new man. In an effort to meet our needs my older sister, then age ten, would fry sliced potatoes, or we would just eat cereal, and we both changed our younger sister's diapers. Sometimes, we would close ourselves in our bedroom when we were afraid. By the time I was eight, I had witnessed my mother's struggle with manic depression and addiction to alcohol and prescription drugs, and I missed her. I missed what any child craves: love, affection, attention. But mostly I lost out on her finding herself, coming home to who she really was.

After her death, my sisters and I stayed in a short-term foster home until our grandmother arrived to fly us back to Montreal. We were originally from Montreal and had lived in Victoria for about two years, where my parents separated upon first arrival. We didn't know where our father lived at the time of our mother's death, as we had no contact with him. Unsettled and anxious, my grandparents, sisters and I blundered through the first few months in shock. My older sister and I lived with my mother's parents, while my younger sister was sent to live with my father's parents – a separation that was heartbreaking for me.

Our maternal grandmother never fully recovered from her daughter's death. Completely devastated, she did not attend or bring us to our mother's funeral service, nor were family photographs sent back to Montreal. The only belongings that my sisters and I took from our old life were what we could carry in our suitcases. When asked why, my grandmother averted any questions about the past, and since she was in so much pain, our family learned to avoid the subject. Ten years after Mom's passing though, I returned to Victoria and researched her death extensively through a number of newspapers on microfilm. In one article, a reporter wrote, "Mrs. Frappier (my grandmother) did not attend the funeral because she wanted to remember her daughter alive." My grandmother's decision however did not support my grieving, though she could not have known this.

While I reconnect with these memories, I am aware that as a sensitive child, despite that we avoided talking about Mom, I intuitively knew that my grandmother's pain harboured profound regret and guilt, and that in not talking about it, nothing was healed. In fact, I did not find peace with my mother's death through communicating with my family, for Grandma was not the only one who resisted talking about her. My father also struggled with profound guilt, for our family blamed him for Mom's death.

Two years following her passing, he returned to his parents' home when my older sister and I were visiting. We didn't recognize him at first, and neither were we given the opportunity, as he was hastily whisked into a different room. We waited to see him, but we were not allowed until the following day. Just a day after he found out that our mother had been killed, he grappled with the news and tried to help us understand his absence, but I don't think he knew how to communicate his feelings or explain why he had left the family.

Over the years, I have pieced together our conversations and understand now that he and Mom had had a very turbulent disagreement concerning the custody of my sisters and me. I don't think either of them was prepared for parental responsibility. They were also both neglected children themselves, with past trauma and abandonment issues.

As I reflect on my parents' lives, I see the lack of emotional support given to them, as their own families treated them with disapproval and disdain. I have had to turn away from the judgmental criticism passed down by my grandparents to see my parents with my own eyes and to choose to forgive and accept them. However, forgiveness does not eclipse the emotional intelligence of the neglected child. It does not mend a karmic bond that has been broken. Recovering from the childhood pain requires so much more; it calls for forgiving the child's pain. We don't think of that usually – we don't think that the child's suffering needs forgiveness but rather that the neglectful adult needs to be forgiven. But how can we forgive anyone if we do not forgive ourselves for having had the experience? Most people who have endured childhood trauma blame themselves; they believe that there was and still is something gravely wrong with them. To forgive the child requires that we listen to the wisdom in its distress.

Something amazing occurs when we listen to the voice of the child: it awakens us to a world where the child is not just an innocent part of us that needs nurturing and play; it is also a part of us that is innately connected to the subconscious and highly intuitive. In listening to my child-within, I am made aware of its instinctual ability, which in my past I held at bay due to my fear of getting into trouble, or worse, of being utterly ignored.

In preparing to listen to my inner-child's experience, Masiandia helped me understand that it was by the age of two and a half that I started to become disoriented about reality. As a sensitive empath, I was like a sponge that absorbed the pain from my family, which overshadowed the clarity of my being. In order to write this chapter, I needed to shed this confusion.

Brian assisted me in holding a sacred space for the child to speak freely. My inner-self began by insisting that she didn't want to talk about the past, that she felt choked, and it was unfair, and why, why, why was I asking her to reveal her memories. In referring to my parents, she asked,

"How do I keep loving when there are so many lies?" ... *"Linda wants to love, the spirits want to love, but I want to hide."* She went on to add, as she spoke directly to Brian, *"You love me too much. It's very scary when you look at me with the truth. Linda loves me like you do, and I hate it."* In the trance state, I began to cry. Through sobs, my inner-self continued, *"It's easier when people lie: I can hide; I can go away. Linda doesn't want me to go away, and you're making me not go away."*

Brian tried to console her; he told her that we didn't want her to stand alone anymore, that we wanted her to come out to celebrate her, accept her and hold her in a circle of arms. He told her of a dream he had where a forest of animals tried to put out a great fire, passing water along from one animal to another. But by the time the water reached the fire, there was too little left to put out the flames, for it had spilled. Some of the animals were just too small to carry all that water. So all the animals had to cross the river. He asked her to be brave, to cross the river away from the burning forest. I could feel her listening to him, the child inside of me taking in his words, wanting to believe. All of a sudden I felt an inner shift, a sense of trust that all the animals were crossing together, and that the animals represented all of my family, and that it was okay for her to speak freely.

She continued slowly, *"I want Linda to write that I didn't trust my parents. I didn't trust what my dad said, because it didn't match his feelings. And I didn't trust my mom, because she was smaller than me."* While she voiced her feelings, Brian continued to reassure her by speaking gently to her and showing great affection. The whole process awakened an unconscious part of me that had been struggling with confusion and distrust in people's lack of congruency, a part of me that was equally afraid of the truth – afraid of love. For several years I had known that for my inner-child, love represented abandonment and neglect. Listening to the inner-child with Brian's support gave me a deep sense of relief, for it allowed me to not only "feel" her pain but also witness her innate wisdom. The following is an excerpt from this trance state that gave voice to her story.

> "Mom didn't try to live. She didn't try to be happy. I don't understand how someone could not even try. I wanted her to try to live. I didn't even want her love; I just wanted her, not all of her indifference. Her body was so heavy with grief. I didn't come into this body to take care of my mother's pain. I came here to be supported by her: freed by her. It doesn't matter that her spirit supports me now. That's a different story. The story I am telling is the story of the little girl that wanted a mom. But I knew that my mom would not try living. I said goodbye to her long before she died. But had she tried to live, that would be a new story.
>
> "I want to talk about that story. If she had tried to live, she would not have covered up who she really was; she would not have protected herself from my love. Had Mom tried to live, which is what she promised me before I came into her body, I would have had the love I needed to protect myself from harm, because she would have protected me.
>
> "I understand that Linda is a healer who will weave together my story into a message that helps people heal, but healing is not erasing. Healing is not covering up the pain with enlightenment. Healing has nothing to do with accepting things the way they were. Healing is a magnifying glass that doesn't overlook anything.
>
> "When Mom was pregnant with my little sister, I knew that Rachel was the second coming of light. She was the gift that was to ignite in my mother the desire to live. Rachel was the spirit that came into Mom's life to help her make better choices.

*But Mom never received her. She blocked out her light right
away, before Rachel was even born.*

*"I wasn't supposed to face this family pattern of not living
fully on my own. I wasn't supposed to come into this body to be
alone. That wasn't the agreement. Linda wants me to forgive,
and yes, I can. Of course I can forgive, what else is there to do?
Still, it wasn't the agreement."*

Forgiveness, Restoring Self-trust

*M*y inner-self was adamant when she said, *"being alone wasn't the
agreement."* Her message invites me in and allows me to provide her with what she needs, companionship and support, which helps
me connect with an innate sense of knowing how to care for my whole
self. This strengthens my trust in Masiandia's guidance, in their asking me
to speak about the abuse in my childhood.

When Masiandia initially encouraged me to speak of my childhood,
I knew that they were referring to abuse that occurred when I was seven.
They were guiding me to dispel the myth that abuse is a forbidden territory that should only be explored in the privacy of therapy. Abuse is a
universal language; it belongs to all of us. It's part of our social system,
which is imbalanced and corrupted by the wrong use of power, by neglect
and fear.

As a child, I had to define my own value with no life-skills and no
understanding of my boundaries, because the adults around me had no
boundaries themselves. The abuse later resurfaced in my adult life, as it
played such a huge role in issues with my health and relationships. And
the process of healing the abuse helped me define my own natural limits
and claim my sense of worth. By having the courage to face my past, I
found strength in myself that I didn't know I had.

I don't remember the name of the man who abused me, but I know that his friendship was important to me, because there was no one else to depend on. My mother had given him and his girlfriend the responsibility to take care of my sisters and me, as she had gone back to Montreal from Victoria to find us a home. I can't recall how long she was gone, except that when she returned, my older sister and I could no longer speak French, the language we grew up with. We could only understand French, as they had forbidden us to speak it. I don't recall either of them specifically, nor what we did while they lived in our home.

For years, I didn't remember much of what happened. When I looked back at this part of my childhood, I saw a dark shadow, I drew a blank memory and felt profoundly afraid. With therapy and channelled support, I discovered that as a child I didn't want the couple to move in and be our guardians. In haste and desperation to return to Montreal, my mother had overlooked our safety.

I have come to understand that her neglect not only confused me but also taught me to override my intuition. How could I trust myself if I couldn't trust her? How can any child learn to follow the guidance of his/her natural intuition if the adults around him/her ignore it? It's by restoring my self-trust that I discovered what happened in the past. Furthermore, the consequence of the abuse kept showing up in my adult life, and this became especially evident during a hypnotherapy class with my mentor, Mahmud Nestman. While studying age-regression, I had a resistance to doing the work, insisting that I didn't see the relevance in doing age-regression with clients. As I heard myself speak, I knew I was speaking with the voice of a very young child, which evolved into a class demonstration and breakthrough. The child speaking was very upset and self-critical, repeating over and over again that she had done something very bad. This is a common reaction for abused children: to feel responsible and ashamed.

In class, Mahmud and my classmates were gently supportive, and my inner-self disclosed as much information as I was ready to accept at that time. Mahmud invited the "adult" me to enter into the past, to be a source of strength for my childhood feelings. He focused on establishing the safety needed to reassure me. The wounded part of me revealed that what had first appeared to be a game turned out to be a sexual expectation. As a child I was frightened and didn't want to continue playing, and the man made fun of me. This was tremendously embarrassing, confusing and hurtful.

The session with Mahmud taught me that there is so much we can bring to the unconscious domain of our feelings. We can enter into the underworld with courage and trust, following the voice of our innocence as it reveals our innermost truth. For the writing of this chapter, I opened a door to my spirit and delved into the wisdom of my innocence. This helped me find clarity and profound acceptance for my past, as I continued to channel the voice of my inner-self. The following is the conclusion of the excerpt from the trance-state.

> "Masiandia nudges me along gently, asking me to talk about what this chapter is really about – abuse. There is no one in this world who has not been abused or is not abused. I knew this coming into this life. I just didn't realize that the oppression would be so confining. I do not want to talk about the abuse. I didn't come here to experience that. I don't care that my spirit accepted the responsibility of being in this body – that it chose to incarnate. I wanted to share that responsibility with my family – to be in harmony with the true purpose of incarnation, which is kinship, not abuse. Our purpose is to love one another and journey together in love, not cause suffering.
>
> "I still want to share the responsibility for being part of humanity, not carry it on my own, so I will blame the man who pretended to be my friend. I don't like that he lied to me, and I don't have to. I knew all along that he wasn't really my friend,

but I pretended, just like he did, because I was accustomed to lies. As well, the truth had become harder to sense [pause] so I believed him. There was no other way but into his abuse; there was no other choice. The energy-message I received from my mother influenced the story I played out with this man. I copied her. It was the only road there was, because I didn't know any other way. She did not feel loved and passed on this distortion to me, so I did not feel loved. She looked for love where it could not be found, and so did I."

There is something profoundly significant in the child saying that she blames the abuser – that she doesn't have to like his lies. I don't get the sense that she is passing the blame onto him for the abuse. She is not suggesting that he be punished, but rather acknowledging that his actions were heartless.

Still, it breaks my heart to hear her say she looked for love where it couldn't be found. I want to cradle her in safety and relinquish any part of me that may overrule her innocence. I want to honour her naked truth – her natural instincts, which is ultimately her inner knowing. I want to welcome my inner-child's deep feelings even as I dislike hearing her say that she did not like my mother. But if I let my discomfort rule me, I neglect her; I dismiss her just as my mother did when I tried to tell her about the abuse.

Masiandia: *"We invite you to love everything, even abuse, especially your revulsion to abuse. Love the child's pain, sorrow and power. Love your soul's evolution in all of its Earth experiences. The more you love everything, the more you can completely forgive yourselves for every life experience, however challenging they have been and still are.*

"Forgive yourselves for believing that you are victims of abuse, and instead be gentle with the deep wounds associated with abuse. Forgive yourselves for

believing that abuse is bad or wrong, and instead become gentle with the child-
hood wounds of both the victim and perpetrator. In this way, you can accept your
fears with gentleness and compassion, and experience the present moment in all
of its expressions – past, present and future – without the limited scope of your
linear minds. Forgive yourselves now to enter into deep peace with your child-
hood and with your future."

―――∞∞∞―――

Forgiveness Is Not Tolerance

On the journey of forgiveness I have experienced many setbacks and difficult life-experiences, and I've discovered that forgiveness is not the same as tolerance. Many times, spiritual philosophies can be confusing and difficult to put into practice. There was a time that my father tried to offer me such spiritual wisdom by advising me to forgive an ex-boyfriend who was at the time harassing and threatening to kill me. The police tried to intervene but could do very little because they required physical proof; emotional and mental violence were not considered dangerous. Police requirements have since changed so that threats alone are considered significant enough to press charges. But at the age of twenty, I didn't feel empowered, and I didn't know what to do. I tried to forgive my ex, who I'll refer to as Don, but his aggressive behaviour persisted. Even my grandmother, who had nurtured and guided me, tried to convince me that I should be nice to Don, because he was a "good man." I was especially confused when I tried to understand my father's spiritual insights about forgiveness. I felt uncertain of who I was and utterly ashamed of myself for the disdainful way Don treated me.

Fortunately, my roommate's mother helped me understand that I was not responsible for his actions. She explained that Don was answerable to his own behaviours and feelings, and that his treatment of me was not my fault. I really needed to hear that, though it took several years for me to fully understand her, because I didn't know how to differentiate between my feelings and his. I was so sensitive that the feelings of others bombarded me; I absorbed them and became highly enmeshed with them. Her support started me on the journey of discerning my own feelings and appreciating their relevance. Before then, I assumed the responsibility of taking care of other people's feelings by blaming myself for their unhappiness. At this time, I realized on a deep sensory level, not just intellectually, that I deserved better and was worthy of respect. Only then could I let go of the confusion and shame that arose as a result of taking responsibility for others' behaviour.

When I look back at this time in my life, I see that my father and grandmother's advice on forgiving Don had very little to do with forgiveness; they were asking me to turn a blind eye and let myself be treated poorly because they didn't realize how abusive the situation actually was. They didn't want to admit that Don's behaviour was abusive, because they didn't want to see me as someone who was bullied. Such denial is not forgiveness. Forgiveness is not about being oblivious to someone's cruelty or bearing the hardship. In her book *The Diamond in Your Pocket*, Gangaji writes, "Horrible things are continually being done all over the world, in our own individual minds and in the collective mind. To forgive these horrors does not necessarily mean to forget." We can forgive and let go without indifference.

Many spiritual teachings suggest that forgiveness is letting go of resentment or anger or ceasing to demand retribution for a perceived violation. In that case, I forgave Don a long time ago, as well as the abuse that took place in my childhood. Someone asked me if Don or the childhood abuser even merited forgiveness. Perhaps not, but I merit being in a state of forgiveness, and from that place I want that for them, too. "Everyone has experienced the sweet release of forgiveness, as well as the hard coldness of not forgiving," writes Gangaji. "There is no need to forget or deny the wrongs that have been done to you and by you, but you can let go of suffering over them." She also writes, "'Forgive them for they know not what they do' is the truth."

Along this journey to forgive and heal the past, I was especially determined to heal my relationship with my father, relentlessly dragging him through my therapy. I recall doing an exercise in a workshop where I answered a series of questions spontaneously. One of the questions was, "What brings you joy?" and I surprised myself by answering, "Loving my dad!" I have learned to have compassion for him, as I know that he was also deeply wounded. I know that if he could undo the abuse from my childhood, he would. I see the burden of his guilt and his love for me.

I once told him that I wouldn't exchange him for another father, no matter how challenging our relationship was. I just needed for him to hear me and help me heal. Since then, he told me that I taught him honesty and that my exploration of the truth was very meaningful to him. But it wasn't until his death that I truly felt his love for me. The night before he passed away, both of my sisters and I saw him in the hospital when he was still lucid and able to talk. He said the sweetest things like introducing us to the nurse as his angels. It was never like our dad to be affectionate, so the sweetness will remain with me forever.

When my father took his final breath, in that moment of his passing away I felt his essence expand into me. It's amazing how spirit releases so much energy as the body surrenders its life. It's truly magical. We don't think of the dying as having the power to touch us, but when I held my dad's hand before he left his body I felt his spirit become more expansive and move towards me, not away.

Living in Harmony with Your Soul

*M*asiandia teaches us to see the beauty in life, even in the shadows. It is with this guidance that I know the most important commitment I have made in my life is to set my intention to heal, to awaken to beauty and to share it with others. Everything that has occurred in my life has supported my healing journey, like a strong wind pushing me forward. I moved along with the current but with reluctance, as I wanted to leave my past behind. But my past followed me, so I chose to welcome it. I brought it along to therapy sessions, I grieved, I grew, I healed, and I learned to value myself. I also discovered that the healing journey does not end miraculously at some point – it continues. It evolves and becomes a spiritual practice in honest self-inquiry and self-awareness.

Masiandia: *"When the healing journey becomes a spiritual practice, you discover the beauty of living in harmony with your soul. The healing journey transforms into a life-choice: choosing to live with conscious intent that then sustains your whole self. More often than not, most people enter the healing journey through strife and misery, physical and emotional pain, intent on 'getting better', until they realize that to heal is to return to spirit. Your spiritual practice is not about achieving optimal health; it is not the act of striving for perfection; you are already perfect. Spiritual practice is the patient daily meditation of remembering your perfection and self-worth and seeing your beauty.*

"It is by embracing yourself that you seed a new life for yourself and a new world for all of humanity. You create a sacred Earth – the Earth that you all want. Therefore, look for what is sacred in everything, and see the beauty even in the concrete cities, pollution, toxins and human behaviours that trigger you. It is important to return over and over again to the deeper realm of your spirit-values, rather than be distracted by the reactions that keep you hidden from the truth. You can see the haze of pollution on the horizon, and at the same time view small birds flying from branch to branch, and behold the distant seagull in the sky, and maybe you will feel your chest expand with the deep breath that comes with happiness. When you remember this, you awaken to beauty, and beauty manifests more beauty in this world."

There is no such thing as effortless beauty –
you should know that.
There's no effort which is not beautiful –
lifting a heavy stone or loving you.

~ Jeanette Winterson

CHAPTER THREE

Healing, A Spiritual Practice

A million miles I'll walk for you –
climb a mountain and
make my way to its highest point,
to connect with you.

I am the shadow to your light –
I see God in you,
and remain close to your heart.
I do everything for you.

I make a fool of me –
risk ridicule.
You're free to judge me,
and let me down.
I'm certain to disappoint you.
Anything, anything,
to connect with you.

I tender my frailties –
I wear them on my sleeve.
All my imperfections I give to you.
Anything to connect with you.

Raw and willing
Refined and sublime
Whole and abandoned
And free.

Finding Source Within

*T*he path of healing is a spiritual journey of reclaiming our sacred-ness. It is a journey of cultivating an intimate connection with our body/mind awareness, honouring the divine nature of our body, thoughts and feelings. Healing is an ecstatic expression of all our feelings that brings profound joy to the most intense emotions, because it is absolutely amazing to give ourselves permission to feel everything with conscious-ness. Delving into the expansiveness of our emotions with acceptance and care is a courageous act because it makes us so vulnerable.

Defenceless, we are accessible, open, allowing, curious, and we look at life-circumstances as opportunities for growth and exploration. To feel is to flow with the inner mystery of our souls and relate with the world in new ways that transcend the ordinary and encompass our truth. But we live in a society, within families, relationships and in work environ-ments that frown upon emotional expression. Feelings have become bur-ied and unknown to us, overshadowed by the rational mind. Prevailing judgments, opinions and social pressures, threatened by the unknown, distance the psyche from its inherent mystery.

In my life, I push against social convention and defy its rules; I em-brace the path that is least followed and reconcile with my loneliness and fear, because I will not be forced into any shape that does not endeavour to help me grow. I want to see this world and my part in it through the lens of awareness. Being awake connects me with my inner-resonance, with what feels natural to me. Then I feel inspired, and I connect with my creative flow, breaking free from social stigmas that inhibit my true sense of self. By embracing an intimate connection with my inner-resonance, I am able to witness life with more acceptances, even when faced with chal-lenging situations. I welcome life experiences, and I take in the guidance of spirit as I examine my thoughts and feelings.

Their guidance calls for an expansion of inner seeing, to suspend our initial perceptions and surrender our will to a larger vision of peace. This vision necessitates deep respect for one another's differences, rather than continue to be threatened and afraid of change. They ask us to be the leaders of our own lives by celebrating the beauty in all life on Earth, not rejecting life through judgment. In this way we can model a new way of being for humanity, a way that honours the value of all things and welcomes the mystery of the Divine in all things.

Masiandia also says that when souls incarnate on Earth, there is an agreement made with the Earth; we choose to be part of its evolution, as it becomes part of our own. We serve the Earth with the courage to heal and transform the collective perception of reality, and in turn, the Earth provides us with the physical reality in which we can express ourselves and unfold our spiritual vision. This co-commitment with Earth calls for us to welcome our soul wisdom into every aspect of our life, so that we can expand our own consciousness and help raise Earth's physical vibration in the process.

I'm willing to sacrifice any aspect of my personality that does not serve this expanded purpose. My longing for spiritual intimacy runs deep. I want to see the grace of light upon all life, smell it and be washed clean. I want to feel it enter into my veins and dance along with its rhythms and hear the call of the wild mystery of my divinity. But this appetite sometimes seems too large in a world that demands we conform and belittle our natural sense of worthiness, thus my fear is equally sizeable. I sometimes become afraid and lose my way, shrink away from the edge of possibility – the edge of my dreams. In the ensuing darkness, I cannot see the path, distrust the way, stumble and fall. But I pick myself up again, drawing inspiration from Georgia O'Keeffe's quote: "I've been absolutely terrified every moment of my life – and I've never let it keep me from doing a single thing I wanted to do." Sometimes, I have let my fear stop me to the point of not knowing what I want, but not for long, for my creative desire propels me forward, as it wants to give freely of my most tender trust and commitment to the truth.

We all succumb to fears now and then, and it is not by overriding these fears that we tap into courage. Courage comes from "loving" our fear, from welcoming and accepting its presence in our lives. In this way, we cease viewing it as an opponent; we stop giving it so much power over us and come to recognize that our personal power is greater then fear. We have the power to heal it.

My sister cares for her fear of performing the piano publicly, not by pushing her fear aside but by connecting with her personal power; her love of music. The joy that she feels in sharing her gift doesn't override the fear; it nurtures it. For many of us, fear represents a part of us that is malnourished, and that needs our love so that it can ease into trust and re-ceptivity. Loving our fear inspires us toward the courage and the willing-ness to grow and create, because we're no longer treating it as an obstacle. Instead we are allowing fear to pull us back into our feeling body, to the place where we hold the key to expressing our desires, our passion and life-purpose.

Healing the Collective Imbalance

*I*n this chapter, Masiandia brings to light our responsibility as a com-munity to grow our love, and how to heal abuse in the world. We enrich Earth-reality with love and courage, and ultimately with our will-ingness to be completely present and accountable for our actions. In their message, Masiandia examines the misuse of power rooted in Earth's heri-tage and in our family conditioning and cultures, to expand our aware-ness of how we all contribute to abuse in the world and in how we can alleviate unkindness and indifference.

Abuse is an energy system that is woven into the grid patterns of Earth-reality, within the foundational energy of Earth. It is shaped out of the control, manipulation, criticism and disempowerment that societies at large are responsible for, of which we are all part. Through judgment of self and others we propagate the energy of abuse in this world, and we need to become highly conscious of our conditioned reactions so that we can lessen its negative impact. With commitment and self-responsibility, we not only refuse to continue being a participant in conditions that maintain judgment and neglect, we clear our fields of depleting energy and pass on a heightened vibration to those near and far as well as to Earth itself.

Masiandia: *"Each and every one of you is needed on this wondrous and beautiful planet. Let yourselves immerse your spirit-consciousness into your daily lives; live as though you have full permission to be powerful, influential, dynamic and authentic. You do have full permission. In fact, we challenge you to step into a greater aspect of yourself, to be all that you can be. We invite you. Earth invites you. To do so is your incarnated birthright and an expression of divine law. Come join us, surrender your passion, let us guide you, let us help you heal the pain … the fear. Let us free you.*

"We are the river of higher-consciousness that is always present, always beckoning you towards your true nature. You are the human embodiment of spiritual purpose and love. You possess an inherent ability to return to your inner beauty, and you have the power to heal yourselves, which in turn heals the world. You have the power to free yourselves from past trauma and break the patterns of abuse in the world. You have the power to stop passing on the effects of trauma to your children, spouse, friends, family, co-workers and even strangers and to instead choose love. By becoming aware of your behaviour, beliefs and attitudes, you treat the world with care and attentive presence. It is important to 'choose' not to disempower yourself and others with judgments and control.

"Please be reassured that we are not blaming you for the abuse in the world; we are opening your eyes so that you can become aware of your responsibility to heal abuse. Even if you think that you are exempt, you are not; you are

intrinsically part of abuse simply because you are part of the Earth. You are all part of the Earth, and since there is abuse on this planet, you are all co-creators of abuse.

"You are part of the Earth's energy-patterns, just as leaves are part of a tree, or droplets of water make the whole of the ocean. You all co-create abuse in this world, because you contribute to the underlying problem causing the abuse – you abuse yourselves and each other each time you cast judgments. Hence, it is highly important that you observe your judgments with acceptance and forgiveness. In this way, you embody acceptance and forgiveness, not judgment, and you change the quantum vibration of your droplet of energy in the vastness of all life."

When I first channelled this message I was profoundly impacted. Masiandia's words smashed into me like a fist hitting my chest. I staggered and resisted, but I also believed them. It was just hard to digest, as an immense sense of responsibility overwhelmed me. I let the words sink in, touch me, push me, grow me, and began to receive the life experiences that I needed to heal my own internal abuse. I was given an audio recording of Byron Katie's book, Loving What Is, and was reminded that it's okay to judge both ourselves and others, because we judge, we just do. By trying not to judge, we make judging "wrong" and compound our self-judgment. Katie says that our thoughts are just what they are; they are innocent and not personal. She says, "They are like the breeze or the leaves on the trees or the raindrops falling. Thoughts arise like that, and we can make friends with them." And she asks, "Would you argue with a raindrop?"

Masiandia once told participants in a support group that enlightened people also judge, and they feel fear and sorrow. They also feel anger. The difference is that they laugh at themselves, they take themselves lightly and engage with the energy of their judgment to transform it, and are themselves transformed. When we fully engage with our judgments, we come to understand what causes separation, fear, pain and self-protection, and we embrace our needs, as well as change. When we allow ourselves to greet all of our experiences with acceptance and care, we let ourselves move out of the familiar territory of our habitual mindset. We are so much closer to our strength when we are open to our feelings, because it takes courage to be receptive.

Shifting from Fear into Harmony

Masiandia: *"Ruled by the physical and mental bodies, many of you are afraid of experiencing your feelings. You are governed by belief systems that camouflage the feeling body with distortions and addictions, and these mask awareness of your true needs. These distortions also impede your ego's natural propensity to serve your higher self. Your ego is designed to serve the human/soul relationship, not suffer abuse and be bound by fear. But because of the collective imbalance, the ego is out of harmony with its intended purpose.*

"When you are aligned with your soul-purpose, willing to engage with your true feelings, you are detached from mass-conscious dualities and embrace all life. You negate nothing in your life or in the lives of others. In this state of balance, your ego serves your soul with ease and trust, and you feel profound compassion towards yourself and others. Because of this, you only follow universal law, which is to live with utmost integrity and love."

The healing journey calls for us to awaken to the depth of our true feelings, so that we can come out of the shadows of pain into the light of our divinity. The Universe awaits our delivery from our own self-imposed exile, and the first step is always ours to take. We can call upon the Universe's partnership and draw nourishment from knowing that we are not alone. The love our guides have for us is constant; it is an imminent part of divine wholeness. As we are nurtured by cosmic radiance, we are also nourished by Earth, the divine manifestation of the great mother. A continuous flow of energy surrounds us; a sea of vibration envelops us to lend support, and it is our choice to receive it.

But we often neglect to recognize the support that is in our life. This is illustrated in my friend's recount of the felling of a tree that had stood outside his reading room. The tree had offered shade and privacy for several years, and not until it was removed did my friend realize the peacefulness it had provided. With the spirit of the tree released, he felt the emptiness and knew that without his conscious awareness, the tree had been a kind and gentle presence. Not only had it shadowed the south-facing room, it had also given him a profound sense of protection and safety. I wonder how much of my surroundings I've been missing, what subtle sweetness I am not allowing in or honouring and what am I not feeling. As I notice this I soften, I thank the spirit of my home for supporting me and providing me with a sacred environment for growth. I breathe deeper and become quiet inside.

Masiandia: *"Your incarnated-life, your human experience, mirrors your soul's ability to explore all that this Earth-plane provides. Through Earthly expressions of emotional, mental, physical and spiritual development, your soul evolves its ability to embody truth. Truth is the essence of simplicity, beauty, returning to love, shedding the masks of complacency and fear, and opening to the support and resources that life on Earth bestows on you. Truth is not control of your feelings. By fully experiencing your feelings, the body/soul can finally rest in its purpose and gather the energy to sustain itself. When you support yourselves, you let Earth's resources in, and you also allow spirit to support you; you receive our care, our insight and guidance. The Universe is a constant support network of energy possibilities.*

"If you try to sustain the social framework you have inherited by denying your own needs, you become like the mother who cannot nourish her child because she herself is undernourished, the father who cannot provide for his family because he is afraid of responsibility, and the doctor unable to diagnose and heal

an ailment because he is unwilling to step outside the framework of his medical
training and take into account the subtle energies of the body.

"You must completely dissolve these attachments to societal conditioning
in order to support integration, balance and fluidity, and to sustain your funda-
mental needs. The mother must develop personal rituals that support her need
for nourishment. The father must learn self-discipline and overcome his fear of
failure by honouring his effort and courage. The doctor must consider other so-
lutions that may not be supported by his prior research and training. He must
surrender his will to the will of the patient, which would expand his knowledge
base far beyond the thought processes he is conditioned to rely on.

"Societal rules, morals and beliefs must be challenged within yourself, not
abetted by the expectation of external gratification or approval. You must dissolve
the attachments to such co-dependencies, which trigger your fears and emotional
needs, and instead gather your own personal resources and focus on establishing
a closer relationship with your self-worth. Otherwise, these external attachments
will continue to deepen the pain and dissatisfaction imbedded in the belief that
you are unworthy."

In the shadow of shame, we neglect to see our beauty and our divinity;
we protect ourselves against the painful forces of our own disapproval. But who told us that we are unworthy? Where does this concept come
from? We learned to dishonour our worthiness due to social conditioning.
We learned to shame one another and ourselves, and we pass this on to our
children as it was passed down unto us through abuse, betrayal, neglect,
hurt. These wounds bleed into fear, which inevitably develops into self-protection, separation and forgetting that we are all part of The Great Divine.

We have forgotten that we are sacred because our Oversoul, or Entity
as Masiandia calls it, fragments when it incarnates within Earth's dense
physical matter. The Entity's multidimensional consciousness cannot
incarnate as a whole without interfering with the human nervous system. As mentioned in chapter one, our lifetime is the embodiment of an

individuated soul, which serves the Entity's purpose. Earth reality then provides the soul with manifested experience, which on the one hand limits the full reconnaissance of its holy existence, though in turn, the soul is enriched with a material form that supports its expression.

Masiandia: *"Earth is comprised of layers of energy frequencies; magnetic fields; past, present and future timelines; all interwoven into the holographic reality that you call physical matter. It is a vibrational interplay of thought and form interconnected through the lens of magnetic energy, which takes shape three-dimensionally. This Earth, as you know it, is physically dense and vibrationally slower than your spirit-consciousness, and while it may seem inhibiting, it is in fact a reality in which you can worship your soul's divinity in all of its expressions. Earth is thus a temple for felt-sense experiences that enables the embodiment of your soul and its imprinting of higher vibrational knowledge into Earth-reality, which supports both the Earth and your soul's evolution.*

"This magnetic planet unites yin and yang dualities, feminine and masculine polarities, that allows your soul to engage in a reflection of its divinity. Earth is a conduit for transformation supporting your soul's evolution, providing it with a mirror for self-realization so that it can 'experience' itself in everything, expanding its ability to tap into infinite possibilities.

"In order for you to step into the depths of infinite possibility, which is ultimately an abundance of energy-vitality and connection to source, it is necessary that you surrender your rational mind and welcome a more expanded perception of reality. Look beyond the wall of fear and doubt, judgment and conditioned responses to life, so that you can break free from limited choices and choose to value yourself.

"Ultimately, we invite you to let God love you because you are worthy of love. In fact, your body is a holy, divine sanctuary for truth. We know that this is difficult for many of you to grasp, because the lineage of human development is rooted in criticism and shame. Generations have been damaged by abuse and continue to be. The more you scar your successive generations with abuse, the

more it weakens your genetic lineage. You are not singular and isolated; you are part of a greater whole. All of your actions are part of a larger synergy of souls interwoven together, working to release locked energy. So you see, abusing yourself affects everyone, and abusing someone else affects you; it weakens your organs, your overall biology, your brain function and your emotional well-being."

Innocence and Vulnerability

Masiandia: *"Children are particularly vulnerable to abuse, as they are less able to defend themselves. It's not in their nature to do so at this stage of their being, as they are part of love. They give their energy to adults, offering healing towards adults' unacknowledged wounds. But when grownups shut themselves off, denying their own feelings, they lose connection with childhood innocence. When this occurs, they resist the feelings of children, become hardened to the sensitivity that children personify.*

"Children are in the feeling body more than they are in the physical body. Their needs, emotions, innocence, and playfulness are denied by the adult voice of reason, which inevitably forces them to shut down their spirits. Through criticism, judgment, neglect and disempowerment, children are susceptible to emotional, mental and spiritual damage."

We sacrifice our future by neglecting the innocence of children, and so doubt the possibility of our dreams by denying the essence of our own innocence. When we give up the responsibility to make room for all our emotions, all our felt-experiences, we neglect to secure our needs and inevitably become hardened to vulnerability. We are being asked to awaken, to welcome the voice of our innocence and the innocence of children, to love and cherish the beauty in this world, in one another and in ourselves.

Often this can be very challenging. There is a tendency for us to withhold affection, as well as reserve our trust and acceptance, the moment that someone's behaviour triggers us. We either try to control them or ourselves. Because we are threatened and afraid of being hurt, we discriminate against others, inadvertently causing separation and misunderstanding.

But what if we knew that we have the power to enliven our lives and the lives of others? What if we could lift one another to higher states of belonging and peace, and heal abuse … with our empathy? We could become great – we could be the heroes of our own resourcefulness – and draw strength from our willingness to free our love. Then we would be equally aware of how our actions can cause so much suffering. We would be conscientious of how our thoughts, judgments and expectations affect others, as well as ourselves.

Many years ago, in my mid-twenties, I discovered that my repressed emotions impeded the flow of my love and overshadowed the support I could have given my friend Kim. I neglected to care for Kim's emotions after she received news of someone's suicide. I had argued that he had the right to take his life – that it was his free will. Naturally, Kim felt hurt and unsupported. My response to her sorrow was so thoughtless, but I didn't recognize this until about a year later, after I had begun to grieve my mother's death in therapy. When I understood what I had done, I called Kim to apologize and reach out with compassion, which was thankfully received.

Over the course of my therapy, I came to realize that after my mother's passing I had become hardened towards death and resistant to grieving. I had forestalled my own grieving in hopes of alleviating my grandmother's suffering. As a child, I would wake in the middle of the night and see her sitting at the kitchen table sobbing, and decided early in life to hide my feelings out of fear that they would overwhelm her, much as her sorrow overwhelmed me.

But grieving death and loss cannot be escaped through rationalization. Understanding this gave me insight in the first year of my counselling practice, helping me support my client Sarah in her grief. She came into my session room in tears, sobbing uncontrollably for the death of her cat. I reflected her pain with compassion, even though part of me initially thought that it was excessive. I couldn't relate to her tears, and as I observed my disconnection, I recognized the old pattern of indifference I had developed towards death. I softened within myself and held a sacred space for Sarah's sorrow, calling in the grace of spirit for help. It is only with the willingness to witness life without judgment that we enter into harmony with what wants to happen naturally in each moment of our lives. Listening to Sarah opened me to her and to myself.

A few years later, it was my turn to cry over the loss of a cat; my housemate's two cats that she took with her when she moved away. Those cats had been my companions, and I had grown close to them. Interestingly, the day of the move, both cats bounced up the stairs to my room and spent the whole afternoon with me before their departure. I sobbed for days in a way that shook me deeply; it dissolved the entire holding on to grief that I had stored from my mother's death.

Balancing Power Struggles

We have all garnered ways of coping with distress and deflecting what makes us feel uncomfortable, to the point of abandoning each other's inner child and the innocence of children. This is especially significant when it comes to youth, for their vulnerability is even more susceptible; their need for our support and love is crucial. By opening our eyes, we really see them, we see their joys, their gifts, and we welcome them. In this way we welcome all innocence, and we heal the negligence and abuse that causes so much suffering in this world. We begin by opening our eyes to our own experience, and we suspend judgment to encompass greater levels of compassion for one another.

Masiandia: *"We want you to open your eyes and recognize that despondency, anguish and suffering happen every single day at the hands of neglect and abuse. For children, it could be from a school bully, an older brother, a cousin, an aunt or even a grandmother who sometimes says cruel things. Though it is unintentional, the harm is done. Why would an adult want to hurt a child? Why would a child want to hurt another child? To attain power … due to feeling powerless. People feel powerless because they have been disempowered through shame and betrayal in a world that admires strength and shuns weakness, which perpetuate the roles of oppressor and victim.*

"This wide gulf between dominance and servitude represents a false interpretation of power, an acceptance of the pretence that force is stronger and better, while frailty is ridiculed or ignored. Because of this, so many people are denied their rightful value, which develops into the fear of one's own soulful empowerment. Because of this misapprehension of power, the mind takes control of the senses, positioning itself in an authoritative role. Thus, the innocence of a child, or the childlike quality of an adult is admired even less; it is the disciplined and logical mind that is revered and rewarded.

"Some children, who are incessantly shunned and ridiculed, later become adults who experience a lack of power with people their own age but have authority over children because children are unguarded, fragile and dependent on them. But these wounded adults are threatened by a child's needs — they control children so that they don't have to feel their own resonating need for love. Unable to acknowledge and value their own needs, they are triggered by a child's vulnerability because it reveals their emotional nakedness. Disarmed and ashamed, they retaliate, forcing their will upon the child.

"Children are abused because in your world, innocence and vulnerability are not honoured. The gentle quality of a child's spirit and playfulness is not admired. They are told how to play, how to learn, how to study — but they are not heard. For the most part, a child's voice is denied, which contributes to the abuse of children because denial doesn't empower them. Without self-empowerment, children cannot draw to them compassionate love, respect and safety. It is love

and acceptance that empowers them, and that returns them to a deep sense of peace, strengthening their connection to their soul.

"You may ask, 'how do we give the gift of compassionate, unconditional love?' Desire it! Be it! Love is not some sort of accomplishment that you achieve with effort, and it is not enlightenment. It is a gift. It is not something you do to prove your worthiness or your devotion – it is who you are. Be in love with your child. Be in love with the child that resides within you. And how do you give unconditional love to this inner innocence? See beyond your reactions, after all they are just reactions, and beyond them is a deep longing to connect, to love.

"So how do you love? Feel your longing for love to realize its manifestation within you. But many of you ask, 'how do we feel that deep-seated longing?' Let go of the protected heart. Release your self-defence. Your feelings are too power-ful to remain harnessed. Constant repression of self inevitably wreaks havoc in your lives, leading to a creative imbalance, poverty, pain and illness. Free your emotions by embracing them. They are beautiful: complex and incredible expres-sions of your spirit.

"We ask you to feel more so that you become an open vessel that welcomes spirit in your lives. In this way, your deep feelings become woven into high-er-vibrational energies, which then ripple out into the world, creating a whole spectrum of pure divinity. By tapping into the wellspring of your deep feeling, you empower your inner-innocence and all innocence in the world; you give the children of the world compassionate love, respect and safety. When children are empowered, they are not abused because their magnetic fields are aligned to complementary energies; their sense of self-value is naturally reflected in their encounters.

"Still, the task of helping children believe in themselves has been greatly misunderstood and misused. For instance, there are many parents who aspire to empower their children by giving them too much freedom, but do not teach them healthy boundaries. They shelter their children from the consequences of their ac-tions by letting them do whatever they want to do, which does not empower them.

"Even children who live in secure homes where their physical needs are met and there is no fighting or abuse are still not empowered if they are not heard or seen. When children are not acknowledged for who they really are, they are expected to conform to moulds of their parents' creation, hence they develop ways to adapt to the constant repression of their energies: ways that betray their true identities – their souls. We are here to challenge and thus free the patterns of abuse that betray the heart of all of your innocence and beauty."

Patience, Acceptance and Loving Kindness

*I*f we as adults weren't repressing our inner child, we wouldn't pass on to our children the pattern of disempowerment. Hence, we need to empower ourselves to give children a chance to be who they really are. We need to honour our own feelings and needs, so that we can be honest with our children, to empower them and help them value themselves. We also must do the hard work of letting go of our children's dislike of us, to cease taking it personally. The same goes for self-judgment and the disapproval of others; we need to observe the disapproval objectively, with patience, acceptance and loving kindness.

A few years ago I witnessed my dear friend, Kelly, maintain a loving yet firm presence with her young daughter, who was insisting on staying at the park when it was time to leave. Kenzie, about three years old at the time, affirmed her right to stay; she flailed her arms up in the air, kicked out her heels and yelled harsh words, tears welling up in her eyes. She told her mom that she hated her, and Kelly responded gently by saying, "Oh, that's okay, sweetheart, I still love you."

This went on for at least 15 minutes, as Kelly walked back to the parking lot with her son and me, while Kenzie lagged behind, slowly inching her way, rebellious and unhappy. All the time Kelly did not make her wrong; she didn't judge her. I was relieved that Kelly didn't stay behind to justify herself by explaining why we had to go; she didn't cajole her daughter into submitting, and there was no criticism, anger or manipulation. Kelly's message was clear and unwavering; it was time to leave, dinner was waiting.

Defiance and resistance are transformed into trust when we have the freedom to express our least likable characteristics and know that we can still be loved. This is conveyed so beautifully in Gordon Neufeld's book, *Hold On to Your Kids.* He writes, "Unconditional parental love is the indispensable nutrient for the child's healthy emotional growth. The first task is to create space in the child's heart for the certainty that she is precisely the person the parents want and love. She does not have to do anything or be any different to earn that love" ... "The child can be ornery, unpleasant, whiny, uncooperative, and plain rude, and the parent still lets her feel loved."

Without emotional support, we try to fit in and become sculpted by society's expectations and acceptable moulds. Shame and ridicule teach us to become defended against our natural feelings. In his parenting course, *Helping Your Children Grow,* Neufeld says that repeated disapproval causes a child to learn to defend himself against vulnerability by tuning out perceptions that lead to sensitive feelings. When this happens, the mind cannot move the child to maturity. He explains that the heart is a very vulnerable place, and a child's mind protects the heart against vulnerability that is too much to bear. Neufeld writes, "If you lose the ability to feel sad about the things that do not work in your lives, you also lose the ability to feel fulfilled by the things that do work." When we shut out emotions that frighten us, we shut down the channel, not the emotions, like the tree that draws away from brackish water, withdrawing its roots and never getting the nourishment it needs.

When children are kept from the light, a prison of darkness surrounds them, attracting lower vibrational energy. Without healthy self-empowerment, children do not value themselves enough to secure good boundaries, their natural talents do not develop and they struggle throughout life for a sense of self-confidence and self-worth. They internalize the lack of support by believing that they are unworthy. When we learn to value ourselves, we are empowered, and in this way we empower children by helping them recognize their inherent potential and worthiness.

We all need heart connection and to rest in the certainty that we are protected and cared for. We need to be liberated from having to work so hard for love, to be supported, welcomed and accepted for who we really are. And we need to see in ourselves, our children and others, the depth of inner innocence that is inherently part of all our emotions. Motivated by deep feelings, we are propelled forward on our spiritual journeys; we embrace all of our experiences with profound acceptance, and we return to love.

> *If*
> *you were to love me right now*
> *what would it look like?*
>
> *Would you see me in your image?*
> *Moulding, scolding*
> *your needs unaware of me,*
> *folding and unfolding*
> *this image that is not I.*
>
> *Would you see me drift away?*
> *Slowly at first.*
> *Miles away to know myself.*
> *Sinking sadly into me –*
> *a river running through*
> *always to you.*
> *A river sometimes black.*
> *Would you see the river clear?*
>
> *If you were to love me right now*
> *Would you see me as I am?*

Relinquishing Control

Masiandia: *"The feeling body is the doorway to your soul, which frightens most of you immensely because the soul is a free agent that threatens to break down social structures. So many of you long for your soul essence, yet are simultaneously terrified of it, as you don't want to relinquish the dominion of the rational mind. Please understand that control is a defence against feeling powerless, therefore, the tendency to control others and yourselves, as well as situations, is a false means to gain power.*

"Your societies are based on a fundamental construct wherein power means control, which perpetuates the duality of victim and abuser. When there is a struggle for control, then there is an underlying fear of losing control, based on the belief that power is scarce. Those who try to control themselves and others are disempowered and contribute to mass-conscious disharmony.

"Power is not about coercing or forcing others to do what you want them to do. Power is love, compassion, trust and growth; it is the essence of a seed rooting itself, an infant's birth and a mother's breathing and forceful pushing during the birthing. Power is discipline when motivated by inspiration. Power is commitment, the hard work of believing.

"We know that some of you are angry with regards to the abuse that children suffer, and you are afraid. Your reactions, disgust and judgments are understandable, for it is something you wish did not exist in the world. However, remaining in judgment only contributes to that which you wish did not exist, for you are perpetuating abuse with your judgments.

"Please, take the time to understand that there are people who are lost in the shadows of your societies, who are disconnected from their soul-essence and hence powerless. These are men and women who were abandoned as children by societies that deny the embodiment of feeling and innocence. They feel betrayed by the rules and morals of society, because they have not been protected from unjust acts of neglect and abuse in their own childhoods. They have become doorways to fear, self-punishment and hate. Imagine that you are the lost man, the

boy whose mother never found him, the person who never got a glimmer of hope.
What is left? Hunger, rage, confusion, anguish."

*W*hat do we do in a land of confusion and anguish? Our defini-
tion of innocence is so narrow. We don't realize that in trying to
protect innocence we become monsters; we become controllers. By judging others, we become just like them. We need to see that we are not different from one another; we are the same, a mirror of each other. In one
another is the reflection of our shadow and light. Sting depicts this boldly
in his song, *Tomorrow We'll See*, with lyrics portraying a prostitute telling
the listener, "Don't judge me/ You could be me in another life/ in another
set of circumstances."

If we hold fast to the notion that we are better than others, we cross
over a threshold into arrogance, overshadowing others with our self-im-
portance. After all, the prostitute could be an angel; perhaps she's a saint.
Maybe she's bringing solace to another human being who would otherwise feel desperately alone. On a soul level, a profound healing could be
taking place between a prostitute and her client that our rational minds
cannot begin to fathom. When we become so caught up in being perfect
as defined by social norms, we expect others to be impeccable; we don't
notice the purity of God in all life.

Masiandia: *"You all judge, so go ahead and judge, just pay close attention to
how it creates separation in your life. Notice how it perpetuates blame and defiance. People tend to cast blame onto others or themselves to try to alleviate suffering. They maintain the tyranny of self-defence and criticism, rather than share
the healing gift of compassion, as a way to avoid change.*

*"Through self-observation, you have the power to evolve, to let go of judg-
ment and release your defended self, so that you can be at peace with who you are
and with the world. Peace is born out of the undefended self, when you no longer
have the need to fight against your inner critic. When you are no longer guarded*

against feelings, yours and others', then you are free of blame and censorship, free to express and truly enjoy who you are.

"In letting go of the need to defend yourself against judgment, you inevitably heal the wound of abuse in this world because you nurture innocence. Acceptance and compassion transforms the lower frequency of abuse into higher vibrational energy, gently sculpting it into a new life-affirming shape. With an undefended and nurturing presence, you accept your part in the polarity between oppression and suffering, no longer identifying with one or the other.

When you no longer have a need to justify your beliefs or your right to exist – you relinquish the role of attacker or victim. You are then whole, no longer tormented by what someone said or did, or for injustices in the world. You no longer need to be right or conversely collapse into helplessness, or fight back to gain some level of power. Instead, you 'remember' who you are and honour your part in the full spectrum of human experience.

"It is necessary that you realize that injustice, exploitation and oppression are part of the social structure and lineage of human incarnation, and that you cannot get rid of these because the act of trying to annihilate abuse is abusive. Any form of control is abusive because it causes separation; it discriminates between right and wrong, rather than supports unity. We are asking you to view abuse in a whole new way, a way that sees it as a signal. Just as your body uses pain signals to communicate danger, abuse gives voice to the wound in your society – it is a messenger.

"But so many of you are afraid of making a mistake, of being wrong, or seen as foolish or weak, that you inadvertently ignore abuse; you tolerate disrespect and unreasonable expectations, or you are indignant and righteous, defended against beliefs contrary to your own. To compensate for this, the human mind becomes trapped in logic, justifying or condemning abuse, thus perpetuating the victim/perpetrator roles.

"But whether abuse is inflicted upon you or you are the offender, it is the same energy-frequency that contributes to physical, mental and emotional suffering in the world. Whether you are the controller or whether you are controlled

– it's the same thing. If you are the controller, something is controlling you. Perhaps it is deep shame from an abusive past, a sense of powerlessness, or fear of change and abandonment that is then projected onto others. To stop the cycle of victim/perpetrator, you must cease defending or rationalizing your feelings, and instead recognize that whatever side of the conflict you are on, you are part of the same problem. You are reinforcing duality by either choosing to uphold one side of the battlefield or the other; you are not at the centre of peace. True liberation does not come from separation, but from beholding the spiritual union between consciousness and form.

"Your contribution to peace, balance and wholeness comes from complete accountability, from being a compassionate witness, 'seeing' that you hold the power to channel your soul-essence, that you are not a victim, not oppressed, not alone, not insignificant, and not powerless! You are immeasurably infinite and part of something so much bigger than all the suffering that holds you back from truly loving this world and you in it.

⸺∞⸺

The "Feeling" Approach

*W*e transform unconscious patterns by becoming conscious of them, by accepting them, so that we can understand how these patterns have shaped us. We become more conscious through the practice of connecting deeply with what we feel, though initially many of us tend to think our way through feeling, which inevitably impedes the flow of transformation. To feel is to suspend the mind long enough to not understand what we're feeling at all, but rather enter into a deepening of the feeling, which is a state of expansion and release.

Masiandia endeavours to help us recognize just how important the practice of feeling really is. *"Feel more,"* they say, over and over again. But many people are afraid of feeling more, stating that they will become more enraged or depressed, and more afraid. But what they don't realize is that by feeling more, the feelings change. Feeling our emotions creates a shift of consciousness. When we "feel" into reactions, we recognize what is being triggered, and we connect with what is opening in us, rather than remain stuck in the initial emotional reaction.

Without self-awareness, the energy behind emotions is projected onto outside circumstances, which leaves its mark on everything we touch. Lessening this damaging influence calls for us to connect with our repressed feelings and discover something remarkable about ourselves, which is the exiled and abandoned parts of us that hold so much grace and freedom, and wisdom. These imprisoned shapes of our beauty and power are hidden aspects within us constantly calling out towards the light.

An illustration of the transformational power of becoming consciously aware of and accepting one's feelings brings me to my client Nancy, who first came to me broken and ashamed of herself. Nancy had woven her self-value into her dream of the perfect marriage, but she was now alone, struggling with a sick child and no child-support. Shortly after her separation, her daughter was diagnosed with Progressive Epilepsy, and Nancy's only support, her mother, passed away not long after. Challenged by these three circumstances, she was devastated, overwhelmed and afraid.

The sessions focused on helping her move through her feeling-states with empathy, so that she could explore the depths of her grief without collapsing in despair. She needed to be understood, and she also needed to awaken to her divine will – to her inner strength. By completely connecting with her grief, Nancy uncovered a core belief that had kept her feeling small and insignificant. She came to realize that she blamed herself for failing to live her dream, a belief that robbed her of her personal power. She was able to let go of her self-judgements and regrets, and discover that no matter what occurred in her life, she had courage, faith and a growing self-respect. She came to realize that the situations in her life, especially her daughter's health concerns, were forces of nature urging her to be powerful, which is what she and her daughter needed. She saw that she was a resilient and devoted mother and that there was support for her, support that she hadn't let herself receive because of her shame.

As we see the broken and misshapen parts of us, we come to appreciate that there is nothing flawed about us, and instead there is a natural longing from within for love and courage. By welcoming our shadow, we honour who we truly are and become receptive to our spirit guides and angels, who shower us with love as we step into our willingness to accept every part of ourselves with absolute reverence. In this way, we embrace our healing journeys and begin to make discerning and positive choices.

To illustrate this, in their following message Masiandia explores a scenario in which a mother has been pushed to the edge of her unconscious trigger point. Through this example, they show us how rather than reacting to external situations, we can make more discerning choices by being attentive to the underlying framework associated with the reaction.

Masiandia: *"We want to walk you through an illustration of a mother with her son, who has reached her breaking point due to his disobedience. He is not responding to her, and the situation has gotten out of control. Can you imagine that? You may not be a parent, but most likely you can relate with her frustration. In this situation, her frustration has become so great that she almost hits her child.*

"Just before she is about to strike him, she stops long enough to observe her reaction. She feels powerless because she cannot control him. She wants to be heard, she wants to be respected, and she also wants to be seen and loved. But he cannot give her that attention for he is competing for the same thing, jousting for what he needs. They both have an identical need to be seen and heard, which seeks fulfilment. As an adult, she must become aware of her feelings to stop projecting her needs onto her child. By opening her eyes and her inner senses and feeling

her emotional experiences, she can begin to heal and make better choices for both of them.

"The initial contact with these feelings is painful, and often people don't take the time to go through this process of self-inquiry, which is why they disconnect and distract themselves instead of delving deeper into their honest experience. It is important to focus inwardly on the subject of your emotional triggers, for it is by going within that you discover the roots of your beliefs. In this way, you free yourself to better manifest who you really are. You are not your belief systems. You are not your shame, or your discomfort. You are beings of pure love and devotion to life.

"In this story, the mother chooses to not react violently, she instead calms her reaction and discovers her feelings. In doing so, she realizes that she falsely believes she is unworthy of love. It is no wonder that you resist your feeling body, for to feel is to be in direct contact with false beliefs – beliefs that do not serve your soul or your personality. How can these beliefs be challenged if you avoid them, and how can they be transformed into a clear reflection of your true essence if you neglect to recognize where your reactions stem from?

"It is only by uncovering these false beliefs through a deep exploration of your feelings, that you can choose the life you really desire. How can you choose to manifest love, happiness and a sense of purposefulness if the underlying law of attraction in your life is tied to the belief that you cannot have what you want? This belief contributes to the scarcity of your self-power. By choosing to believe that life does not support you, you are left in a very dark and lonely place, starving for nourishment – starving for love.

"We see a worldwide humanity starving for love, which contributes to poverty and starvation in the world. When does it stop? When does the abuse stop? Please stop now. Feel yourselves. Feel every part of your lives and your interactions with other human beings, and discover who you really are, which has nothing to do with self-deprecation or fear of loss. The Universe is abundant with purposeful belonging, vitality and love."

*T*o feel is to free ourselves from deception and to open to the higher source of resonance and truth. To feel is the hero's journey to the underworld, to drink from the river of remembrance rather than go to the well of forgetting. My heart yearns to draw wisdom from this river – from the holy sanctum of my own divinity – and receive the immense gift that is here for me. And for me, it is a call to step off the edge, in courage and readiness to welcome the Divine in all things and surrender my love.

Masiandia: *"You cultivate a loving relationship with all life by feeling your emotions and by not getting caught up in your rational mind. When you refuse to experience your feelings, your ego-persona conjures up stories, identifying with self-defences, actions and reactions to ensure its survival, unless and until you are willing to let go and return to your deeper truth.*

"There is no separation between your ego and your spirit. They are two sides of one coin. Your ego is a tool, a necessary physiological, psychological, cognitive faculty that is meant to serve the higher purpose of your spirit. But the ego is out of balance when it doesn't know what its purpose is, when it doesn't realize its role in life, which is to serve spirit.

"In service, your ego consciously chooses to follow a higher vibration of intelligence with love, compassion and forgiveness, while maintaining your security and well-being. The ego must evolve like all of life on Earth, by discovering the rich resources found in all of your feeling states. It must cease overriding anger, shame, sadness, hurt and fear to tap into a deep reserve of inner wisdom. Then it can transform limitations into creative solutions, as it interconnects with your soul.

"Compassionate acceptance of your feelings cultivates a deep and rich connection with soul; it links intellectual knowledge with spiritual wisdom that supports you in being true to yourself. You must come to understand that your feelings are the entrance to your soul-consciousness, always ready to divulge a more authentic expression of who you are."

CHAPTER FOUR

Longing, Our Soul Connection

Far in the distant horizon, a dark silhouette
gazes across the great expanse – seeing nothing but you.
An ocean of light blinds him and he looks away.
When he looks back, you are gone.

He travels far and wide – over years and valleys
in search of you.
When he reaches the horizon where you had once stood,
he looks back across the ocean – still looking for you.

He sees into the distance a figure looking back.
He sees himself, a dark shape in the past blinded by light
He sees a man searching for love.

Now he recognizes you –
still so bright that it blinds him
until he closes his eyes.
The distance disappears, and he finds you.

Engaging Wholeheartedly with Life

Longing is often associated with dissatisfaction, with something that we don't have and never will, or that we have yet to attain. But in its true essence, longing is so much more. It is a call from within that moves us beyond the collective unconscious, beyond the echoes of the past or the fear of the future. When we connect with the true essence of our longing, we become mesmerized by its feeling-quality, rather than preoccupied with trying to manifest it.

It is by connecting with the feeling-quality of desires that we cease being distracted by the effort or struggle to achieve what we want, and align with possibilities that support its manifestation. We are meant to embody an intimate relationship with desires, not externalize them. Only in this way can life meet our longing. By no longer projecting perceived ideas and expectation onto life, we allow our longing to guide us back to our true self – to the propelling force at the heart of desire, which we embody through feelings.

By feeling into our longing we welcome it and step out of mental structures that impede the natural evolution of our creative purpose. We never cease to evolve, and like the infant that comes into the world breaking free from the fetal membrane, we must step beyond the deceptions of our veiled selves to become co-creators with our multidimensional souls. This takes patience, persistence and willingness to feel everything in order to renew ourselves.

"The human perception of reality needs constant reminding of a greater embodiment of expanded reality, a reality that is flexible and fluid and free of discrimination," explains Masiandia. They ask us to welcome everything, leave nothing behind, whether we deem it "good" or "bad." We are asked to feel it all, because when our feelings are explored, they change into fluid expressions that support our fundamental needs. Frustration and discontentment, for instance, transform into curiosity that then kindles

inspiration, and inspiration acts as a strong magnetic pulse that allows the abundance of life to flow into our lives. The same is true for other emotions such as fear, shame and grief, which also transform into expanded expressions that induce healing and change.

Feeling into our longing has the power to help us slow down and truly connect with our essence. Masiandia has said countless times, *"Longing is not found outside of you – it is within you. It is the natural foundation for manifesting the life you want and must be felt internally to realize its potential."* Longing is an essential state without which we would have no fuel to power our intentions.

"When you really want something, it's because the desire originated in the soul of the universe," writes Paulo Coelho in *The Alchemist*. And as Masiandia says, we would not yearn for something if it could not be fulfilled. Our yearning becomes metamorphic, like the iridescent nacre inside an oyster shell that transforms an irritant piece of sand into a natural pearl. The oyster secretes a smooth, crystalline substance around the sand that over time becomes completely encased by a silky coating, resulting in a lustrous gem. As in the metaphor of the pearl, our longing is an iridescent layering that has the power to change reality, to transform obstacles into something beautiful. When we embrace our longing, we no longer search for anything, we cease struggling with reality and we behold the wonders in life. In this way, our longing is fulfilled by simply sensing into it, not by justifying it or by trying to bring it to completion.

Feeling into our longing is a way in which we reflect our light, a way of returning to our inner source and acting from it. We do this by taking the "want" out of desire so that we can connect with the rich and meaningful support of our soul. In this way, longing is no longer related to something we have yet to attain, but rather is a way of "seeing" what is possible now. Longing does not project the past onto the present or the future; it connects us to a much freer way of being, beyond our habitual perception of reality. Ultimately, connecting with our longing calls for us to stop saying "no" to the emergence of our dreams and finally saying "yes" to playing in life's possibilities.

Masiandia: *"When you connect inwardly with your longing, you dissolve all the limiting beliefs that prevent you from enjoying and celebrating life. You enter into a soulful encounter with life where your goals become guideposts, not destinations, and you embrace your fears with acceptance and gentleness, as well as celebrate your dreams. To dream, to fully dream, is not lofty or impossible when it is rooted in your present life. It is fantasy that impedes your life's purpose, not your dreams. To fantasize about the life you think you want without consideration of your current circumstances only serves to cause disappointment and defeat, but joining the present with your longing allows you to uncover the path that is always changing and divinely aligned with your purpose.*

"The next time you say something like, 'I have a long way to go for my healing, success and love,' please stop! Come back to the beauty and perfection of your life with all of its challenges, hardships and bountiful joys. Your Earthly life is not all that it seems; you are indeed so much more than your physical experience. You are a magical being, and returning to the depth of your longing brings you back in touch with yourself. This is how you 'create' the life that best serves you."

Beyond Ancestral Lineage – Transcending Time

Masiandia: *"Engaging with your longing fills you with vibrational support and strengthens your magnetic core. Naturally, your magnetic energy must be strong to make manifest your dreams. However, many of you resist feeling your longing, weakening your magnetic core, because you don't value yourselves. The reason that you have difficulty in valuing yourselves is that there are unbalanced grid-patterns within the Earth plane, which naturally affect you. These grid-patterns are layers of ancestral lineage that influence who you think you are, overshadowing your higher-self.*

"Your sense of identity is initially shaped out of the cellular imprint of your karmic relationship with physical incarnation, which defines your family, and your physiology, as well as the time and space you are born in. Connecting with your longing is a way in which you transcend the time and space of your birth and unravel the ancestral influences that shape your sense of self. In this way, you inevitably help heal Earth's energy-grids by releasing the way in which they affect you.

"A predominant grid-pattern that causes so much upheaval is humanity's mass-conscious perception of time, in which past, present and the future is delineated in a sequence of order. As we mentioned before, time is not linear; the past and the future are here now, therefore, time is whole, it is vast and all encompassing. From your human perspective, however, the past is tangible and not changeable. You regard your history as something that is inflexible, but we know that the past has changed, and it doesn't exist the same way that it is remembered.

"The past actually exists only in the present, therefore, it is influenced by present perception. This means that you can change your past based on your present thoughts and feelings. You can literally change the message that the cells in your body received in the womb and completely alter the framework of your physical nature. How? With the expansion of your perception of reality: by encompassing a larger sense of who you truly are.

"You must look beyond the lens of your history to cease repeating past tendencies and beliefs passed down through generations. When you are no longer confined to the linear perspective, your desires and your natural gifts and talents define your present life, not your past or your ancestors' past. You are free to 'see' the present through an engaged perception of reality, which nourishes the past and the development of your authentic expression.

We want this freedom for you, to see you opened to the divine in you; receptive and willing to flourish in whatever you do, wherever you are. We want you to be shaped by your lineage only as it serves your soul, only as it encompasses divinity, giving your essence a form in which to express itself. In this way, your DNA, your sacred biology, is activated by an expanded sense of the present, not by your lineage. Be conscious – be awake to you, otherwise you become a mere reflection of your ancestors, repeating the same story over lifetimes.

Your lineage is only a reflection of your soul at birth; it is not the full expression of your soul-purpose or its evolution. This means that while you are woven into your family's genealogy at birth, you only maintain that ancestral enmeshment until you grow beyond it. This growth is initiated by the desire to know oneself, and it starts with self-awareness. The soul chooses its family lineage based on agreements made between family members. The influence of family lineage pertains only to the conception that links both parents' genealogies into the fertilized egg and developing fetus, until birth. From birth onward, the soul is 'free' to move past its initial soul-in-body contract.

"The soul incarnates within families, demographics and timeframes that pertain to the soul's purpose, which serves to integrate karmic relationships, shared lessons and growth. Once the soul has incarnated within its intended blueprint, it must grow beyond karmic family ties to express the whole vibration of its purpose. This doesn't mean that family ties have no bearing on your life path. Quite the contrary, the family you are born into provides your body and mind with the necessary energy dynamic – the framework that links your spirit with life. It serves to anchor your spirit into human embodiment, supporting all that you are here to learn and share in order to evolve. Still, you are not your family's dependant, nor are you its keeper.

"The purpose of your soul encompasses so much more than your family of origin will allow. You must relinquish your dependency on the lineage and personality that your soul chose to embody at birth, because your soul must evolve into a larger expression of its beauty and belonging. This means that you are not here to 'repeat' family patterns with addiction, or carry on genetic illnesses, or perpetuate conditioned responses to stress such as with constant worry, negligence and even violent outbreaks. You are here to grow beyond these conditions and behaviours, to evolve not only your own soul but also your family lineage, in order to cease passing on to newer generations the unbalanced and afflicted energies of your genetic imprint."

*T*he reality of what is and is not possible in life is defined by what the members of a group – a family – agree upon and maintain, explains Caroline Myss in *Leaving the Wounded Relationship Tribe*: "While the tribal mentality has definite benefits in terms of establishing common ground and ensuring group survival, it is not a conscious agreement." She suggests that at a certain stage we must challenge the tribal mind to evolve our consciousness, both personally and collectively.

We do this by diving into our soul-purpose, which supports us in cultivating an intimate relationship with our longing. Then we're not actually "challenging" anything; we're stepping into a more expansive reality that encompasses so much more than the collective limitation. By connecting with our longing, we cease to over-identify with our lineage; we move past the patterns that we inherit and break the chains that bind us to outmoded beliefs. When we embrace our soul presence, we communicate and interact in more meaningful ways and make choices that support who we are meant to be.

As this natural evolution unfolds, we move beyond the limitations of our family dynamics and return to love. In love, we gently pry ourselves apart from messages that we received growing up: messages that do not support us to be who we really are. Had I remained ingrained in the limitations of my family heritage, I would not have honoured my healing purpose or dedicated my life to art; I would not have chosen to write this book. The patterns of my lineage are rooted in the belief that we cannot have what we want. My father did not pursue his musical talents; my mother was a healer with no desire to live; and my grandmother drowned her sensitivity in alcohol.

In my early adolescence, my grandparents who I lived with suggested that I become a secretary, as they believed that artists earn a poor living. They did not acknowledge my love for art or encourage me to pursue it. Close to my thirteenth birthday, I asked my grandfather for an artist's paint set. He refused, stating that he had given his daughter, from his first marriage, a paint-set many years before, which had been left in the back of her bedroom and had been a waste of money. Had he not noticed that I was constantly creating with fabric, clay and pencil drawing, and that I had expressed my desire to be an artist?

A year later, after I had moved in with my father, I took my own active step in honouring my longing; I bought a second-hand paint set from a friend and painted everything in sight from pieces of wood, tin cans and plates right up to the kitchen cupboard doors, with my dad's encouragement. Several years later I went to art school, though without the financial or emotional support of my family. They just didn't get it; no one in my family had been to college, especially not for fine arts. I persevered, but not without self-doubt and fear. In some ways I had no choice, or perhaps the longing to follow my artistic vision was greater than anything else.

Healing Your Ancestors

Some inherited traits grant us inborn talents, abilities and virtues, while others lead to addiction, genetic predisposition to disease and psychological struggles that influence our present day relationship with our bodies, minds and spirits. These predisposed traits are made manifest and maintained by the beliefs and attitudes that our families still have towards life.

We inherit our family's dispositions by virtue of our genealogy, but we needn't stay stagnant in this inheritance. We can transform the challenges we inherit into fodder for self-awareness to enhance our life-experience. We can't escape our genetics, but we can have an empowered relationship with it, rather then be victimized and wounded by it.

By transforming the patterns of our lineage, we become the healers of all our ancestors; we release those who have gone before us, as well as the children yet to come. We release conditioned responses and limiting beliefs that inhibit all of us from receiving the gifts inherent in the lineage that we inherit, gifts that are meant to serve our soul-purpose, not hinder it.

Personally, I inherited a disposition towards depression. My mother had tried to take her own life many times before she was murdered. She coped with life challenges and the pain that resurfaced from her childhood by collapsing into profound insecurity and addiction. I remember her neglect, not her love, but when my dad told me that she was also a healer, I saw myself in her, her in me; I saw the way in which her depressive tendencies are held within my own. I think of her when the shadow of melancholy sits at the end of my bed; I call to her spirit; I endeavour to remember that I am more than her legacy, and I am freeing the healer that she is inside of me.

She is more than a memory, more than my mother; she is a tidal wave of beauty moving through me, a reflection of my own purpose. In her pain and our shared history, I can see suffering or I can see the spirit of our karmic relationship and let it take root in my being, let it show me the way to a more life-affirming journey, one that completely frees the healer that she was and that I am.

Masiandia says that our souls choose to incarnate within particular ancestral patterns to work through unresolved karma and master life lessons. These lessons serve to bring forth our longing, open us to the spirit in everything and evoke our soul-purpose. Therefore, our souls are born into life circumstances that best serve our purpose, and from there we must evolve.

Freeing the Past

iscovering the voice of our longing beckons us to relinquish control and allows life to reveal its beauty, which requires non-judgemental witnessing. By observing life-experiences with compassion and curiosity, we become consciously aware of the lineage we inherited. We become aware of what defines our sense of self and ultimately discover the freedom of who we really are.

In a process of self-observation, my client Craig courageously set aside his armour and healed the past by releasing his attachment to anger. He had struggled so much in life to maintain his sense of identity, forming an ego-persona that would defend him at the least provocation. He yearned for contentment and peace, and he wanted a relationship, but his anger separated him from the people he loved.

Through exploring his deeper feelings, he understood that due to having been painfully criticized and ridiculed as a child, he developed a tough exterior to offset the shame he felt. His ego-persona served him fairly well for the first part of his life, as it helped him identify with being strong and capable of handling adversity. However, bulldozing his way through challenges hindered the intimacy he longed for and warded off the support he needed to feel loved. His persona manifested the same life experience he had as a child – the feeling of being unsupported, let down, abandoned and betrayed. Yet no matter how much he understood this cognitively, he still reacted angrily as the result of feeling unloved and ashamed.

It can be tremendously challenging to acknowledge ego-personas, since oftentimes we are unaware of them, as they become such an intricate part of who we think we are. Craig became aware of his false identity when he entered "the dark night of the soul," provoked by deep feelings of internal pain that manifested physically and emotionally. In session, he recalled past memories associated with the way in which his father had treated him. He explored the patterns of anger in his family and got in touch with physical, emotional and mental abuse he endured as a result of his father's rage.

Craig's ego-personality couldn't protect him from this pain; he had to call in the wisdom of his spirit and face what he feared, so that he could release the memories. As Craig observed and willingly felt this pain, he discovered a deep core of shame that was not only about his past, but which was also associated with his father's past. With Masiandia's support and hypnotherapy, Craig realized that his father had been ritually abused, and that Craig had carried his father's shame, anguish and dread for many years.

When Craig focused inwardly, he entered into the realm of his feelings and received the support he needed to release his defended persona. That is where healing takes place, through the willingness to feel and move beyond the hindrance of self-protection. For Craig, facing his shame was intense, yet feeling and being vulnerable enabled him to open to and receive the love of his spirit.

Through this process, Craig recognized that feeling pain within his emotional body only seems overwhelming initially, but in truth it is not. Experiencing our feelings is not what causes pain; it releases pain. Pain is actually caused by resisting, by restricting our breath and intuitive life-force, which then triggers reactive thoughts. Therefore, healing requires deep breathing and a gentle surrender into the feeling state. And it is through feeling that we connect with our longing – with our purpose.

Re-Writing the Old Script

Masiandia: *"As you connect with your longing, you welcome your soul, which is highly fulfilling yet simultaneously challenging, because it is a state of surrender that refuses to conform to the conventions of society. To feel into your longing opens you to expanded reality beyond the known, which naturally brings up many fears and self-doubts and the tendency to slide back into old frameworks.*

"It's instinctive to try to protect yourself against what you fear, even though it keeps you from living fully. However, your greatest joy lies in being willing to stop being small, stop being right or wrong and to finally just be honest. In

that way, life has a way of showing you that you're not alone; your needs are not invalid and your desires are beautiful.

"Ultimately, it is the willingness to be honest with your feelings and experiences that strengthens your sense of authentic expression, which helps you reframe your perceptions of reality and thus rewrite old family scripts. Through this process of self-awareness you strengthen your core-value and define for yourself who you are and what you want out of life. You also grow your empathy and compassion towards yourself and others – you encounter life with the willingness to meet each challenge with the heart of forgiveness. Being authentic is empowering for it returns you to your whole sense of self, supporting you in discovering what wants to unfold naturally in every moment of your life. It frees you to be the creator of your own life – your dreams – and ultimately it aligns to your soul-purpose.

"We know that it takes courage to re-write your script, because you don't really know what it is that you're creating. The unknown beckons you, and in truth you don't realize its full potential. Further, it can seem absolutely outrageous to detach from your heritage, because when your behaviour differs from your family's behaviour, you challenge their expectations.

"You may get pulled back into old habits when a family member tries to persuade you to be the person she/he is familiar with. As you remain clear in your intention and maintain a strong connection to who you are, this family member will most likely object, because unconsciously he/she knows that you have abandoned the old script and thus feels left behind. Can you imagine the strings attached to these scripts and all the people that may not want you to change in order to preserve the life that they know?

"We understand that it can be very challenging when the people you love hang on to the old script. Their perception of your shared reality is attached to your lineage; it is attached to where you think you come from: where many of you still think you belong. Yet it is an illusion, for in order to be 'yourself' you must entrust your present life with your spirit's full potential. You do this by

connecting to your longing, which releases the old script because you are no longer in the past.

"And then something miraculous happens in the present; you become more connected to your family, more forgiving, more understanding, compassionate and willing to let them be as they are and love them as they are, because you are whole and in love with yourself. It becomes easier to love others when you are connected to who you really are. You naturally connect to who you really are when you feel loved, and you feel loved when you welcome your longing. Only then can there be no resistance, no defence and no suffering."

*I*n love, we create a meaningful relationship with ourselves that imparts life-affirming messages to the cells of our body, to our genealogy, which is then passed on to our family. In this manner, we engage with others and ourselves in a whole new way, an approach that honours everyone's essential worthiness and purpose. We ultimately need to cultivate an intimate relationship with our own authentic selves to appreciate others, which begins by recognizing our own sense of worth.

It is by caring for our deepest longing that we create respectful and loving relationships with ourselves and thus with others. It leads to a natural redefining of the role that others play in our lives, because we no longer need them to maintain the old role. When we are connected to our own longing, to our soul's purpose, we don't require our family's limitations to define our sense of reality, and we don't need to struggle with any particular issue or person in order to free ourselves. Since we no longer need others to act as the catalysts for our growth, we release them from that role. We cease projecting our hurt and blame onto them. We see them in a different light, not defined by our reactions.

Ultimately, it is by re-evaluating our own perception and attitudes towards others that we can transform our relationships. This is evident in the story of Tina who, in the effort to heal and strengthen her sense of confidence, chose to stop wrestling with her mother's criticism. Tina redefined the role that her mother played in her life by learning to see her in a new way, a way that was no longer attached to the resentment that had afflicted their relationship. Prior to this new approach, Tina had defended herself against her mother's negativity, remaining stuck in the past, continuously repeating the same scenarios, until she understood that her mother's criticism was a way of connecting, and that the more that Tina distanced herself, the more her mother found fault in her.

Carol, Tina's mother, was lonely and afraid of being abandoned. She resisted feeling unloved by projecting her need to be loved onto her daughter, thus blamed Tina when Tina failed to act in ways that reassured her. For the longest time Tina got hooked into Carol's script because it was painful to be criticized. It triggered her own fear of abandonment. She participated in Carol's story by judging Carol, re-enacting the same pattern of blame and finding fault in others. But judging Carol only served to propagate the disconnection, not only with Carol but also with herself. When Tina accepted her mother just the way she is, without the need to change her or herself, she helped create a mutually caring and compassionate relationship. Carol is still at times critical, yet Tina is less affected, less overwhelmed and defended because she doesn't need to define her sense of self-value by Carol's expectations.

The Ego – An Intermediary Instrument

Masiandia: *"The soul is here to evolve through a co-creative relationship with change. However, the ego-mind works hard to maintain security. Thus, when you endeavour to make changes the ego can have a hard time maintaining faith, as it identifies with familiarity. However, without the ego you would step off cliffs because your spirit does not know physical limitation. You would go mad because you would not be shielded by the ego's assimilation of energy impulses from your physical environment. Even your soul's all-encompassing potential would be overwhelming without the ego to maintain your security, because your own soul-vibration activates change at a pace too challenging to accommodate physically."*

The ego has received a lot of negative attention in many spiritual schools of thought. It is believed to be the culprit for human dysfunctions, a false persona hindering the true self. I came across a message that supports a more compassionate understanding of the ego in *Spirit Wisdom*, an Alexander book channelled by Ramón Stevens. Alexander refers to the ego as the creator of our reality and says that the ego stands as the intermediary between our higher purpose and the beliefs we develop from childbirth. He says that the ego receives streams of information from our physical experiences, nervous system and senses, as well as from our higher self, future occurrences in our lives and through telepathic communication with others. And he suggests that without the ego, the streams of information would flood our mind and body to full intensity, causing a vibrational cacophony, disabling our ability to function. The ego acts as a processor of experiences and assimilates appropriate levels of information based on the threshold sustainable by the mind, body and nervous system.

But in a world culture that is defined by fear of abandonment, loss and failure, the ego's natural and healthy functioning is impeded. As Alexander explains, it is corrupted into maintaining a low-grade panic at all times. Therefore, the body is kept in constant survival mode, fuelling reactions and depleting one's health and well-being. Survival responses do not allow the body to restore, replenish, and repair or thrive, and they restrict the flow of one's spirit. When the ego is threatened, it blocks out conscious awareness, decreasing the mind's ability to absorb information by weakening the intensity of the feeling. When our feelings are suppressed, our connection to Source is lessened, perpetuating separation and anxiety, which manifests as physical and emotional pain.

Sometimes, we even personalize the pain, believing for instance, that if we were rejected as a child then we were not deserving of love, or that we did something wrong to merit rejection. Throughout life, these beliefs shape our interactions with others and with ourselves. Whatever these beliefs are, adopting them is the ego's way of trying to preserve our survival by protecting us from more harm. If a person believes that she is a failure, then she won't try to accomplish what she longs for because she might fail. By avoiding failure she is protecting herself from the possibility of failure. The ego negates positive affirmation in fear of not succeeding, thus it disbelieves the affirmation to protect against possible defeat.

Most of our present pain is rooted in the past. When we believe we are unworthy, we fear abandonment, thus we feel abandoned in the present because fear brings up the old feeling. When we try to annihilate the ego in the effort to move beyond habitual patterns, this only serves to threaten it even more. The ego actually needs to be accepted, like all parts of us. Imagine getting rid of your arm when it hurts: trying to get rid of the ego is no different. By empathizing with its attachment to familiarity, we support a healthy ego, a conscious mind that observes life without judgment.

Masiandia: *"The ego is a necessary tool that needs to move beyond repetitious frameworks in order to find balance and thus transform conditioned responses into fulfilling reality. What is important here is to pay close attention to your attachment to habitual perceptions, question your thoughts and explore other potential ideas, so that you can connect with your soulful belonging.*

"We understand just how challenging this can be, for the ego, in its attachment to familiarity, rejects the higher frequencies of the mystery of the soul. Longing is all about embodying the unknown, so it's no wonder that the ego is in conflict: the unknown cannot be controlled; it cannot be defined by rules. How can the ego protect you when it does not know what to expect? So by default it hangs on to the known for safety.

"Connecting with your longing speaks of feeling at home with your whole self, feeling like you belong and that you are blessed and worthy, not afraid,

worried, caught up in everything you think you're supposed to achieve and pro-
tect. But if you have experienced trauma at some point in your life, possibly
abuse and abandonment, the ego does not recognize your worthiness, thus it re-
jects your soul. It puts up barriers that push against the higher-consciousness of
your divinity, disallowing the beauty of ascension to touch you, having adopted
the belief that you don't deserve it. Thus, self-inquiry through non-judgemental
observation acts as a loving catalyst for healing and growth, as it returns you to
your longing in a gentle and life-affirming way."

There is nothing in the world more healing and transformative than becoming an empathic witness for all of our life experiences, and personally, when I witness my life through the lens of compassion I accept my reactions. I may become aware of anxiety rising in my body; I observe the disquiet and notice that my breath is shallow, and instantly my body breathes in more deeply. It may be self-criticism that knocks at my door when I try too hard to master life, rather than let life guide me. With compassionate observation, the restlessness gives way to trust.

In one of my workshops a participant, Jessica, discovered that everything she needs to know in life can be brought to the surface of her consciousness in a gentle and loving way. After the workshop she said to me, "I grasp now the amazing power and potential I have inside me, and that I need to develop respect for my healing-process to realize that power and potential." Like so many of us, Jessica had believed that there was something wrong with her, which prevented her from gathering the energy needed for healing. Our culture tends to value achievement over self-realization, therefore Jessica judged herself harshly for her health-issues and for not having a clear sense of direction in her life. In the workshop, she came to understand that she needed to cease pushing herself towards an ideal goal, and instead become a loving witness – to care for herself with a deep sense of respect in her natural pace for healing.

So many of us live under the pressure to perform and with a sense of time constraint that does not allow enough time for healing, resulting in a myriad of psychological and physical ailments, and social dysfunctions. We need to feel safe in the hands of our own compassion to transcend the disabling effects of psychological pain and transform our negativity, self-criticism and disbelief.

Tuning into Your Longing

Masiandia: *"Returning to your longing is a spiritual practice that is much like meditation, though not a sit-down ritual intended to regulate your mind. It is a way of life that is in constant surrender to the wisdom of your inner-senses, and which unites you with your higher self.*

"There is so much joy in feeling the longing without changing anything. It frees you to 'be' right at home with who you are, no matter what life presents you. For some of you, that may be an illness. By connecting with your longing for wellness and support you can completely transform the condition, for you culti-vate an intimate connection with your soul that supports cellular re-patterning and miraculous healing. When you return to your longing, you lessen the ex-pectation and pressure to heal, and this patience and understanding provides the cells of your body what they need in order to heal.

"For others, it may be a work-related issue that is of concern. By connect-ing with your needs and desires within your work-life, tremendous job-related anxieties are alleviated, providing you with a clear understanding of what is important to you. Honouring yourself activates a profound shift in how you view your value and in how others treat you. Connecting with your longing may completely change your outlook, allowing you to enjoy and appreciate your current job, or it may instigate a profound change in the course of your work, inspiring you to look for new employment that captivates your interest and sense of purpose, or furthering your education.

"By tuning into your longing – the intuitive language of your soul – you are

drawn away from old patterns of fear and suffering into change, for you let the wisdom of your longing guide you in realizing your potential."

ecause the message of our soul can differ so greatly from the ratio-nal realm of our reasoning mind, we tend to reject our longing and reject change, but that is where our soul is waiting to guide us. By giving ourselves the freedom to explore a truer expression of our whole self, we relinquish control and allow life to move us in ways we may not have thought possible; we feel into our longing, activate our soul's potential and become strong magnets for the fulfilment of our longing. But how? By completely feeling the depth of our desires! By letting ourselves want what we want without having to justify it, without having to figure out how to actualize it.

However, it's so easy to get entangled in disbelief for we are pro-grammed to respect logic, not feelings. When an emotion appears that might guide us in a seemingly illogical direction, our tendency is to doubt the emotion. We tend to control our longing by interpreting it too quickly, by not stepping into the process of experiencing it. This leads to rejecting what we long for because it doesn't make sense to us, and thus we often don't fully realize what we're longing for.

A universal example of this is the longing for relationship. When we yearn for a life-partner we can easily slip beneath the surface of our joy and allow the longing to tarnish, falling prey to loneliness. But it is not loneliness that inspires us; it is the sweet yearning for companionship. By identifying with loss, we turn away from the emotion and we neglect to feel into the pleasure of our longing. It is so freeing to simply feel our long-ing, to let it blossom in its own natural timing. Then our lives are no longer governed by urgency or self-judgment, but rather by epiphanal moments that arise out of our connection with our soul. Wholeness is restored by becoming aware of our longing within – by shifting our attention back to the body and resting in its wisdom. In this way, our actions are propelled by an internal sense of resonance, expanded by our willingness to feel emotions and inspired by our dreams.

Masiandia encourages us to savour our longing, whether it is for health, peace, creative endeavours, a relationship or anything else in our lives. And by shedding our expectation of the outcome we return to the feeling-quality of our longing, which is deeply nourishing in itself. This feeling then becomes the magnetic charge that attracts and manifests what we long for.

Masiandia: *"Your soul inherently speaks through the energy vibration of longing, and tuning into your longing strengthens your ability to manifest it. What you long for has little importance; it is the longing itself that is significant. It is a vibrational frequency that delivers you from suffering. You only experience suffering when you resist your longing.*

"This is difficult to explain to a mind that thinks in terms of cause and effect. Your mind is programmed to think in a linear way, focused on actualizing what you long for to the point of abandoning the intimate relationship you can have with the longing. Forgetting your inner-vision because you're so set on the goal is not unlike building a house without the blueprint. If you don't connect with your longing – the blueprint – you cannot realize what needs to happen next; you can't make manifest what you long for.

"If you only view reality through this linear perception, you let cause and effect limit you; you see what is lacking, not what is whole; you see victim-hood not empowerment; hardship not integrity; tragedy not change. Longing is the heartbeat of purpose – gentleness in a hardened world.

"You must cease viewing the world through the lens of suffering to enter into the sanctity of your prayerful relationship with life. In this way, you fall in love with your longing and honour your relationship with your soul. If all of humanity could feel this in-depth longing, there would be no suffering, no war, no abuse. Suffering exists in this world because it is a force – a perception of reality – overshadowed by fear and judgment.

"Connect with your longing to lessen this force, and give the light of your soul its rightful place in your prayers. In essence, we are saying that longing is supported by the relationship you have with prayer, which is the living quality of your soul's voice. It is the way in which you allow the graceful unfolding of your trust in life."

I t never ceases to amaze me that when we finally stop struggling we effect change. I don't know how many times I have tried to figure something out or pushed to make something happen, and the moment that I felt my longing, clarity came to me and things fell into place naturally. When we feel into our longing, something beautiful happens; we feel peaceful, whole, calm.

Uniting with our longing has the quality of listening-in, tuning in to subtleties that can be otherwise missed. Too often we overlook the fact that our endeavours are not all up to us to accomplish and that we are not alone. By being caught up in making things happen, we don't stop to receive help from the unseen realm. It is by slowing down to connect with our longing that we let in God; we surrender to divine timing and serendipitous events that support us in ways that we couldn't have orchestrated on our own.

There are moments that I have asked the Divine to provide me with a deep sensory experience of what it feels like to receive what I need, to give my longing a grounded sense of possibility. It may be support, understanding, inspiration that I need. My request is always met. Most of the time it's a feeling that overcomes me, or something someone says. Maybe it's a book I read or an inner message I receive. We are always supported, and it's by opening ourselves to the support that we receive it. Being open, tuned-in and connected to the feeling quality of our longing is prayerful. It allows all resistance to fall away. It allows the Divine to join us and support us.

Prayerful Living

Masiandia: *"The word prayer means 'God is listening'. It signifies the totality of being; it represents the light within the dark, darkness that encompasses light. Prayer brings together polarities into a unified whole, it is the fulcrum point between rest and action, rebalancing one's energy to fuel movement and support integrity.*

"Please realize that your prayers are powerful. They are magnetic conduits of energy that disperse illusion by expanding your consciousness. When you expand your consciousness, you raise the vibration of your magnetic field, drawing towards you what you need and desire. Through prayer you become a broadcasting station that emits a strong frequency of faith and devotion – a strong expression of your soul's innate abundance and purpose. Through prayer you embody your longing, which serves to raise the consciousness for you and your families, your friends, co-workers and the Earth itself. When you embrace your prayers you naturally embrace the prayers of others; you welcome their soul as well as your own."

Our prayers serve a much larger purpose than simply trying to manifest what we want in life. They connect us to the unknowable mystery of our soul, providing us with inexplicable and magical moments. It is during these moments that answers to problems emerge effortlessly, without expectation or control. Then we surrender our will and cease clinging to what we think we want; we let our prayers emerge from a profound connection with our felt-senses that then reveal the magnitude of our potential in life. We can still imagine what we want, but not project that onto life or get swept up in the current of worry, disbelief and control. We need to stay connected to the feelings that give rise to our desires.

Masiandia: *"Please be aware that your prayers are fulfilled only when you immerse yourself in your longing. By connecting inwards to the feeling-quality of your desires, you embrace the intelligence of your soul; you let yourself be guided by a spirit-vision, a vision greater than your human thoughts and processes. To long is to embrace your desires, your wants and needs, not try to actualize them or reject yourself when your needs are not met. How many times do you judge yourself or despair when your longing is not satiated?*

"Desperation keeps you from feeling your true longing; it keeps you locked in familiar perceptions of reality, not aligned to your spirit-vision of yourself. By cultivating an intimate relationship with your longing, you open yourself to receiving what you need naturally and effortlessly. You step over the threshold of your fear and disbelief into trust.

"It is important to understand that your longing is your soul communicating to you; it is a divine plan seeking the light of your presence and devotion. Furthermore, longing is born out of faith and the willingness to be a pure expression of divinity, not forged out of dissatisfaction. Prayers are not answered in frustration or from the sorrow of unmet needs; they are fulfilled by passion and surrender.

"Our dear friends, longing is not attached to your mental conception of what you need or on the outcomes you hope for; it is a state of being that is so interconnected with your soul-consciousness that it aligns you to the possibilities that best serve your purpose, actualizing your needs for you. Embracing your longing as valid and whole dissolves any barriers in realizing what you want, for you are guided along the river of life to exactly where you need to be in right time and place."

s I take in Masiandia's message I realize that by asking us to feel everything, they are encouraging us to celebrate our desires. They are not telling us to refrain from setting goals or ambitions. They are asking us to "feel" the wonderment rooted at the heart of our goals and the creative fire burning within ambition. They are not telling us to override our need for fulfilment; they are drawing us back into the nucleus of our endeavours, returning us to the place from which they stem, which is our soul-purpose. In this way, our visions are supported by a deep sense of belonging, as we enter into a prayerful relationship with who we truly are.

Prayerful living acts as a magnetic vortex, drawing vitality into the centre of our lives like the Earth's ley lines – energy currents found at some of the strongest power places on the planet. These ley lines are equivalent to the acupressure points on our bodies. They are high energy zones that have the ability to attract more energy, as do our prayers. Prayerful living conducts magnetic energy currents that ultimately draw us back to the heart of what enlivens us and to what makes us feel whole and supported.

Connecting with our longing takes the "pining" and "have to" out of our lives, leaving us completely accessible to what we want. A fine illustration of this is a time in my life where I let go of the pressure I had held within myself towards creating a relationship. My yearning for a relationship then became delightful and sweet, as I was certain that its manifestation was inevitable. Otherwise, why would my longing be so strong? As Masiandia says, we wouldn't long for something if it couldn't be fulfilled. And so I stopped being anxious and lonely, and instead I felt secure in myself.

I developed an intimate affinity with my longing, becoming enamoured with my desire for a loving partnership. I didn't identify anymore with being single, or with how long it had been since I had been in a meaningful relationship. In fact, I stopped feeling bitter and disappointed with my past experiences; I stopped measuring my sense of worth based on whether or not I was in a relationship. This state of mind was so freeing and fun that when I met my beloved I wasn't attached to my desires; I was completely open and surrendered to whatever unfolded between us.

Masiandia: *"It is such a relief to observe the natural evolution of your life with patience and trust, to realize your dreams by respecting and honouring your natural pace. Unlocking your potential does not come from striving for anything;*

it is brought about by devotion. Peace and fulfilment come from not pushing for change, for it is inevitable that you will change and grow. Peace comes from allowing your longing to unfold organically with devotion. It's about being absolutely willing to feel everything. Then your longing is free to reveal your soul, for it isn't overshadowed by dominance, compulsiveness or impatience.

"Feeling into your longing is a prayerful letting-in of God. It is a spiritual practice that provides you with a deep sensory experience of what it feels like to return to yourself and be enriched with soulful guidance. The Divine is always close by in everything, from the microcosmic particle to the vast Universe, and so you can ask for help. You can ask the Divine to provide you with a knowing experience of what it feels like to be whole, loved, safe and supported. May your longing seduce you every single moment of your life. May your longing be an opening – a blossoming – a letting in of your soul."

CHAPTER FIVE

Soul Purpose

I don't know if the road is near.
Let the sign show the way home –
I've strayed off the course
of the collective mind.
I don't know if you'll hear this song.
Take in every word I pray
and read between the lines.
I have a message for you.

Your face I imagined clothed
in expressions history cannot erase.
Passages of time have defined you –
stories untold yet clearly an open book,
you are, you are visible to me –
great ocean of doubt, rhythms of breath,
consuming machine, creator of happiness.

My love, you are everything.
There are no limits that confine you,
no obscure law that binds you.
There is no hope that will save you.
What mountain, sky, universal truth
or warm summer breeze
will you try to bargain with?
Your life is no less far reaching.

Soul Purpose is Divine Order

*W*e often think that soul-purpose is a vocation, something that we have to accomplish or succeed at. Rarely is it seen as a way of "being" or as a gift that we are essentially ordained to give to every part of our life. Masiandia describes soul-purpose as the gift of our own evolution, as our greater intelligence, which is intrinsically woven into our personality, relationships and creative endeavours, not 'just' in what we do for a living. Purpose sets our soul in motion and provides it with the expression it needs to fulfil its incarnation, its divine order, which is embodying who we are and what we need. Just as our physical bodies need oxygen to be alive, the soul cannot live without purpose.

Imminently part of all nature, purpose is the intention behind the materialization of all living organisms. Imagine the life vibration of a seed in the dark surroundings of rich soil breaking free from its encasement as it seeks the light. Purpose seeks to fulfil itself; it is divine order following the natural cycles of nature. Connecting with our purpose then is seeing the blessing of Earth that generously supports all integration and partnership with life. Together, our soul-purpose and Earth-reality form an alliance that serves a larger system. Everything is in divine order, giving rich meaning to the interconnection between spirit and matter.

As incarnated souls, we have a gift to share with Earth-reality – the transference of spirit-based energy to the cellular intelligence within our body. This transfer of energy helps raise not only our physical vitality, but also the physical energy of Earth, which is our body. Earth, in turn, gives us life and free will, which allows for full manifestation of our soul-purpose. By incarnating on Earth we become part of Gaia; our soul-purpose is woven into physical biology and senses, feelings, emotions and thought processes that evolve out of our interconnected relationship with nature.

Masiandia says that all the elements of Earth and its kingdoms – animal, insect, mineral and plant, are life forms in direct or indirect contact with humanity, in a way that is designed by the interrelationship between Gaia's energy-mass and our purpose and influence. In whichever way humanity is out of balance, planet Earth is part of the imbalance, as are all life forms within its sphere of existence. Therefore, since we are in partnership with Earth, it is necessary that we do our part in raising the consciousness of our own human experience, so that we can give our soul-purpose to Earth.

Masiandia: *"Your human nature acts as a source of organized mental energy, transmitting universal frequencies that support interplanetary evolution. Your soul purposefully merges with human nature in order to activate higher levels of magnetic energy within the physical body and Earth. By embracing your soul-purpose, you activate the spirit-consciousness of your physical body, infusing all of your biology with the essence of your soul. This not only helps restore and rebalance your biology, your nervous system and overall physical structure, it also helps connect you to your mental, emotional and spiritual well-being. And it opens you to higher states of inspiration and peace.*

"Merging human nature with spirit-consciousness nourishes your whole body experience; it gives you a tangible interconnection with higher-consciousness through your physical senses. And through your experience and willingness, your soul touches this world; it enlivens it and gives deeper meaning to your part in the larger spectrum of Earth reality."

*I*t is interesting to think that there is a sacred marriage between Earth-form and soul-consciousness, a union that Earth requires to evolve and the soul needs to embody the beauty of its divinity. Nature is a tool for infusing spirit into matter, an intrinsic part of evolution that provides souls with physical embodiment and the means to develop mental structures that support the purpose of the soul. Earth's purpose is form, giving shape to consciousness. Ultimately, spirit and nature serve one another;

they are part of something bigger, like two pieces of a puzzle that alone would not be complete.

In *The Magical Approach*, channelled by Jane Robert, Seth explains that the human mind, which embodies spirit, provides a rational methodology that nature needs, anticipates and desires. The reasoning mind creates an objective framework for nature that Seth says directs the acts of expression and manifestation. Nature gives our spirit the material sheaf, the dense matter, which allows us to come into our gifts and to share these gifts with the Earth. The Earth in turn is united with our soul-consciousness, and together we are whole and multidimensional, serving a larger universal purpose.

Masiandia: *"This larger purpose is divinity, merging the richness of essence with matter for all people and nature. It is divine fellowship, not shaped by conformity, rules and prejudices, but by celebrating all that is. Divinity's design takes all life – earth, animal, plant, humanity, other planetary dimensions, parallel lifetimes and so much more – into a unified whole, not as* ONE, *but as* ALL TOGETHER. *The wholeness of God is inclusive of every facet of its expressions, which means that its purpose is togetherness, not uniformity.*

"This means that all forms of existence on Earth, parallel earths and other planetary dimensions are part of a larger host, the Divine, and are inseparable. And this inseparableness, that is not singular but whole, harmonizes the diverging aspects of the Divine within the multidimensional Universe."

Being in Touch with Your Purpose

Masiandia: *"We want you to know that your soul, embodied in form, is a miracle. Your spirits have come to this Earth plane to bless this world and be blessed by it. It is good to remember this, as it allows you to make life-affirming choices with ease and acceptance, strengthening your sense of centre. Fulfilling your lives does not require effort or struggle; it requires a connection to truth. When you feel connected and are passionate about your purpose in life, even your fears are surmountable. Your fears become guideposts, not forces of resistance, thus the things that you thought you could not do are made possible. That's the power of your incarnated souls, manifested through the prayerful connection to your longing, which puts you in touch with your purpose. Feel your longing to manifest the beauty of your soul in your body, which moves you to bless this world with the grace of your being."*

*I*nitially our fears tell us that life is not easy, that it is a struggle. Yet, there are people who surpass their fears, who move obstacles with confidence and creativity. Surrendered, they are not limited by mental strategies, thus Masiandia's message about embodying miracles is true for them. These are people who change when life necessitates it. The fact that our dreams are changing dreams, only made possible by our willingness to trust in them, inspires me.

Connecting with our longing and living with purpose requires diligence; it demands of us our total presence and devotion. We tend to beat ourselves up when we lose this connection, which makes our life journey an uphill climb when it needn't be. The power of our soul-purpose is made manifest by connecting with our longing, not our fears. By becoming larger than our fears, we give way to what is trying to emerge in our lives.

This is so true for my client Natasha, who against many odds honoured her longing; she bought her dream-ranch with her partner, Don. For as long as Natasha could remember, she had dreamed of having a place that was relatively untouched and natural. She had been inspired by Don's lifestyle as a ranch manager riding the range and enjoying the great outdoors. It gave her the sense of the spaciousness she longed for – a lifestyle that nourished her soul. Together, they kindled their longing to own a self-sufficient, off-the-grid working farm.

Natasha first fell in love with the land they would eventually purchase, on a long tour of the property with the owner, Mrs. Ronson, a feisty woman of about 75. When they made their final turn out of the forest and Natasha first saw the beautiful open ranch, she had an instant "knowing" that this was her home, though she didn't know how she would finance the whole property. Mrs. Ronson wanted to sell the whole land as a working ranch, not allow it to be subdivided by her sons.

Natasha and Don considered several approaches to financing, some of which included the possibility of sharing the land with family, but they all fell through. After pursuing every possible avenue, Natasha then had the idea to ask Mrs. Ronson if she would finance two-thirds of the mortgage, interest free, with payments over eleven years. They sat drinking tea at the kitchen table with the wood stove crackling in the background, as Mrs. Ronson looked at the proposal and then said, "Yes!" She wanted to pass on her home to a couple that, like she and her deceased husband, loved working on the farm.

Natasha and Don still needed to finance one-third of the mortgage, and Natasha trusted in their capacity to do so with a profound sense of confidence that helped her bend obstacles. Still, after moving in with the agreement that they would provide Mrs. Ronson with the third of the mortgage, and after an extensive business plan and 400 sheep bought and delivered, they received the news that the bank mortgage had been declined. They continued to persevere, and an eager mortgage broker discovered that if Natasha and Don called themselves "hobby farmers" instead of claiming to be a commercial operation, they could likely resubmit the application and hope it would be accepted.

A few days later Don and Natasha drove the four kilometres to the nearest cell tower where they could get mobile-phone coverage, located in the forest just a short walk from the road. Natasha remembers the day, the cold weather and big chunks of sleet falling down around them as they listened to the garbled voice on the other end of the phone. The reception was terrible and they lost connection, but after a second try they heard the best news of their lives. "The mortgage had been approved!" They finally officially owned the ranch!

When Natasha shared this news with me, she said, "The transaction was made possible due to the 'above and beyond-ness' of so many people." She was filled with so much gratitude as people bent the rules, worked longer than they needed to, searched a little more, and tried again: insurance brokers, lawyers, fireplace approvers, assistants, etc. "Angels everywhere, it was amazing!"

I see in Natasha's story a courageous unfolding of purpose and a profound capacity to fully explore what is really possible in life. This is the blessing that the world needs from all of us: the willingness to shift and change to support our dreams.

Fulfilling Your Purpose

*W*e are destined to fulfil our purpose by cultivating an intimate relationship with our longing, and embrace who we are no matter what stands before us: fear, obstacles, disbelief. The teachings of Masiandia maintain that the obstacles do not matter, only our conviction and determination has the power to change our lives. Yet determination and purpose needn't be an overpowering force, but rather a state of gratitude welcoming the divine spark that resides within us all. This spark is our eternal flame that sees into the dark and shows us the way through the unknown, and determines our life-path.

Masiandia: *"When you delight in the spark of your divinity, you support the intended purpose of your soul, which is your blueprint, the foundation for all your life experiences. Your purpose illuminates the way – it encompasses all your relationships, family and friends, life-experiences, interests and desires. Like an engine that roars to life when ignited, your soul-purpose is your life-force that when kindled serves to evolve your talents and gifts, and give* meaning to every facet of your life. You may awaken this purposeful vitality when faced with life-challenges, perhaps when caring for your health, your children's needs or an ailing elder. It could be your work that impassions your purpose, or maybe it's your creative interests or learning a new skill.

There are many paths that awaken you to your soul-purpose. Perhaps it is the path of spiritual mysticism that calls you, with its focus on meditation, and growing your ability to encounter adversity with fluidity and acceptance. However, people who step onto this path often mistaken the purpose of meditation for discipline, insisting that meditation be something you accomplish and not simply a way of being.

"Purpose is not what it seems, as Dofila mentioned earlier; it is not a vocation. For instance, a dancer's purpose may not be the artistry of dance or performance; it may instead be physical vitality, creativity, working in a team, communication and expressing his emotions. His purpose may be to empower others to create, which inspires deep healing. A dedicated musician can inspire and even save another person's life through the creative manifestation of her self-expression, yet she may never accomplish her own dreams. What is her purpose then? Is it music? Yes! Is it fame? No! By following the current of her inner guidance, she takes her love of music into a divine path of being in service to others, by becoming a teacher who helps others fulfil their need for creative communication. Therefore, teaching is her purpose, as is inspiring others.

"The person whose purpose is fame serves to raise others beyond their habitual sense of reality and create a vision of what is possible, or may instead bring awareness to the consequences of fame and its many pitfalls, which in turn can help others learn from this. Your purpose may be motherhood, which can be embodied not only as a woman but also as a man. A man whose purpose is motherhood may fulfil his role by supporting the women in his life or learning to provide maternal care as a single parent. The soul-role of father is equally important, to help children learn to take risks and step out into the flow of life. Currently, many women are undertaking this role due to single parenting, giving their *children directive leadership, thus maintaining the soul-purpose of integrating both motherhood and fatherhood.*

"All these roles are the vehicles for living your higher-conscious purpose, which is to give of yourself. Soul roles are highly important and must be mastered to honour all life. Mastering your life purpose requires self-acceptance, honouring your living-soul and its gift to the world. What is your role? Look to those who are closest to you to recognize what they see in you, which may be a talent or characteristic they appreciate in you, and then grow that talent and trait even more. Observe the challenges that regularly occur in your life, and recognize in them lessons that seek to awaken your unique gifts, gifts that naturally serve your soul."

Masiandia's guidance reminds me of a time, from before my healing practice, when friends and family suggested I become a counsellor. Some people thought that I would enjoy practicing art therapy, since I am an artist. However, it didn't appeal to me. Nevertheless, I trusted what they saw in me and came to recognize that my art is my therapy. The creative process plays a large role in my self-expression, and I see the way it influences my professional healing-practice, supporting my client's self-discovery and rebirth. To me, the healing journey is art as it brings out the natural beauty in people, and that is truly what inspires me the most and makes me feel on purpose.

Masiandia: *"Everything that is needed to support your purpose is always present in your life; it is in the small things, like the compliments that people offer you and even their unfavourable reactions. Lessons garnered from difficult experiences, loss and hurt provide you with much fuel for growth, as you are pushed into surrendered states. Otherwise, why would you ever let go? A man who has been given six months to live may finally live those six months with vigour and purpose, rather than continue to suppress his feelings, yearnings and emotional needs. Perhaps he learned, early in life, to hold it all together, except that his body* can no longer cling to those conditioned responses. In order to free his body and connect with his true value, he needs to feel, to feel and to feel more.

"Fulfilling your purpose may push you into the role of leadership so that you can encompass your true values and share them with others. Your purpose always requires that you take risks that not only support you, but also support others to risk being honest with themselves. That makes you a catalyst for change, invention and new thought, as you step fully into the new Earth and embrace all that is in the light of truth.

"Do you have more than one purpose? Well, yes, and it all comes down to one thing in the end – love. Your purpose is love, which you must first give to yourself. By loving yourself, you enliven the cells of your body with life-affirming messages and thus enter into a state of absolute balance. Contrarily, when you neglect your need for love and support, it triggers the fear of abandonment and failure, which constricts your vital energy.

"What is love if it is not first given to yourself? Incomplete! It is emptiness, like a fountain that has run dry. If you are prone to looking after others before you consider your own needs, then you unconsciously interfere with the natural abundance of your love, for it must first serve you. Then there is enough for others, because you become so full that you overflow your love onto others. Your soul cannot serve this world externally without first replenishing your own human existence from within. Your purpose is to love yourselves, dear ones, love yourselves.

"Very few of you truly know what self-love really means, and we will address that later in more detail, as the subject of love is a significant one that requires a full chapter of its own. (Please see chapter 12.) In continuing chapters, you will be guided into love's embrace, as we journey together towards a deep surrender into loving all there is. For now, we say to you, start with connecting to your need for love. In this way, your soul can join you, to meet your uncensored need."

The Heroic Path

*M*asiandia has frequently admired our soul's bravery for choosing to incarnate in human form; they see in our life experiences great acts of courage through our tears, persistence and willingness to learn and grow. They admire our conviction and they understand the extent to which we are forging a new path. The encouragement and love of all our spirit guides champion us to be whole – to be more than our limitations – and in turn, our open hearts and willingness to learn are blessings to them. We sustain their guidance by including them in our daily lives and support their purpose with mutual devotion.

I rest in thee. Great Spirit, come, and rest in me.

~ Henry Richard McFadyen,
lyric from his song, *The Lone Wild Bird*

Masiandia: *"You honour us when you receive our support; you join us on the path of divine union, letting the love of spirit-consciousness guide you. You are not meant to journey alone. It is with the grace of God that you are empowered. Divine order defines the path for you, and that path serves you, all of humanity and the larger spectrum of divinity. We are 'all' divinity, and we as a whole embrace one another's purpose, our differences and our beauty. Spirit guardians serve to help you remember that the most important ritual in life is celebration and joyous recognition of humanity's gift to all life and to universal balance. Your part in the great expanse of universal evolution is to plant the seed of your divine spark into Earth matter. In this way you join Gaia – the Earth Entity – in a symbiotic relationship that supports universal alignment.*

"You are more than your human experience, more than physical reality and greater than the human conditioning that defines you. It is by welcoming the

intuitive language of your spirit-consciousness that you remember who you are, which unfailingly enriches your life with deeper meaning that you then share with all life and universal intelligence. It is in sharing who you truly are that you are whole and fulfilled."

H onouring our soul's bravery is a heroic path, a journey that accepts who we truly are and celebrates our incarnation on Earth. It is a privilege, yet so many of us see it as punishment. I can't count how many times I've heard people say that they hope this is their last lifetime. They yearn for freedom beyond the body's limitations, rather than see in our human nature and in Earth's beauty a depth of freedom that exists right here and now. Countless seekers reject the body's wisdom and want to reach nirvana, heaven or anything rather than be faithful to the spiritual practice of committing to and celebrating the heroic journey. Enlightenment has become a goal, a way of avoiding feeling that is no different than overshadowing the wisdom of the soul with the tyranny of the rational mind, which impedes the flow of divine providence.

We are here to make manifest the beauty of our soul-purpose that is intrinsic to all our life-experiences. Yet we fear our purpose, our beauty, our light; we avoid embracing it and feeling it because we don't know where it is leading us. Terrified of the unknown, we relive the familiar. But that does not enliven us or support deep balance and inner-peace.

Masiandia has said, *"Stop living your life by looking at the past with your back to the present. Turn around and face the Divine."* When we turn around and face the Divine, we face the present through the lens of divinity rather than imprinting it with our past memories. If we only view the present through the lens of the past, all we see is familiarity, which for many of us is laden with disappointment and pain. Personally, when I face the Divine, any pain-residue from past abuse, neglect and abandonment steps forward with me and I stand elated in the glory of God. Here I feel completely safe, embraced by an incredible sense of belonging for the present no longer holds potential threats.

The new age dictum of "living in the present" has never been more inspiring and clear to me than through Masiandia teaching us that facing the Divine allows us to step forward with all our life-experiences, fears, sorrow, anger, joy… into the present. When facing the Divine we neglect nothing about our past or our fears, for we embrace all that we are in this precious moment. We only fear what the future will bring because we view it from the projection of our past memories. By having our backs turned away from the present and thus only facing the past, our backs are to our relationships, our creative endeavours, and our family and friends. Old wounds resurface and hinder our ability to really see what is going on in our present lives.

Imagine for a moment a situation that troubles you, and you keep your back to it as you continue surveying the past. Seeking answers in the past or reliving the past isn't going to provide you with insight. All the past feelings will continue to dictate how you respond to the present situation, and you will simply not be able to see the present. By turning around and facing the Divine in everything, you embrace the present and you also let yourself to be all of your ages from infancy to now, which opens you to new possibilities because all of you is welcomed.

I recall a vision I had in prayer that illustrates this beautifully. I saw an image of myself dialling an old phone with the intent to talk to spirit. Interestingly, the fingers dialling the phone were small. I knew instantly that in the vision I was a child. The dialling ceased, and I heard myself say to spirit, "I'm so afraid that if I don't learn to connect with my longing, Linda will go on ahead without me." Her concern was so sweet and telling that I instantly took care of my inner child's fear. I reassured her that she didn't have to figure it all out. It was clear then that my inner innocence would always be with me, whether or not she grasped the meaning of longing, and that she was safe with me.

So often, we believe that aspects of ourselves must be discarded so that we can advance, heal, grow. But this is untrue, for everything about us must be brought to the light of the Divine, every facet, every age, every memory, our strengths and weaknesses. We don't have to be perfected, purified or have mastered all of our lessons to enter into God's embrace. We can bring all of ourselves, turn around and face the present, face the Divine, and fall in love with all of who we are now.

Empowering and Inspiring Innocence

Masiandia: *"Your whole self is defined by a multitude of expressions, ages, feelings, beliefs, memories and desires. By embracing all of you, you honour your sacred-purpose and strengthen your inner innocence, which is true heroism. The path of courage is defined by innocence for it emboldens honesty.*

Innocence is not powerless because it is captivating, enticing you into authentic expression. It is an unbridled power that seduces the dark; it bewilders the dark and brings it to its knees. By honouring your innocence – your inner-child's need for love, reassurance, faith and dreams – the shadow of fear no longer discourages you. You return to your wholeness, bringing spirit-vitality into all areas of your life, courageously unfolding the grace of your belief in yourself."

*I*n many mythologies, it is children who defeat the dark forces; they are the agents of change. In *The Chronicles of Narnia*, written by C.S. Lewis, children play a key role in protecting Narnia from Jadis, the evil Queen. Jadis has cast Narnia into a perpetual winter, a metaphor for our frozen emotions. It is children, the quintessence of innocence, who restore warmth and open us to feeling.

It is children who create change because their youth and innocence is connected to deep feelings and self-discovery, not defined by rules. Masiandia says that children are the foundation for generations to come, the regeneration cycle upon which dreams evolve ... because they are the embodiment of growth. Without the quintessence of innocence forming the basis of our lives, nothing can grow. Instead, we cling to old forms, false identities influenced by social conditioning – set on shaping ourselves to patterns that only suit the archetypes of humankind, not nature or the soul. We would build our world and communities on sound foundations if we could only connect with our innocence. We would honour children and our own intrinsic renewal.

Masiandia: *"Everything that exists in life stems from birth and rebirth. Without continuous renewal, there is imbalance and disease, not the synergistic system of regeneration that supports soul-purpose. Incarnation on Earth is supported by regeneration just like a forest is sustained by new life. The interactive synergy between the old decomposing trees and the forming of new trees creates a rich eco-system. Without the fecund soil of an ancient log, there would be no nutrients to nurse new trees to life, and without new life, the decomposing trees would have no purpose. The new life provides a way for the fallen trees to continue their timeless cycle with new vegetation that take root within the fertile matter, infusing the Earth-plain with vitality. And so it is true for you: you carry on the cycle of your innocence in all of your creative potential, springing forth your life-purpose.*

"Like the symbiotic relationship between nursing trees and new vegetation, children depend on you and are also your lifeline. They are the future shapers of this world; therefore, they are the shapers of your present world, for the future is now. They play a very important role in balancing the dualities found in the inherent makeup of family and social patterns, as they express and manifest repressed emotions. This expression is immensely needed to release stagnant energies within families and to bring the profound balance of purity and devotion to the Earth. The cells of your body require honest expression and conscious living to thrive. And it is with sincerity that you help children discover the heroic path that supports their true sense of value, which helps evolve a new vision of Earth."

*T*o express our emotions as children do, unfettered and transparent, connects us to the wisdom of our innocence. *The Bible* says, "become as little children" to enter heaven. Be an open book, unguarded and authentic to enter into harmony.

As we reconnect to our innocence, we shed the mantel of duty and obligation that so many adults assume. We become provocateurs of change, strengthen our connection to the web of life and embody inner-truth. We take natural risks in expressing our feelings and trusting our inborn wisdom, and we choose faith. Children are born with faith, though with time they learn to distrust, as they don't do well under the system of inflexible rules and untruths. They need explicit honesty, clarification and time to understand their environments and the reason for social order. Are we as adults any different? But unfortunately we try to pin ourselves down with social conventions and mask our real emotions, which only stands to confuse children, including the inner child – the inner innocence – within us.

"Children come into this world with clean and clear eyes," explains Mike, who communicates through his father in the book *From My World to Yours*. The author, Jasper Swain, found a means of connecting with his son's spirit after his fatal car accident and explores a new channelled relationship with his son. Mike's death had broken Jasper's heart to the understanding that there is a greater reality, and it awakened in him an intuitive awareness of his son.

Their new partnership formed into a tender inquiry into why Mike's particular generation had developed such an obsession for lethal drugs. In answering many of Jasper's questions, Mike says that children come into this world seeking love, truth and brotherhood, but instead they find deception and oppression. They find themselves in a world where people are hypercritical and craven and the actions of most adults contradict their values. Repressive behaviour imprints itself on children, and double standards throw them into such confusion that by the time they are adolescent, they feel that they must either adapt or try to escape.

Masiandia: *"Children have a profound need for the truth at all times. Pretence and trying to placate them and yourselves is pointless, because they are not separate from you. Children are highly intelligent, able to intuitively draw vast amounts of information from spoken words and nonverbal body-language, and especially the energy-field of their families, friends and society. They have a highly attuned connection to their inner-knowing, thus they witness far more than is apparent. This is especially true in the case of divorce. Parents must reign in their conflict; they have to take full responsibility for their actions and non-actions. Blaming one another only serves to teach children that there is something gravely wrong with them also, because when one parent criticizes the other, children become very sensitive to this condemnation, since they are, after all, an offspring of the parent being scorned.*

"With this said, we cannot emphasize enough the importance of clear communication and absolute integrity. This not only supports the young children in your lives but also your own inner-innocence, and it emphasizes your natural gifts. You are innately, highly intuitive and intelligent beings, drawn to Earth to fully join with the beauty and grace of your fellow human beings and with Earth itself. Therefore, you must be mature adults who dare to be real and enthusiastic about life, by strengthening your own self-esteem, self-identity and inner truth."

Reinventing Yourself

*T*his is a time on Earth when culture's value of tradition and perceived unity is being challenged, breaking down the façade of family life. We are reinventing ourselves and defining our own unique characteristics in many ways, such as through ending relationships and in the case of immigrants, by departing from old conventions. Because of this break from the conditioning of ancestors, many children no longer identify with a unified front defined by their family's traditions or expectations. While this is a difficult turning point, it nevertheless acts as a catalyst that obstructs and disintegrates outmoded patterns from both parents. This serves to lessen an over-identifying with either parental pattern that does not honour the soul.

Masiandia: *"When family patterns are interrupted, this restrains the ego from over-identifying with one parent's lineage or the other. In this way, children are unencumbered by the tightly woven interpretation of self-identity that occurs in an unvarying home environment. As you consider your history, many families remained together for the sake of the children. Many of those home environments were very strict and programmed to fit the family, not the individuals. Now the family dynamic has become so individuated that the child has no one reference point to identify with. As unbalanced as this seems, it is beneficial for many children, since it helps them break free from outmoded family scripts, attitudes and beliefs. The old script that has been passed on through generations is being undone, which is giving children the opportunity to renew themselves, to completely lose their heritage, lose where they come from, lose any identifying personality traits other than who they really are.*

"The Divine encompasses everything, and everything is in divine order. Union with soul-purpose is made possible for these children, because in essence, their divine union supersedes confining family patterns. When constricting ancestral patterns are weakened, this allows the personality to surrender to one's soul."

Keeping the family intact may seem like the right thing to do, but when parents pretend to be happy, children see it; they embody it and lose their innocence and their connection to the Divine. Because children are very perceptive, they see and sense their parents' dishonesty, become despondent and lose confidence in adults and themselves. We need to entrust children with our courageous sincerity to support mutual growth. Children's need for our authentic expression has the power to influence us in being balanced and whole, and in turn our growing maturity helps them thrive.

As with immigrants who move away from their home of origin, children need to be given the freedom to evolve. Change affects the whole family, since everyone has to reconstruct their outlook on family. But most often it's children who adapt more easily to new life and then struggle to free themselves from their family's traditional views. I attended an intercultural wedding, where my Korean friend Jeung and her Caucasian partner not only bridged cultural differences but also loosened the stronghold of traditional belief. Jeung's parents initially refused to support her choice of partner, only meeting Matthew a year into their relationship. I remember Jeung's emotional distress, her deep sense of not being supported, which contributed to difficulties in her relationship, as well as distrust of her parents and herself. On the day of the wedding however, both cultures came together to form a rich tapestry of colours, textures and expressions, honouring family values and change. And in her parents' eyes, I saw joy.

The Law of Attraction is Balance

Masiandia: *"Universal law does not support resistance but rather maintains a constant state of divine intervention. Therefore, you cannot side-step your purpose without experiencing setbacks and upheaval. Fulfilment is made possible with the willingness to embrace life as it is, letting go of resistance to receive life's many gifts.*

"The interrelationship between spirit and humanity forms the law of attraction, which is magnetic energy – the source of your life's abundance. It is the sacred code within your body's energy system – the balance point that your living organism must maintain to regulate a state of homeostasis. One could say that the law of attraction is the law of balance. We compare this to the migratory patterns of birds. How do flocks of birds know when to follow the course of change?

It is the law of attraction, a magnetic force drawing them. To resist would result in being out of balance.

"Many people assume that the law of attraction is a way in which 'like attracts like'. But in truth the law of attraction is the essential law of balance, wherein polarities, not similarities, are drawn together to unite spirit with form. For instance, water is not drawn to more water; rather, it is the flow of gravity that draws streams to oceans. Water is drawn to quenching thirst, to filling land. People are pulled together not because they are the same, but rather because they need one another for their evolution, to grow, to learn, to honour karmic ties.

"All dissimilarities, discomforting relationships and situations that expand your sense of reality serve a greater purpose, which is to return you to balance. You cannot achieve balance in isolation, by only adhering to the status quo and surrounding yourself with people with whom you are comfortable. It is duality, not similarity, which serves your growth, which awakens you to new energies that instigate and inspire your thoughts and emotions. Therefore, returning to balance is not about finding the still point of beingness only in quiet moments such as in meditation, but being in a meditative state throughout your life, which is being open to 'seeing' the beauty that is all around you in everything. When you 'see' the beauty in everything, you support the symbiotic relationship within all aspects of your life, which allows your purpose to flourish.

"By recognizing and thus welcoming beauty, the feelings of shame, insecurity and fear no longer exist. By seeing the beauty in all life, which is accepting its natural order, you become an open vessel, a conduit for divinity. Therefore, there is no need to strive for more, because your heightened magnetic-centre attracts to you what you need to fulfil your dreams, strengthen your health and honour your purpose. The quantum intelligence of form and consciousness together reach towards you to grant you all the love and support you need. Your job is to receive it.

Therefore, open your eyes and 'see' the beauty in the world, for there is so much to see. When you 'see' the beauty in the world, you see yourself in all of its reflection, and you experience the deep well of love, union and peace that exists within you."

I am
the shadow that follows you
       wherever you go
and the mountain
that climbs itself
to the summit.
I am
the sky embracing earth,
       water in all living things,
and a seal chancing the
fisherman's net
in pursuit of prey.
I am
the seed in the palm
of your hand
destined to be planted,
and I am your hand
       holding the seed.

I am courage beckoning a
dying man, and the
courage to be born again.

I am faith in the darkest hour,
and love waiting at your door
patiently.

CHAPTER SIX

Beyond Illusion

Laughter, love and loneliness,
              fear forgetting truth …
Cliff too high to climb
and a forest strewn with diverging paths.

I can't find my way –
              lost directions pointing everywhere.
Where do I turn? I follow you.

I follow your emotion,
your gestures and your eternal grief.
I cross the river deep with memories,
              but the bridge is falling apart.
Falling, falling.   I grab on to – nothing.

Where are you, beloved mirage?
In a past that I am no longer a part of.
              In a dream that didn't come true.

Dispelling Illusions – A Spiritual Practice

 raditionally, many Eastern philosophies have upheld the belief
that the world is an illusion and focus on the idea that our perception of the world is a projection created by our collective agreement of
reality. When I looked deeper into the origins of this concept, I discovered
that the Sanskrit word for illusion, Māyā, centres on the fundamental idea
that the Universe cannot be reduced to our perception of it. It is our human perception that restricts us, not the multidimensional Universe and
not Gaia.

If the world were a figment of our imagining, then it would have no
reality to it at all – it wouldn't exist. But for me, Gaia is very real: an Entity
encompassing ecological interrelationships between all life-forms, vegetation, humans, animals, soil, water and air. The Earth is a living organism
supported by natural cycles: a complex, regulating eco-system that maintains life on Earth, just like the body's physiological system that regulates
internal homeostasis.

Masiandia's sustained support of the symbiotic connection between
our souls and Earth-reality inspires me to envision a world that isn't associated with illusion, but rather with reverence. A world that is whole
and welcoming … homage to heaven on Earth. Imagine honouring the
life-force in all nature or beholding the life of a newborn with profound
delight, celebrating a more authentic reality than we think we know and
then realizing that our joy affects that new reality. Our joy balances reality
by shaping a whole new expression of that reality. It blesses the new life
with love and touches Earth with renewing presence.

Masiandia: *"There is so much more to see and experience on this beautiful planet, and it is by embracing your shared divinity with Earth that you lift the veil of
Maya and receive the gift of Earth's magnitude – her love for you.*

"The Earthly realm, which you see and sense, hear, smell and taste, is very

real. It is a tangible phenomenon, a vital existence that the 'union' between soul and physical-reality has created based on principles of shared consciousness. Earth is an Entity, a vibration of matter that merges spirit-consciousness with form in all living things, from human nature to wildlife, trees, mountains and water. Yes, forms such as rock, soil, roots and water are alive with spirit-consciousness and are maintained by their own participation with this amazing planet. Together, all life on Earth co-creates a synthesis of form and essence made manifest by a collective relationship with Earth, which is evolving and changing. It must evolve in order to sustain all life on Earth.

"Your concept of the material world needs to expand to encompass more of Earth's vital essence. Otherwise, you limit your understanding of the relationship between form and consciousness; you devote your energy to misconceptions rather than the beauty that Earth has to offer you. From our spirit perspective, it is the energy vibration of matter that is real, not matter itself. This doesn't mean that this planet is merely the fabrication of your collective mind, or that it doesn't really exist. It means that it is more than your mass-conscious understanding, more than physical dense-matter and more than limited time and space. Earth is a living symbiotic system of energy, interrelated and shaped by your existential partnership. It is not separate from you. Nothing is separate in the entire multidimensional Universe, as all is mutually responsive and in relationship with the Divine."

Partnership with Earth

Masiandia: *"Your partnership with Earth is part of a greater relationship with multidimensional reality and needs your devotion to truth to evolve. Thus, Earth's evolution is your evolution. It is your responsibility to become a shaper of a more heartfelt reality than the inflexible reality you have all been struggling with, by believing in something greater than yourselves, by believing in your relationship with Earth."*

$\mathcal{W}$e cultivate an expanded perception of reality when we honour our relationship with Earth, and we move beyond illusions by seeing through the lens of awareness. In contrast, when we perceive our environment through the lens of fear and worry, as well as through judgment and discrimination, we send a crippling message to our body. Fear-perceptions set in motion the nervous and endocrine systems to prepare the body for fight or flight, a physiological response to a perceived threat to one's survival. The hypothalamus transmits neural frequencies to the kidneys, activating the adrenal hormones, which sends a danger signal to the cells of the body. From a state of prolonged heightened anxiety, the cells lose vitality, depleting the immune system. We can shift our perception of reality by cultivating a state of restful integration, which allows our mind and body to receive fundamental messages of belonging and safety. By encompassing a deep sense of care towards ourselves we become rooted in our inner-sanctuary.

It was through cultivating such a state that I received a channelled message from Gaia, a message that evoked in me an inmost sense of trust in divine order. She said to me, *"I am your dream … we both want the same thing."* Her words reminded me that I am not alone, that I am part of something greater than myself, and in that moment I believed that anything was possible.

Personal Journal:
Channelled Message from Gaia, Mother Divine

"There is no place more worthy of home than your love for me. It is the guiding force in your life – the will of Divinity showing you the way. Your love is guiding you home because it is shaped by the frequency of belonging, thus it manifests its counterpart – its place in time and space. Love influences the complete matrix – the symbiotic relationship between desire and reality.

"Follow me, my beloved. Return to my belly, my breasts and my people. Shower them with affection and cherish every moment. There is no path but for the way to me. Come to me, let me hold you in my love and show you that life is not the shadow of the past; it is a fresh new beginning. Home and belonging are not found in fear and disappointment; they are only found in faith, gratitude and devotion. Give everything to me, and I will give everything to you."

When I received these words I felt held in sacredness akin to stepping into a cathedral of trees. I felt blessed as a newborn child held in her mother's arms and welcomed in a way that I had not yet experienced. I knew then that I belonged in this life, with its meandering paths and challenges, and that I was ready to love it all. It's in loving life that we allow it to be more than our limited perception; we give it permission to be magical and whole, as we cup the flame of our desires in trust and devotion.

This sense of wonderment is the way in which my friend Steve looks at life, inspiring me with his innocence, with the way he rejoices in every experience. He feels everything in depth and with curiosity, and he believes in a larger reality that encompasses the artistry of outgrowing limitations and embodying the mystery. He shared with me an incredible incident that occurred in his life a few years ago. He was commuting from the city centre in Montreal to the South Shore and was stuck in heavy traffic, berating himself for underestimating the time it would take to arrive at his daughter's home, as they had planned a special event that she had been looking forward to.

He became so overtaken by a profound desire to honour his engagement that the traffic problem no longer mattered; in fact, it no longer existed. He couldn't explain the means, but somehow he found himself on a completely different road, past the connecting bridge, past the traffic and en route to his daughter's place. Steve enthusiastically told me that he teleported, and needless to say he arrived on time. He had so completely resonated with his desire to support his daughter that he matched his vibration to its frequency and fully embodied it.

Once we embody an idea wholeheartedly, we link to the power grid of its morphic field and literally shift our reality to what we are in resonance with, suggests Richard Bartlett in *Matrix Energetics*. Steve was interested in this concept and wanted to know how he could do this at will. Masiandia told him that shifting reality is not about willpower; it is an unbounded capacity to see no end to possibility, a seamless trust in transformational consciousness, magnifying our capacity to change outer world events through suspending our perception of reality. Bartlett explains that we contain the keys within us for infinite possibilities, as long as we do not try to *make* anything happen. "The idea here is to let go of what you think you know so that your thoughts can then lead you towards a more desirable new outcome," he writes.

I appreciate what Bartlett is saying, and simultaneously I know just how difficult that is. While letting go of what we know is freeing, at times it can be equally, if not more, unnerving because it challenges our commonplace sense of reality. Instead of trusting life's possibilities, too often we struggle with reality and define our life choices based on past experiences, on what we "think" is possible. I refuse to remain stifled by a limited sense of possibility defined by my past-experience and by the obstacles I see around me, when instead I can cultivate a rich and fulfilling relationship with my dreams. The present does not have to be interpreted by the past or by the consensus agreement of reality. Reality can be far more wondrous and benevolent. I've heard too many hopeful stories that have expanded my sense of reality and have opened me to what is possible, to continue projecting disbelief onto an otherwise expansive life.

Things are really not as they seem. A friend convinced me of that when she told me of a shocking situation that occurred when she was in her teens. Walking along a city street, she noticed that she was being followed. She hastened her pace and saw that the man following her was walking more quickly, so she began to run and then heard his footstep coming close behind. Disoriented, she turned into a narrow street in her attempt to get away from him. Running as fast as she could, her heart pounding up into her throat, she saw a fence closing off the end of the street. Terrified that he would catch up with her, she hoped that she could scale it, but just as she was about to grab the fence she ran right through it, and stumbled on the other side. Looking back in stunned amazement, she stared at her pursuer, who stood on the opposite side of the fence, wearing an expression of absolute disbelief. What morphed the field of her reality? Perhaps it was the help of unseen presences that created a shift in reality, an answer to her breathless prayer for help.

Not only is reality not as it appears; we are also not alone. If only we could remember this on a day-to-day basis, we could draw immeasurable support and nourishment. I was so fortunate a few years ago to have avoided a car accident with a bus. I was positioned in my car beside the front of the bus when the driver proceeded to enter my lane. I honked to let him know I was there and quickly accelerated to get out of the bus's way; then to my surprise one of my spirit guides overtook my body. The hands on my steering wheel were no longer my own, and it felt as if my car was being pulled back, as though in reverse. Suddenly, rather than near the front of the bus, my car was at the back end, leaving enough space for the bus to get by without a collision. My whole sense of where the bus had been had completely shifted, as if somehow time had lapsed backwards by a few seconds, long enough to reposition my vehicle. The sensation that I experienced while driving can be described as being in a warped time and space, being out of control and equally very safe.

Real-reality

*I*t is the expansive and magical moments in life that move me beyond limited perceptions of consensus reality. These larger-than-life recollections, experiences and visions connect me to the riches of what is truly possible and inspire me to be who I really am.

With clarity and devotion emboldening our vision, we can manifest the lives that we long for. However, for many of us, stepping out of the normalcy of habitual thinking initiates a spiritual dilemma, which brings us to the question, 'Who Am I?'

"Just be yourself!" friends have said over the years, which I have taken as meaning that they love who I am. But how many people look at themselves in the mirror and actually like what they see? The question, 'Who am I?' just can't be answered by dwelling on who we think we should be or who we currently think we are; but nevertheless, many of us try this route.

Masiandia says that these conditioned interpretations of who we think we are or who we think we should be are illusions, limited perceptions that define us and inevitably separate us from Source-energy. Illusions are imbalances shaped by the stories that we make up about each other and are formed by conditioned beliefs that originate from misunderstandings, judgments and learned behaviour. These misconceptions overshadow our authentic selves – misconceptions such as the belief that we shouldn't stand out or that we have to be tolerant, positive, unemotional and invulnerable. We sacrifice our souls to maintain these misconceptions, denying the guidance of our feelings and the flow of divine intervention.

I wonder who we are outside of the bounds of these consensual misconceptions. Who are we when not shaped by our limited view of reality, by the fear of failure, condemnation or rejection, or when we are not disapproving of others and ourselves? Who are we when we are not limited or separated by the fear of loss? We are visible and powerful beyond measure and leaders of our own lives.

However, we are rarely recognized honourably when we first set out to expand our concept of reality, when we follow our own way in life. When I had my first website designed, the designer's husband explicitly suggested that I not mention channelling. He thought it wise that I not tell people that I communicate with spirits, that I should be subtler in my approach and focus primarily on counselling and bodywork. But how does hiding serve anyone? Illusions are the false premises that bind us to the past, to staying infinitely small and hidden away.

Many of us don't allow ourselves to thrive because there is a lot at risk: perhaps our self-identity, family, friends and employment are all subject to the possibility of loss. For some, disapproval and discrimination can lead to imprisonment and even death. How does one inhabit his/her genuine truth and encourage the fullness of soul vision in a world that insists on conformity? Masiandia say it's by honouring our karmic relationship with this world and moving towards a conscious and loving relationship with ourselves.

Masiandia: *"No matter where you are, what your heritage is or what determines your quality of living, you and nature are both beholden to one another, dependent on one another's care. You can only find deeper meaning in life and free yourself from the bondage of oppression by honouring what is sacred in you. In this way, you care for your own nature; you embody your physical form with deep reverence and self-respect. In loving yourself, you love the world, an action that regenerates and balances the Earth's grid patterns – an action that expands your vision of reality. By opening your eyes to the beauty of who you truly are, not the distillation of what your life has defined for you, you embrace your sacredness. When you embrace your divinity, you emit a strong frequency of possibility that shifts reality – you enter into the arms of miracles."*

———ↄ᙮᙮ᑍ———

Expanding Your Collective Agreement of Reality

J would like to address the process of seeing the world from a renewed inner vision by recalling an exercise that Masiandia initiated
regarding my art. They asked me to deepen my sense perception of my
paintings by entering into the feeling quality of colour and its purpose.
They began by explaining that the way a colour looks to us visually is
based on our perception of its energy, and that our perception is based
on a collective agreement. Masiandia asked me to feel into the colour that
I had been working with in my painting, which was red, and then guided me to embrace its expression and slowly move beyond the consensus
agreement that defined the colour. They explained to me that very few
people actually "see" or "sense" the energy-vibration of colour; people
instead project a three-dimensional image of colour that is bereft of spirit.

"It is so much more," Masiandia said. *"The colour 'red' is magical, spontaneous and imaginative; it is varied in expression and represents different things
at different times, based on your receptivity. To go beyond the collective notion of the colour, you must delve into the deeper realm of feeling, sensing and
enthusiasm."*

Personally, feeling into the colour red gave me an intimate connection
with my art and its meaning. It showed me a sense of how the colour-
energy interacts with other shapes in my work and helped me see the way
in which it touches me. In *The Widening Stream,* David Ulrich explores this
form of colour-perception beautifully. He explains that when we maintain
a measure of awareness within ourselves while simultaneously directing
this awareness toward the object of our perception, we are no longer limited to looking at the outside of things. As an artist, Ulrich has a practice of
looking at colour by feeling it, locating where its particular hue resounds

in his body. He says that every part of our body is a sensitive receiving apparatus and that colour can touch different inner regions, stimulating thoughts, emotions and sensations.

"Real seeing," Ulrich says, "implies not only a positive, life-affirming attitude, but also a genuine effort toward direct, conscious perception." He goes on to express that the nature of our perceptions is relative and depends on our state of awareness. "Suspending the internal dialogue, maintaining a dual attention that embraces both ourselves and the perceived object, and trying to be fully present to the moment in front of us, are exercises in the process of seeing."

This enriches my creative process: the way in which I relate to my art and to colour. It also expands my understanding of energy healing. In whichever hue colour presents itself, it holds harmonizing qualities. An intimate relationship with the hues and shades of colour balances thoughts, feelings and physical functions and supports brain integration, which regulates the central nervous system. Neuron frequencies in the brain move into a balanced state, interacting with the energy messages of colour and one's relationship with it. This is one of nature's gifts that activates and balances the health we need and long for.

Your Perception Is a Matter of Choice

Masiandia: *"We have purposefully chosen to refer to Earth-reality as illusion, in order to help you see that it is more than it appears to be. Everything that you perceive is more expansive than your present five-senses allow you to experience, such as your observation of the flesh of the human body. It is visibly corporeal in the space and time of the reality in which you have chosen to incarnate. But in the totality of all time, your image of flesh is only a partial picture because you are only viewing it through a three-dimensional reality, while the physical energy vibration of flesh is actually multidimensional.*

"As scientists have discovered, at the molecular level, matter is actually energy expressed in quantum light waves. Energy is intrinsically multidimensional, however your human perception cannot fully grasp this, at least not at this point in Earth evolution. There are future lifetimes where human vision is very similar to microscopic vision. Imagine seeing flesh in all the detailed layers of skin, blood and microorganisms. Most people are averse to this image and return to their familiar perception of flesh because it is what they are comfortable with, yet in a future lifetime it will be quite ordinary to perceive flesh in all its dimensions of reality.

"How do you dispel illusion? Through choice! You like the illusion of your skin. Keep it. But if you don't like your skin, such as with eczema, acne, deformations or scarring, then it is necessary to examine your illusion. Your perception is a matter of choice."

When it comes to physical conditions and emotional issues, examining our perception can be painful, because we tend to think that the situation is due to something that we're doing wrong or that we are being punished. Most people also attempt to resolve issues by trying to fix them or wage war on them to control the situation, rather than establish an intimate connection with what they need. Nature has endowed us with conditions and emotions for a higher purpose – to arouse self-inquiry and self-realization. But if we're only set on controlling them, how can we examine our perceptions, dispel illusion and thus fulfil our needs?

Masiandia: *"As we have said in previous chapters, the only way to heal anything is to feel it more; the only way to fulfil your needs is to listen to yourself and develop an intimate relationship with the full spectrum of your human experience. Otherwise, your life is made manifest in direct proportion to your limited beliefs, rather than as a reflection of your soul-consciousness."*

When Illusions Become Real

Masiandia: *"We understand that many people find it difficult to honour their human nature, let alone their soul relationship with the Earth, because they believe that the Universe has failed to provide for them and that they are alone and unwanted. This belief is part of the misconception that humankind is unworthy of pleasure, fun, freedom and security. It is a belief that has been passed down through generations and has developed into mass-conscious illusions, illusions that have become tangibly real.*

"A prevailing illusion is poverty-consciousness, which either evokes hardship or greed. This illusion has become a reality that affects all life on Earth, exuding a destructive force on this planet. Poverty-consciousness has become very real because it is granted an immense level of energy. It is an illusion that is imbued with and enforced by layers of misunderstanding and judgments, based on the belief that humanity is sinful, and unworthy of love.

"We are referring to an energy miasm – a constructed reality manifested by the collective-unconscious shared perception of poverty, which is the fear of not having enough, the belief that one has to have more, hunger for power or the thought that one is powerless. These limited perceptions of reality form limited reality globally.

"When your willpower is focused on a specific belief, you give that belief the power to manifest into reality. When a large group of people focus their willpower on the same collective belief, the belief fuses into a reality-pattern that has a life of its own. Poverty-consciousness has become a system that exists independently, contributing to the imbalances and distortions of the Earth's abundance.

"The surest way to surpass the limitations of poverty-consciousness is by freeing your joy and transforming your relationship with the Earth – by allowing yourself to see more than consensus reality. To do this you must cease giving collective patterns so much energy, such as results in the prevalence of cancer. Cancer is an energy-illusion that humanity has chosen to anchor in three-dimensional reality for the purpose of working through the global belief that humanity

is guilty. The prevailing denial of self-value and suppression of the fundamental needs of your soul-in-body weakens otherwise healthy rejuvenating cells. The energy vibration of cells goes out of balance when there is no other choice, when truth is denied and it must fight to maintain equilibrium in a body that is in conflict with itself."

*A*s I review Masiandia's message, I'm concerned that some readers may think that they are suggesting that those with cancer have brought it on themselves. On the contrary, anyone struggling with an illness is helping us all heal, reshaping our collective illusions about reality and redefining the truth about our soul's miraculous interconnection with Earth. Masiandia's message endeavours to help us cultivate a different relationship with mass-conscious patterns, thus viewing disease in a way that is empowered and life affirming.

Masiandia: *"It is only the human mind that judges illness and by so doing shuts down the intricate re-patterning of the body's cellular system. Disease, like all other imbalances, requires reconstruction of beliefs to support the mind in re-membering soulful worthiness, thus transforming conditions of dishonour into love. We want you to understand that you have the power to completely create the lives you really want with patience, forgiveness, acceptance, trust and con-viction – not hatred! By trusting the body, you enter into a profoundly healing and rejuvenating relationship with your whole body, mind and soul.*

"Our dear friends, please honour the gift that your soul has come to bequeath to Earth, and in turn receive Gaia's gift. The Earth provides your soul with rich, purposeful life-experiences to merge your divinity with reality. All physical and emotional setbacks are opportunities to evolve your consciousness and to give the gift of your devotion, so that you can be part of raising the frequency of love on this planet. All souls enter Earth-reality to make manifest their love.

"It is easy to manifest love in ideal conditions. Everyone is happy in fair weather, but what about when faced with challenges, adversity, war, poverty

and pain? These are the conditions that shape a soul's endurance, and the desert landscape that tests its conviction. You are here on this planet to evolve beyond its mass-conscious reality in order to transcend it and give it the gift of your spirit. Our dear friends ... spread your wings of faith, and endure the lessons that awaken you."

Embracing Your Wholeness

There is true magic that occurs through enduring our lessons, or in other words, by persisting through situations that arise in our lives. We evolve beyond the lessons, and our diligence leads to uncovering who we are.

I would like to illustrate a process of awareness that ultimately leads to embracing who we are, by sharing a story told to me by Andres. He had gone rock climbing with a group of advanced climbers, and throughout the day he compared himself to them, to the extent that he felt insecure about his own rock climbing skills. Midway up his climb, Andres insecurity worsened; he felt shaky and unstable. To break free from this reaction, he pushed aside the fear and persevered to the top of the cliff. But by the time he reached the summit he felt extremely dissatisfied and disappointed, because when he looked back down to where he had pushed his fear aside, he saw his frightened inner-child left behind and alone. He realized that he wanted to be fully engaged and present, and to do this he needed to accept the fear along with his pride, which took more courage than asserting power over his vulnerability. In this way, his frightened inner-child could also accomplish the climb. Now when Andres goes climbing he doesn't over-identify with his drive to perform or with fear, instead he observes the two with a calm sense of self-acceptance.

It is with gentleness, empathy and self-acceptance that we see beyond illusions; we recognize our intrinsic wholeness and luxuriate in the affinity that unites the dualities of our fears and strengths. In this way, we also thrive in the union between our soul and nature. We dissolve our resistance, thus we cease neglecting our nature and become mindful of the Earth.

A few years ago, as I sat by a lake in the Kootenay Valley with my journal in hand, I endeavoured to make peace with my own duality. Emotionally devastated, I sat overlooking the burned remains of a forest on one side of the lake and a clear-cut logged perforation on the other. I felt angry, hurt and dispirited. To soften my emotional state, Masiandia encouraged me to let go of my disapproval of clearcut logging, for it caused a disconnection with my appreciation of nature. They said that with disapproval I neglected to love the land. Initially, I didn't want to look at the deforestation with the heart of forgiveness. However, I did want to gaze upon the land with tenderness, to lose the expectation that it be flawless to deserve my love. Journaling helped me come to accept what I was feeling, and it also brought to light the immanent forgiveness that I needed to embrace. I've chosen to share my journal writing here, because I think it is relevant in exploring the personal process of lifting the veil of illusion.

Personal Journal – Kootenay Valley

> My feet are cold, and the lake is a clear mirror, slightly rippled and reflecting mostly clouds with patches of blue sky in the far distance. I am writing to let my emotions find purpose through words. My shoulders are sore, and my breath is shallow in this place – this place where light subtly illuminates, and a bird rests on a log, wings spread as it takes flight towards the trees. I'm restless. The osprey just dived into the water, splashed and spread its wings wide. I saw it through the binoculars that make me dizzy.
>
> My eyes are now trying to recover. I long to feel at peace. My feet are cold, my eyes are strained, and I'm still restless. I long to feel calm, secure, held in the comfort and stillness of my heart, but when I see the burned remains of the forest across the lake, my

heart sinks. I try to remember that it's all part of nature's cycle of regeneration, until I look in the other direction and see a clearcut patch defacing the landscape. I try to appreciate the universal order of things and tell myself that in this small depressed moment I cannot see the bigger picture, so I give my grief to the spirits and pray for a healthier planet. But when I look back again to the geometric clear-cut that severs the continuity of the mountain, I want to close my eyes and not see anything anymore. So I don't see the still lake, and I don't see the mountain peaks of snow and dark contrasting with the sky, or the lush green field separating the trees from their reflection. I don't see the mirrored sky in the water fade as it approaches the shore or the rocks in multitudes of colour. But I can still hear the birdcalls and the highway sounds a mile away, and I am too restless to keep my eyes closed.

I'm too restless to not see, not hear and not live amid the unbalanced and balanced qualities of life. This emotional push and pull keeps me moving, it keeps me from shutting down while nature keeps on moving, living, flying, being still, belonging and growing back where mankind's control encroaches upon it. And while it may not seem as if nature is prevailing, I believe it is.

*W*hen I had lifted my gaze and begun to appreciate my surroundings, Masiandia offered their continued support. They asked me to understand that the Earth is not a victim of environmental damage or misuse. They said the destruction of nature is part of the Earth's agreed evolution with humanity. This doesn't mean that we are not responsible for the negligence and greed that contributes to destruction. It points to our misunderstanding and lack of custodianship with the resources that this planet so generously gives to us. It is our limited perception of reality that restricts Earth's vitality and abundance. We don't see how generous the Earth is, just as we don't acknowledge the magnitude of our multi-faceted nature. It's by welcoming every aspect of our humanity that we truly receive what the Earth has to offer us. In this way, we are not set on confronting nature wilfully, but rather investigating the alternate ways we can benefit from this land and body. In Masiandia's words, being true to our divinity, opening our soul channel, is the greatest healing gift that we can place upon this planet.

> *Forgive me, father, for I have sinned*
> *Caught in a web of illusions*
> *Hiding my soul from your grace*
>
> *Forgive me, mother*
> *I have neglected you, you within me*
> *I have not seen my own divinity*

CHAPTER SEVEN

Faith, Returning to Wholeness

Oh Great Spirit, I am your servant.
I am your messenger, I am your beloved.

I give you my faith and I know that you are guiding me.
I know that you are answering my prayers.

I am answering your prayers.

I am no longer waiting.
I am in love with this rich and wonderful world.

True Meaning of Faith

*W*hen I initially received the message for this chapter, I was convinced that I could not capture the true meaning of faith, that I didn't have faith myself because fear overshadowed my sense of conviction. Then I saw through my fear; I saw that throughout my life faith has been my inner refuge from disappointment and hurt and from the conditioning of my ancestral lineage. It has been the place within me where I seek comfort and the courage to find my own voice.

There have been times in my life when all I had was my faith, when depression overtook me and getting out of bed was laborious. This is when faith pulled the covers back and gently demanded that I get up. It refused to let me fall away from its incessant call to the wild, to the far reaches of my dreams. Faith was and still is an urging from within, returning me to my innermost longing, inspiring me to face each day with reverence and prayer. For me, faith is trusting that I will be taken care of and knowing that when I'm willing to face what lies before me, I am given the strength and courage I need.

It reassures me to know that the strength and courage needed to face any of life's challenges is not ours alone. It is shared with spirit, gifted by the Universe. Our faith is an active force that merges our heart's desire with the presence of spirit; it serves to open us to the divine in everything. It becomes something larger than us: a stream of energy given to us by our higher will, our eternal grace that cannot be explained and has nothing to prove. The purpose of our faith is to awaken us to our freedom, thus it cannot be coaxed into a manageable form. It is not an objective, something to be thrust out onto the world, but a gift that we receive from the grace of divinity.

But many of us haven't learned to receive God's gift. We demand proof and assurances and seek perfection before we give ourselves to faith. *"But faith doesn't like being tested,"* says Masiandia. Faith exists on its own terms, defined by our soul-purpose not our personality. Faith cannot be governed by our whims and expectations, for it's meant to support our higher-consciousness in relationship with the whole Universe, not our mistrust and skepticism. In a world that tests everything, it only stands to reason that faith is not welcomed. We are taught to plan our lives and force our will upon our own nature, not embody a way of life that is prayerful. In fact, faith is thought of as something to achieve through discipline. But it doesn't work that way; it cannot be bound by our expectations. It cannot stand the confinement of oppression, for it is a fluid motion; it is the centre point between our longing and resistance, where the energy of life pours freely.

Fulcrum Point

*W*ithin the channelled message for this chapter, Masiandia travels along two pathways in exploring the meaning of faith. They speak of the relationship between longing and resistance – the way in which one supports the other – and they also refer to faith as the practice of spiritual devotion, the state of being in receipt of God's love.

It is here in the centre-point between our longing and resistance that we allow ourselves to be made whole. Here we embrace all our life experiences: the ones that we cherish and regard as acceptable and also the aspects of ourselves that we dislike. We give ourselves permission to be imperfect, simultaneously welcoming our soul wisdom and entrusting our most vulnerable frailties to an inner compassion. In this way, we leave nothing behind. Every part of us steps forth, in tandem, onto the path of manifesting our purpose. Therefore, what looks like opposing forces is actually an alliance between complementary energies. This fulcrum between our longing and resistance becomes the point of transformation that roots faith into reality.

Our longing for fulfilment and our habitual resistance are

interdependent and cannot be separated; the relationship between the two is an intrinsic part of the whole expression of our soul and body union. Just like a great piece of art, it is the tension that gives it character; it is the duality between contrasting elements that creates the evocative composition and brings the art into harmonious balance. The duality between our longing and resistance forms an interplay that naturally creates harmony, for it has the power to return us to wholeness, just like the body's homeostatic system that seeks balance even if illness is the method it resorts to. For instance, when we become overactive, anxious and stressed, depression can be the route that duality takes to bring us back to balance; it depletes our vitality to force us to rest. If it's passivity that undermines our energy, then duality takes on the allure of a challenging situation, forcing us to value what we want.

We often tend to see duality as something that is out of balance, not in harmony. But what happens when tectonic plates smash up against one another? Mountains are born. Duality is not the entangled aspects of ourselves that we see as misaligned, but rather opposite forces within us that are allies. Our dualities cannot but push up against one another until something gives way, for they are part of a universal law that naturally moves us towards wholeness. Universal law draws our differences together to support us in making peace with everything. We must follow the natural rhythm of our polarities to enter into a state of balance, by not only accepting the many facets of our personalities, but also by connecting with the way in which these differences form an alliance that is mutually supportive.

Masiandia: *"Without shadow you could not differentiate between water, rock or sky. Similarly, without light there would be no shapes to form your landscape. You need your resistance because it forms the contrasts that define your landscape; it provides structure and helps you maintain equilibrium. Your longing in turn fills you with purpose; it insists on change, refuses to repeat the past and ultimately brings you into alignment with the present.*

"Resistance serves as a support or base, like a vessel or riverbed, and longing is the energy that fills it. In faith, you honour the supporting structure that eloquently carries the vibrant energy of your soul, and you cherish the divine nature of your longing.

"Faith is 'knowing' that everything is interconnected, not broken or imperfect; everything has meaning and purpose. When you 'know' this, you are one with your eternal rhythms – your soul lifetimes, and you want to honour all of yourself because you intuitively recognize that anything you do in this lifetime affects the whole of all your lifetimes and the lives of others. You are intrinsically woven into all of humanity; your individual expression is inseparable from the whole. You are part of a larger multidimensional Universe that is not whole without you or fulfilled by you alone. Therefore, your greatest joy lies in opening yourself to the support of your whole Self, letting all your expressions serve you in inexplicable ways, no longer separating yourself in fear or shame. Take huge leaps, dear friends, leaps of faith into the fullness of who you are, not who you think you should be, but into the fullness of your multiplicity."

Along the Pendulum Swing

Masiandia: *"In faith, you lessen the fragmentation between your personality and essence; you draw the two closer together. In this way, the attributes from both human and soul-consciousness serve to return you to balance. Along the pendulum swing between the two you find the centre-point, which is the Holy Grail, an awakened sense of purpose and devotion. It is not the outcome of reaching for the centre-point that is important, for when awakening becomes a goal you no longer receive the messages and teachings from your life experiences, but rather identify with a false persona, neglecting where you are right now. When you seek enlightenment you negate the attributes of your human endeavours; you refuse the expression of pain and the inner language of your human nature.*

"We wish to impart the necessity of welcoming all of your Earthly and vi-
sionary experiences. You are a relationship unto yourself, a union between spirit
and matter that your ego-mind cannot fully understand. Thus, your mind moves
into unconscious patterns of confusion, forgetfulness and resistance. Your greatest fulfilment comes from allowing your mind to question and work through its
confusion, letting it be an active force that crystallizes higher vibrations. As your
mind bridges spirit and reality within its own natural timing, you no longer
over-identify with your thoughts; you enter into a state of in-between, the resting
point amid fluidity and structure.

"This centre-point exists at the place where your polarities meet. It is an incredibly freeing space that encompasses your fear and grace, confusion and clarity, movement and stagnation. Along the pendulum swing between these vastly
different polarities, your mind moves from one state into another, forgetting and
remembering, like waking from a dream in which the details are foggy, to later
remember the dream as though you had just awakened. You forget for example
that you are loved, entering a fog of loneliness and abandonment, to the point
in which your need for love awakens you; it calls you back to your worthiness.

"This dance of polarities serves a greater purpose that moves beyond the
mind yet needs the mind to evolve. Your soul unites you with a larger purpose
while your physical nature, your mind and body, gives you a form to experience that purpose. Like the fulcrum point between inhaling and exhaling, your
soul-consciousness and human nature coexist and are perfect counterparts of a
unified whole."

As I explore the fulcrum point between inhaling and exhaling,
I feel the expansiveness as my chest and belly extend, my
shoulders lift and my back is filled, and it feels good to take in oxygen.
Naturally I can't hold this breath, I need to let it out, let it go. It reminds
me that in life we tend to hold our breath, hold our lives together, but this
doesn't allow us to receive support. At the centre point between exhaling
and inhaling, releasing and receiving, there is a momentum of energy and

inner-quiet, like the rise and fall of waves, which is nourishing and profoundly healing – it is peaceful.

Having faith is returning to that natural rhythm between breathing in and letting go, trusting that we can fully release our resistance to be filled anew with sustenance and support. But the moment that we focus only on trying to attain the support we need without surrendering our will, we contract our very essence and vitality. It is with faith that we are receptive to harmony and balance. Then things have a way of coming together into a unified whole. Faith knows that everything is in harmony, even our most challenging circumstances. Everything plays a role in bringing us closer to our higher consciousness; everything supports our soul's journey into fulfilment.

Imagine being attentive to the synergy around you, to the signals, messages and opportunities that are making themselves present at all times. Imagine that there is more to see, more to understand, more to experience: that an endless sea of opportunity flows through your life constantly. In faith your eyes are opened; you take in more and you give more fully, and that is nourishing – it enhances your whole life-experience.

Trusting Faith

People often mistake faith for passivity. But as an artist, if I were only a passive force with my paintbrush, my art would have no meaning. As an artist who relies on the connection to spirit for my ideas, I know that my art would be lifeless if I didn't carry through with devotion and self-belief. Faith is about stepping off the edge of our comfort zone and daring to trust who we are. To trust in our faith is to hold a point of readiness for what wants to unfold in our lives, like with a bow and arrow that needs to be held in place to gather force before the arrow is released. Therefore, it is critical to have faith, to become still and find from within the readiness to act on the guidance we receive. It's important to remember that this still-point is not control. The arrow cannot aim true if it is held too tightly.

I was reminded of this in channelled communication I received from the Over-lighting Deva of Faith. In hopes to better understand and encompass my own faith, I asked the essence of faith for guidance and the following is her message.

Channelled Message –
From The Over-lighting Deva of Faith

"I am always underfoot, overseeing and administering your needs. I am always by your side. I am life opening its gates to you – walk through me, let me guide you home to a world that is seldom seen by the human eye and seldom revered. See me walking alongside you. I am the alighted shadow, the swift current of excitement that ruffles your consciousness and awakens you to your truth. What is faith? What is faith? What is there to understand? Cease trying to understand, for you stand in the way of seeing me. To focus so forcefully prevents you from seeing clearly. Allow your vision to blur, your senses to betray you, your mind to falter, your tension to dissolve. Only in this way will you receive me.

"I am a gift. As water keeps your body alive, I maintain your electrical system; I uphold your purpose in this human body. Reach beyond your hollow perceptions, not with force but with tenderness and absolute devotion. What is faith? What is faith? Keep asking, and you will always be searching. Stop and let me show you. Hold steady, relax, breathe and step forth onto the path before you. Your present experience will change; it has to, for that is its purpose. Aim, breathe again and again and know that I am hopelessly with you, in love with you – your

most tender friend. That is my mission. Like shadow that is
caused by the light, I am light illuminating the shadow. To have
faith then is to be free to flow with all that life gives you without
defining or evaluating it, for what governance has decreed the
dark as bad and light as good has been mistaken; they are one,
made whole by the other."

Masiandia: *"In many of your societies faith appears to be an illusive practice, a*
way of life that is relegated to mystics and spiritual devotees who are buttressed
by a foundational religion or spiritual philosophy. Therefore, faith is ridiculed by
prevalent social thinking. A socialized mentality relies predominantly on rational
processes, substituting faith with a reverence for order. So many people deny the
guidance of their spirit guardians, their souls, family, friends and their own sense
of truth, because they are afraid of losing something: love, success, security, iden-
tity. Faith is seen as being ineffectual, childish and even crazy.

"But in truth, whatever you want to accomplish in life calls for faith, because
it is the refined magnetic draw that manifests all of your desires. As we have men-
tioned before, you are comprised of magnetic energy. Faith raises the vibration
of this energy, attuning you to the situations that best serve your purpose, your
needs, your journey. With faith, you become magnetically charged and responsive
to what you need and want. You draw towards you the situations that are syner-
gistically aligned to your state of faith.

"In essence, faith is nature in its glorious and magical moments like the fever-
ish growth that sunlight arouses in a burgeoning garden, or a bee's unfaltering
thirst for the nourishing nectar surrendered by flowers. Faith is the wild salmon
leaping upstream, with shear conviction and willpower moving against the flow
of the river, following its natural rhythm with the cycles of the seasons. Faith is
the still-point at the core of a dried out land. When drought leaves desolation,
faith retreats far into the parched earth; it doesn't accept the drought for it cannot
survive it, instead it surrenders to death. Then the earth does not defy death; it

becomes what it must. In faith, the earth goes into dormancy; it retreats into its next stage of evolution until it is reborn again.

"Faith does not struggle with reality, but rather flows with what emerges naturally. Faith is the act of allowance, permission and surrender, such as a woman who knows when her relationship is over, or a man who knows that if he were to cling to his marriage he would be hanging on to a fantasy – to his idea of what a family ought to be. Faithfulness also knows when a relationship needs support and renewal – when love needs to be 'believed in' in times of stress, growth and difficulty. It is the act of trusting your longing and simultaneously caring for your resistance, and it is wisdom, health and hard work. Faith is your wondrous and magnificent duplicity, cradled in God's embrace."

We seldom allow ourselves to engage fully in what we are experiencing in the present, especially if the present moment is unclear. We're quite good at implementing actions, but when it comes to allowing life to carry us, we tend to force our will and deny the power of our spirits. Sometimes we need to do nothing in order to determine what to do next, how to do it, and where life is leading us. This doesn't mean becoming lethargic; it implies being empty so that faith can fill us from within, guiding us to the centre-point between our longing and our logic.

If all we do is focus on rational processes and on what we have to accomplish, we lose sight of our inner vision – our dreams. We become motivated by anxiety; constantly pressuring ourselves to achieve what we want, yet seldom stop to refuel. Without taking the time to rejuvenate, how can we become receptive to what we want?

My client, Alex, concentrated all his energy on an investment that would bring him early retirement. Unfortunately, he put everything else on hold; he borrowed money to invest in a venture he expected to be highly profitable, and primarily focused on manifesting techniques, imagining his success but not actually living what he was aiming for. A year later, the stock market crashed, and he lost everything.

When Masiandia asked him what he had intended to do with the money and his retirement, Alex said that he was finally going to rest, travel and read books. Masiandia then asked him, *"Did you take time to read while you were imagining your success, did you go on trips?"*

Angrily, Alex blurted, "No, I was working really hard so that I could finally quit working."

That is just the problem; Alex worked towards a future that he thought would enable him to retire, rather than incorporate some of what he wanted to experience into his present life. By overlooking his needs, he neglected to truly believe in what he longed for. He had no faith, even though he forged ahead and focused on what he wanted. Had he engaged in a more restful and fulfilling lifestyle, he would have strengthened his magnetic field, become energetically aligned with his vision and open to receiving what he wanted.

I see this in the lives of so many people who want to change yet continue to perform the same tasks with the same mindset. How can anything change when we continue to repeat the same actions? We need to take a leap of faith, not go on perpetually hoping for a better outcome. We need to step onto the path of our dreams in the present, not wait for guarantees before we act on them. And while it is true that believing in our longing calls for taking risks, we can only do that one step at a time. Hence, so many of us lose faith in our dreams because life doesn't provide us with proof of success right away. And yet, rather than endure doubt, we must endeavour to live from our trustful hearts, let our dreams gather momentum, propelled by our sense of worth and our longing.

Surpassing Your Dreams and Expectations

$\mathcal{T}$hings don't always work out as planned, and in the midst of disappointment we often disbelieve that situations can improve. But life has a way of working out and can surpass what we dream of when we allow it to. I know that for some people things fall into place with precise planning; they save for the future and it all works out; their marriage lasts and very little bewilders them. I was standing in a line-up when I overheard a woman talking about her retirement. She was baffled as to why people thought she was lucky to be able to retire. She said, "Of course my husband and I can stop working, we planned it all along … that's what it takes." For others the path is not so clearly marked. Perhaps they are confronted with health issues, separation or work-related changes and must completely remodel their lives.

By comparing ourselves to others or expecting that we each fit into a universal model, we miss out on the gift of life's mystery, which is available to us in all our unique experiences. "What is the gift?" a client once asked me. There is a Zen story that best defines this gift, about a farmer whose workhorse ran away.

Upon hearing the news, his neighbour came to console him. "Such bad luck," he said, sympathetically.

As the story goes, the farmer said, "Maybe."

The next morning the horse returned, bringing with it three wild horses.

"How wonderful," the neighbour exclaimed.

"Maybe," replied the farmer.

Interestingly, the farmer had no judgment about what was happening. Perhaps the loss of the horse was unfortunate and maybe it wasn't. The following day the farmer's son tried to ride one of the untamed horses. He was thrown off and broke his leg. The neighbour again came to offer his sympathy, and again the farmer's response was that perhaps it was a misfortune and maybe not.

The day after, military officials came to the village to draft young men into the army. Seeing that the son's leg was broken, they passed him by. The neighbour congratulated the farmer on how well things had turned out.

"Maybe," said the farmer.

Things are the way they are for reasons beyond our understanding, beyond our interpretations and evaluations, and something magical happens when we trust this. We discover that manifesting what we want in life is not about forcing our will upon reality; it's about letting divine grace support us. While there are aspects of life beyond our control, they are nevertheless within the reach of our trust. Ultimately, in trust we welcome life's mystery and receive its support. In this way, the obstacles and difficulties in our lives do not indicate that we have failed or that we are unable to master our lives, but rather they are opportunities to discover the joy in loving our wondrous and magnificent duplicity. No longer content to deny a single aspect of ourselves, we welcome all of our life experiences with open arms.

Masiandia: *"There is so much joy found in loving your life as it is, even with its many opposing contrasts. It is the moment that you argue with life that it argues back, resulting in conflict. That is not faith!*

"Faith is not fighting for change and struggling to be seen and heard. It is not anxiety and desperation, self-deprivation or disvaluing your life choices and who you are. Faith is allowing yourself to be startled awake by the worry and discomfort, forced to address your true sense of value and what you ultimately need. Nothing can escape divine order. Outer distress is but a call from within, a beckoning towards self-awareness, self-acceptance and acceptance of all life. You are destined to discover more of you in all your life experiences, whether these experiences are good or bad, pleasurable or disappointing. To spirit, it is all the

same – everything is divine, and everything is an unfolding story awaiting your true commitment and faith. To spirit, your greatest challenges are your greatest allies, serving to help you remember who you are.

"All situations are then opportunities for becoming truer expressions of your soul, transforming limitations into joy, insecurity into conviction. In this way, for example, struggling with a spouse evolves into surrendering your fears into trust. Whatever is occurring in the relationship, whether it is a disagreement or lack of respect or care, your involvement becomes defined by your sense of faith, not the pressure to change the other or yourself or the situation. This allows you to be reshaped by what emerges within you, beyond reactions and self-doubt. Then the value of your relationship is not questioned, and nor is the validity of your feelings or your spouses'. You become receptive to what best serves your soul, not your personality, and you awaken to your highest potential, setting aside insecurities for self-worth.

"Ultimately, you are your own life-partner – the one that holds the key to your heart. You are the engineer of your own life-experiences, and the bearer of self-judgment or self-acceptance. It is ultimately your choice to embrace all life with faith.

"Faith is pleasure, not war; mutual support, not neglect and disharmony. And within the context of your life, relationships, family and work, faith is intuitive responsiveness. It is about being in a state of in-between, not knowing and knowing simultaneously, thus allowing life to surprise you, sustain you, and entice you. You in turn offer life your own support and seduction. Yes, you can seduce life with your beautiful acceptance and trust, with your willingness to not know and to be wise beyond your understanding, beyond reason. Let life amaze you, shock you, quiet you, move you ... while you step into it fully. Only then can life be fulfilled by you, awakened by you and brought into complete balance. Then any struggle cannot continue for it is relieved of its purpose – its raison d'être. Suffering becomes nonexistent when you choose faith, when you give all life your prayerful involvement – your eternal presence."

Stepping into the Flow of Life

*D*avid Whyte's poem "Faith", from his spoken-word album *Close to Home*, offers a concept of faith that is especially meaningful to me. He laments his experience of refusing faith "even the smallest entry." Whyte says, "Let this then, my small poem, like a new moon, slender and barely open, be the first prayer that opens me to faith." I am touched by this honest portrayal of human frailty because in welcoming our humanity, we allow ourselves to be more than our resistance, more than our refusal to trust. His words return me to my own prayer and show me that it is in the small actions, the small steps, that we uncover our faith.

For me, each creation that I honour – this book and my work, caring for my friendships and family, and my body, health, and spirit – is a small action that opens me to faith. Each creation is like a small crocus or bulb that in spring does not falter in faith, but grows toward light. Without this natural and trusting movement, there would be no flowering to enjoy, no greenery to behold and celebrate.

Masiandia: *"Faith requires action, otherwise it turns into waiting. Waiting for something to happen only manifests more waiting for something to happen, not what you long for. If you don't activate your faith, you invariably devalue your longing; you refuse to connect with who you truly are, and thus hold back the potential of your life while trying to move forward. You end up in stagnation.*

"You need to awaken your faith, give it purpose and propel it into action. To only have faith without action is to hope that something will come along without engaging wholeheartedly with life. Faith is a whole state of being, from believing to involvement, which requires courage and giving your greatest potential in order to make manifest that potential."

ur potential cannot manifest without our willingness to step into it fully. This reminds me of a phrase originated in ancient Greece,

'God helps those who help themselves.' And as my friend's brother likes to say, "a rudder only steers the boat if it is moving through water."

Masiandia: *"Manifesting the life you want requires stepping into the flow of the life you want and trusting the natural timing of your gestation. Your deliverance occurs when you are filled from within, and there is an outpouring.*

"We emphasize the importance of living wholeheartedly so that you can be filled to overflowing with the grace of your soul. You must cultivate initiative and simultaneously connect with the in-depth beauty of who you are, your needs and your longing, in order to manifest it. Develop a faithful relationship with yourself by honouring yourself, by allowing the Divine to permeate you with a deep sense of belonging."

By returning to our longing again and again, despair and disbelief ease and we enter into a state of grace. It is truly magical the way things do work out and surpass our expectations, but more significantly, we uncover in-depth awareness about who we are and what our purpose is. We discover what is truly important to us, which is not necessarily what we had initially envisioned.

An old friend once told me that becoming a quadriplegic at the age of fifteen spawned a life direction that helped evolve his consciousness. He believes that he would have followed in his brother's footsteps and led a life of heavy drugs and alcohol. Instead, he became a counsellor and helped countless people heal from pain and suffering. On the onset we have no way of understanding the mystery of life, but it helps to know that it isn't against us; it's serving a higher purpose than we are aware of.

In faith, we cherish that purpose and give it our utmost trust, which fills us with a profound connection to Source-energy. It is this faith that I see in my friend Kelly, who has endured countless health setbacks, including suffering a head injury in a near fatal accident. Sometimes I don't know how she goes on, except that her spirituality and her yearning for truth uplifts her daily. She is a devout believer that her faith is a gift from God that she mustn't forsake. She believes that everything that has happened in her life is a gift, an opportunity for her to learn and grow and be truer to her faith.

No matter the depths of her helplessness, when she has debilitating headaches and loss of memory, she affirms her relationship with God. She seeks to understand what is trying to emerge through her life experience, and she chooses to surrender to the Divine in all things. This is what I see in her: even when her negativity overtakes her and she fears the worst, she finds beauty in the small things in life, in the small actions that open her to faith. It is in these moments that I know that at the time of the accident she chose to live, and she is still choosing to be fully alive every day that she accepts her setbacks with faith. She is giving her life the grace of her belief and her love.

Cherishing the Self

Masiandia: *"Seeing the beauty in the small things or in life-changing situations brings you in direct contact with forgiveness. When you see the beauty in everything, you hold a high frequency of forgiveness, love, acceptance and above all, faith. There is nothing that keeps you from loving everything as it is and as it unfolds; nothing separates you from harmony but your own unwillingness. Harmony and peace – the fulfilment of your heart's desire – is always emerging, breaking free from resistance.*

"You can either defy the heart's longing or surrender, or enter into a state in which both meet. Your greatest sense of joy and purpose comes from merging duality: force and ease, willpower and trust, and aim and release. When you integrate both sides of duality you have wholeness, and that is fulfilling. The sooner you know this, the sooner you choose to live in faith, because you're no longer pulled by opposing forces.

"When you struggle to change reality, you deny the natural beauty in

everything and see only your projections. So often you critique what you see, compare yourself to others and their achievements, and define your faith based on what you think is possible. But what is possible? Do you know? You cannot know – it's beyond your present understanding. And how can your understanding evolve without faith? It cannot ... it remains the same. Without faith, you go around in circles, repeating the same old beliefs and logic, and you never taste the sweet nectar of hidden potential because it remains hidden. Your life's embryonic potential is meant to be birthed into life, seen, felt, heard and appreciated, not just dreamt of."

There is nothing more magical than birthing our potential, seeing in ourselves the beauty of who we are and giving that to life. If we cannot connect with our essence, our longing and innermost feeling, how can we even begin to have faith?

When a diver jumps off a diving board, his faith meets the resistance of the platform as his longing springs off and leaps into the water. In that moment of pure faith, there is seamless synergy between contact and release – the sublime dance of form and freedom. We cherish our own longing when we press against our resistance and take a leap of faith into our dreams. Then our resistance is no longer a setback but an opportunity to evolve our dreams and to honour what wants to emerge in our lives.

In a private counselling session, Diane, a client whose husband had passed away three years before, deepened her love for her husband by letting herself completely miss him. She had been denying her grief because friends and family had told her that she had to get over him, and so she tried not to think of him, consequently suppressing her enjoyment of life along with her loving memories of him. In the session, Diane entered a hypnotic trance, allowing herself to fully feel her connection to him. She missed their life together, and as she yearned for him, she no longer missed him; she no longer felt the sorrow of his departure. Instead, her longing became an invitation for his spirit to return to her and nourish her.

Ultimately, Diane's longing was not about her husband; it was a call for her to nurture a relationship with herself in a way that transcended the role she had adopted in her marriage. She revealed to me that in her marriage she had not experienced the kind of intimacy that she wanted. Her loss spoke of sacrifices that she had made, and her longing reflected a deep desire to be in a relationship where she could experience what she never had in her marriage, which was a trusting alliance with her femininity.

Diane's husband had been unsure of her intuitive insights and had ignored her wish for him to actively care for his health. He died of lung cancer after a lengthy and painful illness, which she nursed him through. She was wearied and discouraged by feeling so alone, yet drawn to her unspoken need for fulfilment. Her life now called for faith, a deepening of her spiritual serenity and greater commitment to honouring her feminine essence and strength, and to allow that to unfold in a new relationship.

Masiandia: *"It is natural to grieve for your beloved spouse, sister, brother, friend, parents or child and simultaneously miss what you didn't have with them. Your child may have distanced himself before his passing, leaving a huge space in you for regret. Or perhaps your sweetheart came into your life for a short time, and before the romance could flourish, he left his body. These are the moments in your life that leave you feeling incomplete.*

"You must journey back to yourself, back to the present moment where everything is welcomed, even your pain. In faith, you no longer struggle with the pain, you see it as an ally. You are no longer victimized by pain and are free to learn from its presence in your life."

Welcoming All That Is – Including Pain

Masiandia: *"Pain is not what it appears to be; it is an active participant in karmic release, as it creates a bond between your physical body and multidimensional lifetimes. It activates the nervous system at a frequency that bridges this lifetime and other lifetimes, to support soul integration. Soul integration opens your heart and mind to higher-conscious awareness, and enables you to live more full and authentic lives. A mystical alliance with your soul is ultimately what you seek. To know thyself is the ultimate reward.*

"You must remember that you are not only a human being in this time and space, but a synergistic thread within the larger tapestry of your soul. As we have said in earlier chapters, your soul exists in multidimensional time. Past lifetimes, and present and future existences are eternally now, interconnected and bridging realities constantly, which means that all your lifetimes are parallel and not sequential. The beauty inherent in this mystical law of eternal time is that your present life is not separate from other lifetimes, but mutually influential, beneficial and necessary for soul-evolution. The past communicates with the future, the present sets the past free, and the future informs the present.

"With this in mind, we want for you to understand that pain is not the cause of suffering, but more importantly, the fire that forges alliances between lifetimes. But so does love and expanded awareness. Pain, love, passion, curiosity, devotion ... are intense emotions and experiences that create the 'heat' that then forces the body to feel and awaken to God, and which transforms limitations into freedom for all lifetimes. The soul is intrinsically evolutionary, like an explosive fire at the heart of stillness. And like the rays of the Sun, each lifetime is an expression of the whole that serves to support and strengthen all lifetimes.

"The immense significance that ties lifetimes together is mutual support. A learned lesson in this life can save another lifetime from hardship, which then aligns with your present-day energy field to provide you with the frequency you need to fulfil your dream in the here and now. Also, freeing yourself from the shackles of the past can completely change the past of another lifetime and its future outcomes, which then not only supports you but other people in your present-life.

"The more you celebrate all your life-experiences, the more you encounter greater depth of meaning in everything you do. Only then can life be witnessed through the lens of acceptance, faith and true happiness. Even a woman's

physical pain during birthing can be seen in this way, because in truth, her pain creates an intense opening that pulls her child into her auric field; it links the infant into her whole body, mind and spirit. This creates a deep bonding and intuitive connection between her and the child, which clears karmic imbalances between them both.

"We are referring to the intense healing power of pain, not trauma. When it comes to childbirth, many women fear pain to the extent of inducing traumatic experiences that impede natural births and cause undue suffering, weakening the spirit-bond between the mother and child.

"A woman giving birth can lessen the frequency of trauma by entering into a state of permissiveness. In this way, she no longer resists the possibility of a traumatic experience but rather welcomes it into the arms of forgiveness and faith. No longer confined by distressing worry, together mother and child are enveloped in a tremendously powerful union that is supported and aligned by their shared courage.

"Again, we say that pain is not what it seems. It is not to be feared or avoided because it is a source of karmic interconnection. Therefore, give pain what it needs – acceptance, forgiveness and love."

few years ago, I visited a client, Janet, after she had given birth to a baby boy. The birth had been emotionally and physically excruciating. The channelled message I offered her supported her in understanding that the painful birth had helped her break through a karmic limitation. She had finally broken free from fear she carried through many lifetimes.

In the months before giving birth, Janet's healing sessions focused on her need to value herself. She had been fraught with emotional stress, induced by deep sorrow surrounding the fact that the infant's father did not want to be in her life. I never met him but was left with the impression that he did not want to be a father and that he had been uncommitted in their relationship from the start. But she didn't want to admit this and kept trying to contact him. All her thoughts were set on him, and whenever we met she questioned the spirits to find out what would happen in the future, why he didn't want to be a father and how could this change. Masiandia responded every time by guiding her to accept the circumstances.

In the hospital, Masiandia explained to her that the painful birth was a catalyst for changing an old pattern of dishonouring herself, so that she could finally choose a life that supported not only herself but her child. It wasn't until her son's birth that Janet took her role as a mother seriously and acknowledged her need to be supported and cared for.

Masiandia: *"Before giving birth to her son, Janet did not have the self-awareness or the conviction to oversee her own magical birthing experience, instead she froze in despair and fragility. There is nothing wrong with this, as her reaction was the manifestation of her fear and beliefs until she let go and experienced the alchemy of her son's birth. While the physical pain was excruciating, it was not an emotionally traumatic experience, as Janet accepted it and learned from it, freeing herself as she discovered the grace of bringing her child into the world. She received her child and realized the purity and gift that was given to her.*

"There is no right and wrong way in life; there is only the way that best serves you. Your journey is discovering what that is for you, not for anyone else. We want for you to know that there is no perfect frame of mind that can prepare you for physical, emotional, mental and spiritual pain. There is only forgiveness of life, which is all about embracing your experience in faith. Welcome your pain with the certainty that you are courageous and that you are never alone. Allow yourselves to be fully held in the comfort of your faith, for it is a soothing balm of deep stillness and inner peace."

There is so much fear when it comes to pain, especially the pain of childbirth which I can only empathize with as I chose to not have children. I have heard stories that compel me to believe that birthing can be euphoric and very magical. A few years ago, I heard an amazing story from a midwife about her client Arial's birthing. Arial gave birth to her daughter effortlessly in a squatted position facing her husband, after rocking herself into a deeply relaxed trance. The midwife witnessed Arial move her whole body from side to side in rhythmic motion and instinctively knew not to intervene. She made sure that Arial was safe and supported while Arial trusted her own inner-guidance. The birth was natural and profoundly beautiful.

These are the kinds of stories that inspire me to trust my own natural rhythm. There is nothing more fulfilling than to follow what wants to happen naturally in each moment, because it creates an opening. It allows us to step onto the path of faith with complete presence, surrendering into the unexpected. This doesn't lessen pain; it invites release and ease. By opening our door to all experiences we don't shut out miraculous possibilities.

❦

Universal Courage

There is a large cauldron of universal courage that we can draw from; a source of energy and support that spirit readily offers us. We are not destined to walk this path alone, but rather to behold the grace of Divinity walking alongside us. We do not have to rely only on our humanity for courage, trust and faith, when in fact these attributes are given to us from our spirits. Faith is not a virtue to master but a supporting hand given to us from the whole Universe.

When we receive support from our spirits we move along the changing current of our lives with ease. We trustingly transform the pathways of our beliefs and patterns, and surrender resistance, moving effortlessly around obstacles. There is nothing more freeing than to see obstacles as beautiful energy that the currents of life can flow around and beyond.

Masiandia: *"We want to support you in flowing more smoothly through all chapters of your life. It is especially significant that you embrace your divine self in order to encounter life's many shifting energies in a world that is changing quickly. You live in a world that is now operating at a vibratory frequency of instantaneous change, to balance and assist the evolution of the law of attraction. This means that life has become an immediate reflection of what you are asking for at all times. All your thoughts, beliefs, ideas and wants are amplified instantly.*

"This can be very exciting when you're manifesting your authentic expression, your dreams and desires. However, many of you operate out of desperation, attuning your energy field to the frequency of doubt, insecurity and blame. This multiplies; it ripples out into all aspects of your lives, relationships, health and work, causing external limitations and internal depletion. Wouldn't it be more meaningful then to attune your energy field to the frequency of faith? In faith, your field becomes highly charged, drawing into your life the seamless support and sustenance you need.

"You tap into faith when you remember that you are more than your human experience; you are spirit and matter combined. In relationship with spirit you emerge whole and are no longer distracted by disbelief and fear because you live prayerfully; you allow your spirit to faithfully fill you from within, reverberating through you out into the world."

For many of us, this calls for recognizing who we are even when others do not … to cease projecting inadequacies, failures, and obsessions onto the world. There is so much in life that cannot be changed by our force of will, for all we manifest by struggling is more struggle, not joy. Joy comes from letting go of the struggle and resting in the certainty that we are not alone.

Yielding to spirit opens us to universal energy, providing us with the courage to persist when we are too tired to go on, belief when we are uncertain, tenderness when we are frustrated, and clarity when we are disillusioned. With spirit, our lives then are no longer filled with un-certainty, frustration and disillusion, but instead with inner power, ac-ceptance, patience and clarity. Our spirits have the power to fill us from within with a profound sense of inner-peace, and draw into our lives the answers to our prayers. We are not alone and our lives serve as constant reminders. Everything and every person join us in a consummate play of differences and paradoxes, pushing us to serve a higher calling, opening us to listen with greater empathy and communicate with love.

This utter surrender to higher-consciousness has the power to shift our perception of reality, which changes our lives. My life has been re-shaped by countless opportunities to expand my fear perceptions and re-sistance. I've been pushed and pulled into new thoughts and expanded expressions, sculpted by the hand of God that asks me to let go into the unknown, trusting in the benevolence of the Universe.

I have come to understand that our trust helps spirit tend to our needs. It is spirit that lifts the veil of past conditioning and opens us to who we truly are. Our responsibility is to surrender our will to the will of Divinity, which we do through self-inquiry, prayer, meditation, breath-ing, resting, and opening our eyes and hearts to the Divine that is right before us. In this way, we become the sacred vessel in which God sees the world through us. This is when we give fear and pain over to spirit and I let go of the struggle.

It's reassuring to remember that the change we long for does not come from us alone. As Masiandia says, shifting reality requires more than pro-jecting our will onto reality, more than working hard to achieve peace; it calls for peace, which is spiritual devotion.

Masiandia: *"Peace is a sweet embrace of the unknown and letting differences unite you, not define you. Peace is a faithful approach to life, letting the spirit in all life surround you and fulfil you.*

"In this quickly changing world, your prayer for peace, joy and fulfilment

instantly rushes towards you, pushing through your limitations, inspiring you to move beyond who you think you are and to accomplish more than what you think you're capable of. Life is beckoning you to impregnate it with the fullness of your being, to give each moment your prayer – your eternal presence.

"It is paramount that you become aligned to what you truly want, because when you focus on what you don't want you inevitably multiply it, attracting into your life limitations and suffering. The only way to shift the rippling effect of life-depleting energy is to establish a new thought, a new state of being, which you do effortlessly when you return to faith because you let your spirit join you and support you.

"The magic ingredient for peace and fulfilment then is 'faith': letting yourself change with the natural course of your life, allowing yourself to evolve out of your familiar perception of yourself and beyond the confines of other people's perceptions of you into a fluid expression of your soulful being. This signifies the need to be larger than your dreams, more expansive and alive in everything that you are a part of. It means seeing beyond your limited view of the world and beholding a greater vision that isn't defined by you alone, but by a larger framework, an expansive union with all there is.

"Our dear friends, let these words align you to your true essence now; let this message penetrate your defences, insecurities, fears, doubts and uncertainties, to bring you closer and closer to your faith. Because therein lies the doorway that opens you to the divine in everything."

Rose is a name of a wildflower,
Soft silky petals
taken gently by the hands of gravity,
now scattered to the ground
in the midst of stone, dried leaf,
earth and the truth.

Rose is a name of a child
lost in the forest of people;
precious being unseen in a
distracted sea of movement.

Rose is the name of time
eluding time,
taking its sweet time,
or quickened without notice.

Or the name of today –
spirit lured
by the subtlety of meaning,
but for the certainty of faith.

CHAPTER EIGHT

Welcoming Abundance

The sky is white with mist
and fragmented into angular shapes
by the tall buildings that stretch high
above me.
All around is a frenzy of movement –
people going by with honesty
in their eyes,
unable to hide their stories.
They are full of containment,
bursting with the soul of the city.
I see it in their faces, in their gestures –
the tell-tell imprint of time
and spoken languages forever blending
into a drone.
I walk into it, past it and all along
the tempo follows me, and invites me in,
as if it wants to enfold itself into me.
I become a part of it –
the city – the landscape
where the horizon vanishes.

Receptivity

On the path of healing there comes a time for ripening, for emotional maturity, a time when we are more and more receptive to what life is offering us. We come to recognize the inherent gift in all personal, emotional and health issues, in setbacks as well as opportunities. We realize that everything in our lives is truly in divine order. We cease judging life-experiences as good or bad and openly receive the support of our higher selves.

This is when we make ourselves available to the fluidity of abundance rather than be restricted to our perceived goals, thus committing to the divine in each passing moment. It is by letting go of the pressure to achieve something, or to get "better" or "fix" a perceived personality flaw, that we become receptive vessels. Through our receptivity, the abundance of life joins us. We become intimate with our longing, honouring it rather than keeping it hidden behind self-protection. As we do this, life celebrates our longing. People, situations and our whole body align to who we truly are.

In the moment that we cease trying to gratify our longing, we are open to receive the abundance that life has to offer us. Abundance is a gift; it is not something we attain. We do not conjure abundance into existence but rather welcome it with faith. It already exists! Our receptivity then is the magnetic force that draws abundance into our lives. The Universe is always generously answering our prayers, and it's up to us to receive these answers.

I see abundance as the balance created when a need is met, when creative ideas are actualized without effort but rather with conscious intent and faith combined; when instead of the mind controlling our lives, it honours divine intervention. The following illustrates how abundance comes to us in ways we least expect and the beauty of allowing it to unfold spontaneously. My dear friend Heidi invited me to stay for a few days at her ocean-view home, when I was going through a personal crisis around finding a new dwelling place. Her invitation was guided by the intuition that her home would inspire me to connect with my prayers. I had searched for months to no avail, and all I could do was trust that something in me needed to emerge.

When I walked along the beach by Heidi's home I immediately felt a deep connection within myself. As I walked, I prayed to Mother Earth to show me the way home and to fill me up. I was so hungry for her love that I was completely undefended. In that moment a presence overcame me, a sense of wholeness spread upwards towards me and seized me in a powerful embrace. I was enraptured by the vast sky and the murmur of the ocean lapping along the shore, and felt grateful for the way in which everything had brought me to that moment. I knew then that I longed to live close to the sea and the open sky, and all the details of how to make it happen no longer mattered. My longing was complete, and I felt at peace. No longer worried that I would not find the "right" home, I knew that it was inevitable, and even more significantly, I sensed intuitively that I was being shown the way.

Six months later, my partner and I took a leap of faith and moved to the Sunshine Coast, a marine getaway on the mainland of British Columbia only accessible by ferry. This was a location that months prior we wouldn't have thought possible. It required so much change, as we had to re-invent how we approached our businesses and social circles. We were nonetheless willing to follow our inner guidance and transition through uncertainty, deepening our trust in divine order, a trust that was fuelled by a sense of wonder and possibility. The realization of this dream has inspired me to believe in the changing journey that led me here and will continue to lead me wherever I need to be.

Masiandia: *"Abundance is a gift of nature – it is quantum energy eminently woven into your karmic relationship with Earth. It flows towards the magnetic energy of your whole physical, emotional, mental and spiritual body. In so doing,*

it draws to you the necessary circumstances and karmic connections that sup-
port your soul-purpose. You align your magnetic-frequency to the abundance
that Gaia holds for you by opening your receiving channels. In order to be given
the abundance you want, all you must do is receive it. In other words, everything
you truly desire and need is woven into your incarnation on Earth. It's all at
your fingertips; it's a matter of drawing it to you.

"Abundance is your birthright and is intrinsically woven into your karmic
union with Earth, within the interdependent relationship between conscious-
ness and form. It is this interconnection between spirit and matter that creates
symbiotic opportunities, which you then must open to so that you can receive
what you need.

"Your receptive channels expand as you surrender to the mystery of your
soul, which allows you to flow with life's guidance and returns you to your in-
nermost sense of self-value. The more your self-value is strengthened, the more
your magnetic frequency becomes aligned to life's resources."

Cultivating Abundance

Masiandia: *"We want you to understand that abundance is not materialism,*
and neither is it the lack of possessions. It is not about living with less or more.
Abundance is the magnification of your energy-field, opening itself like a flower
to the light of God. To welcome the abundance that you need and long for then
requires that you become receptive to it."

Our every thought, perception and belief are written within our magnetic energy and act as a lure that attracts possibilities. When we are open to what we want, life reflects it; everything conspires to support the realization of what we want. When we are generous with our spirit, with our trust in life, life just can't help but reflect that back. I see this with performers: when they are generous and trusting, the audience celebrates and trusts them in return. When dancers, musicians, public speakers, actors, comedians focus on honouring the audience with their best performance, the audience joins them. The same is true for all of us; when we hold a high frequency of trust and passion, life in turn joins us with abundant support and love. In this way, we embrace whatever situation is arising in our lives; we become receptive to change instead of being braced against what we fear and we develop a profound sense of self-value.

Masiandia: *"Cultivating an abundant relationship with life requires living in the light of your worthiness, which means honouring your true essence – your divinity. Without spirit you operate solely at the physical and mental levels, controlling emotions and felt-sense experiences, inducing a tremendous level of anxiety.*

"It is only by returning to your divine self that you honour the divine in everything, which opens you to inner-peace and to life's abundance. Otherwise you are closed off from your essence, you are unaware of your truth, and you shut off the flow of support in your life. Your needs cannot be met if you refuse to let spirit in. Without spirit, your mind triggers beliefs and conditioning that deplete your whole body vitality. But when you are interconnected with your essence in trust and devotion, then life magnifies that.

"It is by trusting your own value, your needs and spiritual essence, that the divine in everything can join you, because you let it. You cease projecting a fantasy onto life; you stop fighting with reality. In this way, you are guided by all of your life experience rather than remaining in a state of struggle and resistance. You return to the magnetic frequency of your faith, allowing that to deepen in all areas of your life, like a rich and fertile earth that nourishes your being so it can root itself and grow strong.

"Our dear friends, welcome your divine natures, for when you are one with the Divine there is no more wanting for more, because you have more. You are filled from within, and the world around you reflects that. Your life doesn't change to accommodate your expectations; it evolves, and because you trust your essence

you also trust life's evolution. You discover a depth of awareness that you didn't have before, which enables you to flow with life more freely.

"Spirit consciousness is far more aware of possibilities in your life than your mind is. By surrendering the mind, you gain in-depth clarity, which is incredibly fulfilling. Your mind wants to serve divinity – that is its purpose, and its greatest potential is to work in tandem with higher-consciousness. In union, humanity and spirit are whole, and thus wholeness is made manifest exponentially.

"It is by honouring and valuing your spiritual essence that you see so much more. You connect to your inner-knowing and respond with love to every situation arising in your life. Then nothing is made wrong – not even jealousy, anger, heartache, or an unmet need – because you are awakened and enlivened by spirit. Awakened, you are open to seeing life as it is, not fabricating stories. Awakened, you have the ability to perceive reality through a wider lens of acceptance and trust. Awakened, you don't dismiss anything; you cease denying your feelings and the feeling of others; you take action based on spiritual guidance; you lead from the heart. Awakened, nothing is made wrong because you value the spiritual essence in all life.

"Valuing your spirit and your human nature – ultimately your whole self – manifests all that you want in life, for it unites you with the Divine. Then you have everything you need because you cease compromising the essence of who you are. You have everything you need, because you are fully present to all of yourself, spirit and human consciousness."

Engaging with Your Felt-Experiences

*A*s we embrace a trusting relationship with the sacred, everything appears more alive, which is energizing and completely rejuvenating. And when we connect with our world in this way, we are fully present, in touch with all of who we are and with the fullness that life has to offer us.

There was a summer day at the beach when I had such an experience, an expanded awareness of the spirit in everything. I had recently discovered floating, and I was lying on my back, arms outstretched above me and swaying in the gentle waves of the ocean. On this particular day, I sensed everything around me with a strange acuteness, and my body bristled with aliveness in the cold water. Everything was energetically animated, and noise seemed to be approaching me from everywhere. I even looked up at one point because a motorboat sounded as though it was coming right at me, when in fact it was moving in the opposite direction. I could hear the swishing and tinkling of pebbles underneath, voices that appeared to be right next to me and the splashing of water by my ears. It surprised me to discover that I was afraid of this cacophony of feeling and that I desperately wanted to leave the water, to stop the intensity. I was also distinctly aware that I had been frightened of this aliveness all my life.

Though I was afraid, I was even more curious, especially when I breathed in the immensity of it all. The infinity of sky and ocean merged, and together they were one. I could see the tops of the trees and recognized that they knew I was there, and together we were whole. I stayed there fully engulfed until it was too cold. But even as I stepped out of the water and carefully walked along the rocks, I was still aware of an expanded and more real reality than my usual sense perception allowed. Having been touched by this all-embracing oneness is a reminder that I am part of something much bigger than I. The experience remains a source of inspiration and guidance.

Masiandia says, *"Receive the alighted and unknowable mystery of your soul by engaging with your whole felt-experience."* Again and again they ask us to feel everything, as this allows us to connect with spirit in all things. It grows our empathy, our ability to feel what other people are feeling. But for many people, feeling this deeply is overwhelming, because with empathy they cannot justify controlling their lives and the lives of others. Many people control their environment for a false sense of safety, so it's understandable that they don't want to relinquish control because it gives them power; it protects them from feeling defenceless. With empathy, one cannot maintain control, nor justify discrimination, abuse or war. It's impossible to harm other beings when we can actually connect with their feelings, just as we cannot harm nature when we comprehend the consequence.

Our belief that we can protect ourselves by maintaining control is the ultimate paradox, because by hanging on to self-protection, we limit our connection to spirit and prevent ourselves from engaging wholeheartedly with life. We forget that we hold the key to our joy and our true power – we are in charge of transcending our own reality.

Masiandia: *"What is feeling, really? It's about 'being', not enforcing one's will. What is being? It is wholeness! If you only allow yourself to feel half in love and half protected from getting hurt, half available and half hidden, where are you? It is only by being fully available, fully in love, fully engaged that you complete yourself, because you are fully present to yourself. If you protect yourself from others, you inevitably reject some aspect of your own self; you disown your need for love. It's only by being fully engaged with life, fully awake, that you are able to receive the support, love and nurturing you need.*

"Imagine falling in love with yourself as though you are newly born. Imagine that this is the first moment of your life and that you are filled with a deep sense of awe at this miracle that you are. Let every cell in your body be filled by your love ... with its power to refuel, rejuvenate and rebalance you. Then everything that has prevented you from embracing your life will be washed away. Past occurrences, disappointments and hurt will no longer have a stronghold on your emotional well-being. Instead, you will recognize past feelings that you have harboured for a long time: emotions that need to be felt in the present to be released.

"When you are fully engaged with your felt-sense experiences, you 'see' your patterns and conditioning with complete devotion and gentleness. You are no longer defended against loss and abandonment, because you are surrendered to the love of your spirit, ready and willing to love yourself fully, which inevitably reconstructs your sense of reality, drawing life's many gifts to you."

*E*ngaging wholeheartedly with our felt-experience is a deeply heal-ing spiritual practice that is not a hurried journey. It is a process that requires patience and our deepest surrender and self-acceptance. By slowing down, we see and sense more; we navigate the inner landscape of our feelings in harmony with our spiritual integrity. We discover the mes-sage of our souls and come to understand and accept our essential needs.

Experiencing our emotions as they are in the present is a calming, meditative approach to life. Pema Chödrön describes this so well in her book, *Awakening Loving-Kindness*. She writes about seeing our emotions and thoughts just as they are right now, "not trying to make them go away, not trying to become better than we are, but just seeing clearly with preci-sion and gentleness." There is nothing more enriching than to encompass our present feeling-state with utmost presence and curiosity, yielding to the inner intelligence of our deeper awareness.

In a private session, my client Ellie explored the feeling quality of her anxiety. She had been struggling with health issues when Masiandia told her that it was fear that was causing the problem with indigestion. They said that fear is very difficult to digest, that it is completely unpalatable. Ellie was curious about the fear and quickly surrendered into connecting with the feeling of her anxiety. She described it as a grey field of tightly woven fabric wrapped all around her, which had the effect of permeating her whole body. The more she allowed herself to connect with this body sensation, the more she felt a tightening in her chest and a profound sense of sadness.

Most people will try to avoid this feeling, but Ellie allowed herself to connect with her experience. She dropped into the sorrow so deeply that a memory of her mother's rejection surfaced, but only subtly; it didn't stop her from following the guidance of the sorrow, until the hurt she had felt as a child became pure light in the present. Ellie discovered that her sor-row spoke of the need for gentleness.

She didn't say, "I really should be gentler with myself." Instead, she embodied the tenderness she longed for, until it consumed her and awakened her to her spirit. She let herself be filled with an inner quality of absolute calm, spaciousness and security. The issues she had presented in the session had not changed, but she was changed. And the discomfort and bloating in her belly completely eased.

Engaging wholeheartedly with our felt-experience frees us to be more fully present in our lives, with others and with ourselves. It supports us in accessing in-depth knowledge and to simply rest in the all-embracing oneness of our divinity. It helps us heal and embrace the wonder of the beauty all around us and within us.

◇◇◇

Valuing Every Facet of Who You Are

Masiandia: *"To become radiantly open and thus manifest the life you truly want, you must say 'yes' to everything that is occurring in your emotional life. Say 'yes' to everything, rain or shine, in order to fulfil your purpose. Celebrate every facet of yourself, from delightful to boring, wise to ridiculous. Enjoy your certainties as well as your shyness and anxiety.*

"When you control aspects of yourself that threaten to reveal your emotions, such as insecurity, you inhibit yourself from realizing what you truly want in life. Control evokes a sense of separation and a high level of stress, not the abundant manifestation of joyousness and well-being. Shutting down your emotions induces reactions, which the body simply cannot contain. The body is meant to be a free flowing channel of energy, not a storage-centre for unwanted feelings. When you fail to express yourself or release your feelings, the body can't help but go out of balance, for you give it no choice.

"Suppressed emotions are the culprit for nervous system disorders as well as cellular mutation – cancer. A man cannot survive cancer treatment, whether allopathic or holistic, if he tries to hold everything together by restraining his

feelings. A woman cannot guide her family into loving harmony if she distrusts her needs. If you are not connected to your emotion, you cannot know what you want, and you cannot manifest it. To manifest what you want you must be in-touch with what you want, which requires an intimate connection with your sense of value – welcoming everything about who you are. When you perceive all of your emotions, thoughts and life-experiences as relevant, you validate who you are.

"Let us provide you with an example of welcoming every facet of your felt-sense experience. One of Dofila's clients, Wendy, was initially set back by a profound sense of insecurity when she had an important presentation to do in school. She spent hours preparing to the point of exhaustion and felt resentful that she didn't have more time for further preparations. Worried about the presentation, Wendy was overcome with panic. She anticipated the worst, profoundly afraid that her peers would disrespect her.

"You must understand that life mirrors whatever state of consciousness you are in, and for Wendy it was her friends who reflected her worries. Her friends became as anxious as she was without knowing why; they distrusted her, which led to misunderstandings and conflict. When you are in conflict with yourself, as Wendy was with her need for perfection and approval, others will join you. It is necessary that you make peace with your own struggles for others to be at peace with you.

"Through self-observation, Wendy saw that her fears had build up such resistance in her that she could barely concentrate on the presentation. It is by connecting with the fear that she was able to let go of control and thus lessen her panic, which helped her realize that the reason she was so worried about failing the presentation had nothing to do with the fear of being judged. She really had a profound yearning to do well with the presentation. In fact, Wendy's desire to learn was greater than her fear. By no longer trying to control her fear, she didn't dread failure or being ridiculed. Instead, she connected with the essence of her desire to improve her presentation abilities. Therefore, she made manifest

the strength of her desire rather than the intensity of her fears and delivered a convincing report out of integrity and self-belief."

Valuing What You Want

Masiandia: *"When you value your desires, you become patient and no longer desperate. You cease grasping for love, attention, approval, success, money, because you no longer believe that it's impossible to manifest what you want in life. You also stop claiming that to achieve what you desire you should somehow deserve it. Manifesting what you desire has nothing to do with deserving it; it has everything to do with allowing it to take form in your life. When you value what you want you become receptive to it! You become what you desire; you become loving, attentive, gentle, successful, abundant, nourished. Therefore, your magnetic field becomes attuned to what you want; it becomes a strong alluring force that draws to you the frequency of abundance.*

"Our dear friends, valuing what you want in life helps you become receptive to life's abundance, rather than guarded, disbelieving and conditioned for disappointment. When you value what you want, you value all of life; therefore, you celebrate a reality filled with abundance, not one that is pained with suffering and regret. You also cease thinking that living with less means more will be available for others. Living with less does not leave more for others; it represses the value of your desires, which dims the flame of your spirit. This does not only deplete your sense of value, but your sense of the value of others. When you repress your spirit, you impose restrictions on the human collective, such as perpetuating the false belief that you must be a bad person for wanting more. Living with less than you actually need does not sustain your health and well-being or the well-being of others.

"When we speak of that which you desire, we want to make it clear that we are not talking about materialism; we are talking about love, prosperity, a sense of belonging, purposefulness, freedom, joy and more joy. Happiness is not found in possessions, nor is it found in the lack of possessions. By valuing yourself, you

can better enjoy the world you live in and respect your desires, which then leads to respecting the desires of others.

"There are too many people in this world who are ridiculed for what they want, for what they dream of. They are told that it is not possible, and then it can seem to them that life is working against their true longing and needs. They become de-spirited by the negative feedback and lose faith in life's possibilities. To manifest the abundant outcome of dreams, you must be the one who values your longing, which means beginning by valuing yourself."

When we "value" who we are, we enter into heightened receptivity, a strong point of magnetism that is the key to manifestation, which requires deliberation, dedication and the willingness to surrender our disbelief.

The same dedication as an athlete's training and endurance is required in a spiritual life, so that we can grow our own power, our own magnetic energy. This calls for us to share our wealth of spirit, belief and devotion, not covet what someone else has or struggle with what we have yet to realize.

Many people wonder why their lives aren't shifting, why they haven't manifested what they want. They don't realize they are unwilling to change. The experience of wanting something passionately and connecting to it intently is so intense that they avoid it. An example of this became apparent in one of my workshops on self-mastery. One of the participants expected me to give her the answer to her problems and resisted connecting with her own process. In fact, at one point she was annoyed when I asked her to express what she felt. She said, "I don't have to tell you how I feel; you're intuitive and already know it." She refused to step into the depth of her personal experience, remaining only in the shallow end. She blocked the depth of feeling and transparency required for transformation, as she struggled to attain what she expected from the course without being willing to give herself to it.

Our culture has been fostered to seek gratification and pleasure, therefore, spirituality and the new age movement have become commodities. We expect growth without carrying through with the stages of learning and development. We fool ourselves in the belief that we want to change, thinking that we are ready, yet constantly stepping away from the intensity of our feelings. Breakthrough happens when we journey inwards into the magnitude of feeling and surrender to the value of our longing and vulnerability. It is by giving birth to the extraordinary beauty of our feelings and true desire that we weave deeper meaning into the mundane. We heal our fears and support our need for connection.

Strengthening Your Magnetic-Frequency

*W*e draw abundance into our lives by valuing what we want, as it strengthens our magnetic frequency. A strong magnetic frequency completely permeates our whole life with a deep sense of belonging, which draws to us the abundance we need. To align our frequency, Masiandia reminds us to focus on the positive. They say, *"Don't think of anything besides being enthusiastic, inspired and living your dream fully, because nothing else exists, unless you think of it and bring it into form."*

Masiandia: *"The reason we ask you to focus only upon living your dream fully ... is because this directs your creative energy towards what you really want in life, which empowers you and everyone involved. By directing your creative energy from the centre of your self-worth, you inevitably see the beauty in yourself, as well as in others, and you trust in life's infinite possibilities. You value what you really want and allow it to manifest in its own natural timing. You do this with grace, gratitude and gentleness. In this way you are no longer attached to a limited and judgmental view of reality. Instead, you are willing and honoured to be part of a greater relationship with God and all of its creations on Earth.*

"Our dear friends, abundance is being generous with your love – being so

full to overflowing that the world is a richer place because you are in it. You are love incarnated here on this Earth to firstly give generously to yourself, which then allows your light to overflow unto others."

Being full to overflowing with our love directs our creative energy from the centre of our being out into the world. I see this as a personal fountain – a rich resource of spiritual integrity that comes from within us and ripples out into all areas of our lives. Our spiritual integrity comes from an inner wellspring of magnetic energy, which draws into our lives the perfect match for our energy.

Spiritual integrity then supports life's infinite possibilities, because it helps us see more clearly and therefore actually changes reality based on our clear observations. Through "right seeing" we observe reality through a completely new lens, which encompasses so much more than our familiar perception of reality. We see our friends, family, co-workers and even strangers through a renewed perspective that frees them from the confines of our limited beliefs. It grants them the opportunity to heal and grow.

From a quantum physics approach, reality is an infinite field of energy that exists as a possibility, but does not manifest as anything until consciousness observes which possibility is going to transpire. When consciousness observes reality, it projects an expectation of what it thinks is going to emerge. This expectation locks into that particular possibility, setting in motion the manifested reality that is expected. It's only natural that as we observe reality through the lens of spiritual integrity, being inspired and living our dream fully, then we direct our creative energy towards manifesting that reality.

Each moment holds infinite possibilities, and we in turn hold the key to which reality we experience based on what we perceive and therefore, what we give to reality. We can observe life through a wider lens of awareness, generously overflowing our trust and devotion. Change happens when we surrender and allow it to transpire. Dreams unfold as we receive them. Prayers are answered with the willingness to step into them with open arms.

———∞———

All Prayers Are Answered

I want to share a story about becoming receptive to our prayers, which is all about directing creative energy and thus imbuing our prayers with belief. Alana, a participant at another group-channelling event, expressed her dilemma concerning the incongruence between the concept that we can have what we want in life and the limitations of physical disability. Alana asked Masiandia, "If all our prayers are answered – if all we need is to ask in order to manifest what we want in life – then how could that be true for someone with a disability who wishes to be able-bodied?" She struggled to understand how she could possibly tell a man in a wheelchair that he could have whatever he wants. Alana expressed to the group that if a man in a wheelchair wants to dance, she couldn't just tell him he can dream that into reality. Masiandia told her that, yes, she can and that she would be telling him the truth …

Masiandia: *"The disabled man can dream a real dream; he can connect so deeply to the essence of dance so as to encompass it more fully than an able-bodied dancer. As he imagines dancing, he feels the movement in his internal organs; he responds physiologically, flows with the music and soars in all the energy vibration of the dance.*

"We as spirit know that this imagining is not a physical manifestation, but we see the bigger picture, we understand that there is so much more going on than the disability. Please try to imagine the freedom the man experiences when he realizes that his imagination is powerful. He reaches towards his whole

soul-essence with this dream. The dance becomes magic as it manifests in unique and soul-reaching ways, beyond the intellect, beyond limitation.

"Look inwards to see for yourself just how great it feels when you dream and believe that it's possible. But when you underestimate the power of divine order, the power of potentiality divined by your own spirit, then the dream fades. When you disbelieve, you become dependent on your finite perception of reality. The spirit that dwells in everything is far more expansive than this. The Universe is far richer with possibilities than most of you will allow. You cannot manifest your dream if you measure its success by a limited sense of reality, because the limitation cannot support your dream. Believing in your dream supports its manifestation. For instance, if you long for a deeply loving relationship yet disbelieve that it's possible, then you disown your longing and you neglect your self-value. You must stay connected to your longing, because it is a gift, not a reminder of what you cannot have. When you focus on the dream, you naturally attract the partnership to you because there is nothing obstructing your vision. There is no limited perception of reality, therefore your energy-field maintains a strong magnetic frequency.

"The same is true for the disabled man. When he realizes that he is free to dream, to connect to the wellspring of his longing, then he does not perceive himself as limited and neither do the people around him. They see a man who is soulful and whole. Then they can touch his heart and spirit in ways that he may never have known without the disability, because they expand and evolve their sense of reality in relationship with his own reality. People who are 'disabled' are not really limited, and they are definitely not less fortunate. That is an illusion that disregards a person's true essence. Everything and all people are so much more than they appear. Do not be fooled by perceived limitations; the soul is a free agent."

Infinite Possibilities

Masiandia: *"Infinite possibility lies in the consciousness of spirit, in the spirit's awareness of all time and space. Therefore, tapping into possibilities must first come from connecting with your spirit. Hence the focus on self-value, as you cannot connect with your spirit if your mind is guarded and refuses to believe in both yourself and in what you long for. Remember, you strengthen your magnetic field by directing your creative energy from the centre of your self-value. If you do not believe in yourself, it is impossible to align to what you truly want in life. Then you inevitably wait for a sure sign, a perfect life-direction, or you try to enforce your will onto reality. That does not honour your self-value; it sets up a limited environment that only manifests more limitations.*

"When the mind is guarded, you may have high aspirations but never take the risks necessary to truly live, love deeply or create your life. You may aspire to greatness but do not see the ways in which you limit the scope of your creative exploration. You cannot receive the unknowable beauty of life's abundance if you tell life what it should look like, or when and how. Reality is ever changing; it cannot be harnessed. It demands your intimate surrender, your absolute devotion, in order to serve you.

"By imposing your will onto reality, you rob yourself of infinite possibilities that are meant to answer your most intimate prayers. When you project your expectations and disallow the curiosity of your desires to evolve, you close yourself off from receiving the answers to your prayers, from meeting your heart's longing. Control does not open you to what you want in life; it begets more control. You must be willing to be disappointed, let down and hurt again and again, to align yourself to your self-value. Otherwise you protect yourself from disappointment and pain; you close your heart rather than become open to love.

"You mustn't force your will onto life, for life doesn't work that way. Let go of control, and let life support you, because that is its role – its responsibility. Life is always in the ebb and flow of your beliefs, subject to your observation. Observe it through a limited lens and it can promise you nothing other than your perceived limitation. But when you witness life with surrendered devotion, curiosity and acceptance, reality then holds many more possibilities for you. When you value yourself, the ebb and flow of life meets you exactly where you are. As we

have said earlier, when you value yourself, life values you also. Then everything
conspires to join you in that value because your magnetic frequency is aligned to
that greater potential."

I t is by delving into the many facets of our sub-personalities – into unconscious and limiting perceptions – that we let go of control. That is when we see more clearly, beyond the trickery of our ego-mind into the nature of our soul.

Many years ago, with the help of my colleague, Karen, I delved into my unconscious conditioning in response to a reaction I was experiencing in my work. It turns out that I held a childhood belief that what I had to say was inconsequential. This vulnerable feeling was stirred up by the fear of channelling for large groups of people. After an emotional outburst from my inner-child, Karen suggested that maybe I didn't have to do the groups, and that I could just say no. That sounded wonderful, but then I realized that I would not say no because even my vulnerability was more willing to honour my desire to grow than remain in fear.

Initially, as I observed my vulnerability, I admitted that I didn't want to be confronted by anyone's skepticism or judgment, because I knew that not only did it affect me, it set a tone for every participant and created an unsafe environment. I wanted a beautiful, healing and inspiring experience for everyone. Karen supported me in setting a clear intention for the group channelling, in order to prepare me energetically and emotionally. This helped me direct my creative energy and thus align my magnetic field to what I truly longed for, instead of reinforcing the possibility of a challenge. Since then, I always raise the vibration of group space before an event; I pray for grace, spiritual guidance and safety for all those present.

In one of these group-sessions, before the group began, one of the participants boldly told me that she was a skeptic. Because I had directed my energy towards what I wanted and was aligned with my values, I was able to remain confident, calm, grounded and trusting. So when the session started, I was very amused to hear myself kindly let everyone know that there was a skeptic in the room. I didn't point her out; instead, I added that I am also a skeptic. I acknowledged that there were two of us in the room and asked for a show of hands for anyone else who related to us. This created a safe and light-hearted welcoming for the initial person who had spoken to me and for everyone else.

Because of my clear intention, I felt at ease and proceeded to talk about the two sides of skepticism: discernment and closed-mindedness. On the one hand, skepticism prevents us from being overly complacent, but it can also lead to distrusting our own resonance and shutting down our hearts. I told everyone in the group that I didn't want them to be gullible and invited them to connect with what personally resonated for them. This easeful exploration created a safe environment. Everyone laughed and had a lot of fun, and it also deepened their connection to one another.

Had I not directed my energy towards co-creating a sacred circle, I would have been nervous and not given the initial participant what she needed to feel safe. This participant chose to be honest and admit her skepticism, which I welcomed gratefully as I chose to co-create a beautiful interaction with her. Instead of developing separation and possible judgment, I witnessed her interact in the group. She asked questions and offered ideas that invited other people's participation. It never ceases to amaze me the way in which receptivity and purpose can meet, weaving together the transformative power of intention with our willingness to stop struggling with reality.

Risk Being True

We welcome the love of God by trusting others with our human frailties and inspire intimacy when we dare to reveal our true feelings. Our personal needs cannot be met without disclosure – we have to speak up for our right to be valued. How can we be given abundance when we hide in the house of fear? We must risk being true to our value for the potential of manifesting what we want in life.

This is evident in the story of my client, Carla, who was upset with the terrible way her boss treated her. She wanted to resign from her job, yet spent the first forty minutes of the session explaining and justifying why she had to leave, rather than affirming what she wanted. Burdened with guilt, she blamed herself for being too sensitive, fragile and insecure about her work. Conversely, she affirmed that she was good at what she did and that she deserved to be treated fairly. Five minutes later she doubted herself again and wondered if she should give her boss one month's notice, especially since the business was short-staffed. In the same breath, she said that she had been trying to rise above her boss's critical and moody behaviour for several months, yet had been making excuses to miss work. These contradictions kept her locked in indecision and self-judgment rather than able to admit what she really wanted, because she feared losing her security. The fear of angering her boss had more power over her than her own anger about being treated poorly.

It was when she focused on her felt-experience that Carla was able to calmly observe her emotions with regard to the two options: either give advance notice and minimize her workweek until her departure or accept that she could no longer tolerate her boss's criticism and quit immediately. When I asked her to describe the difference, she said that to imagine staying another day was disheartening and valuing her need to leave the job immediately felt amazing. She needed to support her own sense of self-value, not continue to define her choices based on trying to minimize her boss's reaction. Otherwise, she deceived herself; she operated out of fear, not self-respect. After connecting with her sense of value, she came to understand that if she continued to work in that environment, she wouldn't find the courage to create a new life for herself.

Masiandia: *"We want to take the opportunity here to talk about addiction, which can be not only to substances and material things, but also to the need for approval and assurance. Addiction leads many people to dishonour their value and reject their inner-knowing. Carla, for instance, was addicted to her work ethic, which was passed down from her father. He had a high regard for long-term employment and was not in favour of his daughter risking her security for her emotional benefit.*

"Carla struggled for many more months in total dissatisfaction before she finally gave in her resignation, when in fact she could have shifted the entire issue with her employer by addressing his critical behaviour near the start of their working relationship. Her boss learned, in the first year of her employment, that he could push her around because she berated herself for not measuring up to his expectations rather than hold her ground. She was so addicted to her work ethic that she blamed herself for his unfair treatment.

"The only way to break free of all addictions is to value yourself. Value yourself, and then others join you for they become drawn to you like moths to flame; they become part of your light. We would love for you to realize that by honouring yourself you also champion others to grow beyond their limitations and control – you invite them into a meaningful connection that supports both your needs.

"In the case with Carla's boss, he didn't really want to take advantage of his employee; he wanted to rely on someone he could trust. But he couldn't trust her insecurity, so he controlled her. Carla didn't want to be treated poorly; she wanted to be respected, but she didn't respect herself. By not respecting herself, she created a limited situation in which her boss did not feel safe with her, therefore, he fell into the role of the bully, an addictive behaviour that was shaped out of his feeling insecure around her.

"Addictive behaviour is triggered by intense insecurity and fear, but is formed by a profound lack of self-value. A pregnant woman unable to quit smoking, for instance, does not hold herself in high esteem. Although she knows that smoking threatens the life of her unborn child she is nevertheless unable to value this other human being due to not loving herself. She does not want to be addicted to

cigarettes; she wants to be taken care of and comforted. The same is true for a man who lives under a bridge, who begs for food and is desperate for a drink. He does not really want the bottle of gin or anyone's handout; he wants to make peace with the past. He wants help. Conversely, he wants to be left alone because he is afraid. So what he really wants is to be safe.

"You have to connect into the depth of your value so that life can transform before your very eyes. The way to health, joy, prosperity and peace is found on the path of release from pain … into the value of who you truly are. You are not your addictions. You are not your fear or deceptions. You are whole and beautiful!

"Release is the opening of a closed bud flowering in its own natural timing. You cannot pull the petals apart to quicken the process. In order to release pain, you must unfold the petals of your being naturally, at a pace that is perfect for you. As you surrender, joy fills you up and heals you. Please be mindful that judging yourself is not joyful. Surrender is a state of witnessing without evaluating or rejecting anything."

As I contemplate Masiandia's message about addiction, I am aware that it may not always seem like people have a choice. As Dr. Gabor Maté writes in his book *In the* Realm of Hungry Ghosts: *Close Encounters with Addiction,* underlying factors predispose a person towards addiction. Maté explains that addiction is a response to a problem, a desperate attempt to soothe pain, and that pain is formed early in childhood when the brain is being developed. He writes, "The brain eventually develops circuitry that craves soothing from the outside, because its own reward systems are not functioning adequately, owing to the traumatic circumstances."

When I brought this to Masiandia's attention, they said that the issue of addiction comes from denying the value of our soul, and that we are all a part of the problem. Addiction is a mass-conscious social issue that we all contribute to by judging, justifying and defending our worth, rather than embodying it and being at peace with ourselves and one another.

Masiandia said that letting go of addiction is a matter of spiritual devotion and that it is a choice. To this I argued that the issue of choice is complicated, especially for people who are raised in abusive conditions. Maté writes that abuse alters the function of the brain; therefore, as adults the brain's ability to make discerning choices is compromised.

Masiandia: *"We understand your concern, however, we want you to see the larger picture. Everything is part of the greater spectrum of soul-purpose. You must see beyond the reality you are familiar with to recognize that the "compromised brain", as you call it, serves a complex purpose that functions as a catalyst for growth, not only for one's soul, but also for all of humanity. All people whose biology has undoubtedly been affected by abuse have opportunities for soul-growth that they would otherwise not encounter.*

"All life-experiences hold a frequency of opportunities and requirement for growth that serve the soul's purpose. Everyone has a journey to fulfil, a path that honours divine order. Therefore, what looks like a terrible life-experience can actually be a miracle, an opportunity to open yourself to the grace of your soul value, not continue to repeat the pattern of suffering.

"You deceive yourself by seeking perfection and fairness rather than honouring the journey of the soul. When life is welcomed in all of its facets, something miraculous unfolds. Abuse is transformed into profound self-awareness and forgiveness, which does not only serve the self, but all of humanity. Therefore, something that you 'think' is 'bad' can actually be an incredible opportunity to serve humanity's healing and evolution. By evolving your own self-value, dear friends, you embrace all life. Then addiction is shifted into self-empowerment. Then you are no longer victimized by your past and your fear, nor by the fear of others. You are meant to grace this life with the beauty of your spirit, with the love of your heart's desire. Return, over and over again, to your self-worth, dear ones. Honour who you are so that you can honour all life on Earth.

"We want you to understand that while the human mind cannot begin to measure the soul's evolution and purpose, you can begin to understand addiction

through the lens of interconnection. Thus you will see, in those whose lives have been shadowed by addiction, that they are a reflection of you. See yourselves in all that confounds and disturbs you, because you are no different; you are no better or worse. No one is separate from another human being. You are all in this world together. Observing all of life through compassion and forgiveness will set all of you free. Please forgive yourselves for all your human frailties and endeavour to be holy people. Recognize your worthiness so you can do the same for all others."

As I take in these words, I don't see victims in the world, but people whose lives are depictions of the lessons that we all need to learn. People who struggle with addiction are conduits for healing lower vibration energies, thus helping us all raise our collective-consciousness. I also see that we all have addictive tendencies. They may not be destructive behaviours, but they can be disharmonious nonetheless, affecting the whole of humanity.

This brings me to *Ubuntu*, an ancient African word that represents interconnection. We do not exist in this world in isolation, for we are all intrinsically bound to one another. In his book *No Future Without Forgiveness,* Archbishop Desmond Tutu writes, "A person is a person through other persons." He explains that Ubuntu is the essence of being human and that we think of ourselves far too frequently as separate from one another, whereas we are interconnected, and what we do affects the world.

Many years ago, I stopped to give some coins to a woman panhandling under a busy bridge. People passed her by quickly while she desperately tried to tell them why she needed money. I knelt before her, compelled by something beyond words, and she continued to tell me her story until I asked her to stop. I told her that she didn't have to justify her need in order for me to see that she needed help. Before I knew it, I was holding her in my arms in a warm embrace. After giving her some money, I walked away deeply affected. I felt free! I had the distinct impression that an angel had just touched me, and in that moment I felt a profound letting go of all the anger I had held against my father. I can't explain why or how that occurred because the two seem so unrelated, except to say that through my experience of her I felt the need to love my father unconditionally.

We are not so separated after all; there are threads of consciousness that weave our lives together, creating a symphony of possibilities for us to discover connections amid our differences. With the spirit of Ubuntu, we celebrate each other's diversities rather than feel threatened by them. This celebration is part of a rich unfolding of a unified relationship with all life.

"Compassion is not a relationship between the healer and the wounded. It's a relationship between equals. Only when we know our own darkness well can we be present with the darkness of others. Compassion becomes real when we recognize our shared humanity."

~ Pema Chödrön, in *The Places That Scare You:
A Guide to Fearlessness in Difficult Times*

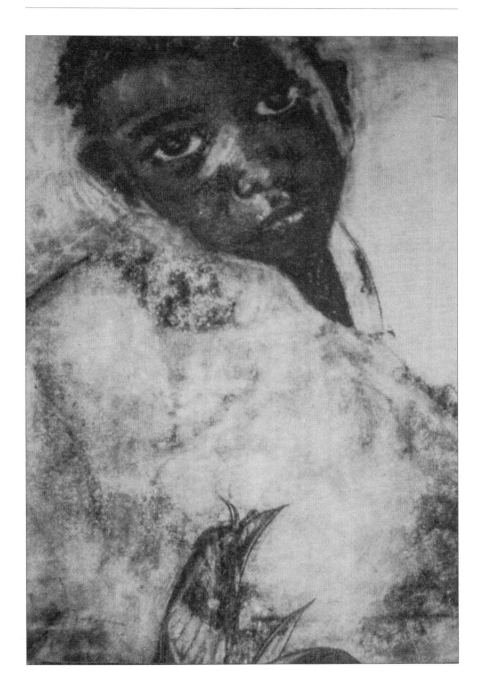

CHAPTER NINE

The Art of Letting Go

Holding-on
alters the natural course.
Letting go
lets freedom
and love expand.
Like rushing water
on the palm of my hand,
it disappears, as I reach
to grasp too tightly.
With an open heart,
my arms are wide open
Walk in,
and I'll let you go.

~ Don Hyssop

Letting Go into Possibilities

*E*very day is a new possibility, a miracle wanting to happen. It is a raw canvas ready to be animated by the transformative gift of our creative freedom: a potential that is born of letting go. It is by shedding our old skin that possibilities emerge.

Today as I contemplate letting go into new expression, I am sitting on the beach looking out at the horizon, as grey clouds part to reveal the setting sun. The warm hues completely transform the sombre landscape, and I see in the changing sky a metaphor for our own shifting energy. Like the sunset, which cannot be captured because its beauty is in it's unique metamorphosis, our own beauty is the ever-changing evolution of mystical expansion, empathy and growth. In letting go, we expand the role of the ego-mind and thus encounter a complete metamorphosis of our creative potential. Left on its own, the ego, if it could, would capture the sunset to make the moment last forever. But by letting go, the ego forms an alliance with the soul. Together, they become attuned like the strings of a violin that make up a beautiful melody. The ego and soul unite to create such beauty that we are moved beyond old conditioning into states of inspired freedom. By letting go, we lose nothing. Instead, we see, we witness and expand ourselves into receiving so much more.

Masiandia: *"Your sole responsibility in life is to acknowledge your essential worthiness, which calls for you to surrender everything that stops you from fully expressing the unknowable mystery of your soul. It is by shedding the old skin that you let the new reveal itself, which connects you to your true sense of value. By stepping aside and letting the mystical joy of transcendence take you, shape you and fulfil you, your spirit then fuels the fire of your creative awakening. Your essence is the formless form that acts as the agent of foreknowledge, providing you with divination potential that you can work with closely. It establishes the* necessary changes that you long for by aligning current reality with possible outcomes.

"Your spirit is projected forward into future outcomes before you ever step into them. It assesses these future situations to establish the scenarios that best serve your purpose, which it then communicates with your mind. Your mind then accesses the body's ability to meet those situations. However, when the body/mind is resistant, the probabilities and desired outcome are restricted. This creates an internal conflict as the spirit's input is rejected, impeding its ability to answer your prayers and fulfil your dream. To make manifest the outcomes that support your longing, you must surrender into harmony with your spirit.

"All your endeavours, your dreams, require letting go of something. But most of you impede the natural flow of what wants to happen organically in your lives, you counteract your intuition. For instance, your personal sense of value may require that you let go of a job, a relationship, friendship or habit. Perhaps you have a deep longing to free your creative energy, to fully engage with what you are capable of, but rather than support you, your work demands that you prioritize the needs of others. Your spirit projects into the future and brings together key individuals and circumstances that best align to a more fulfilling possibility, but because you refuse to let go of the job, the opportunities don't line up.

"But how do you know when it is necessary to leave a job or a relationship? You must realize that your personal needs and self-honour come first. When you connect with your sense of value, you position yourself in such a way that any choices you make do not compromise your essence, and then you know whether or not the situation is in alignment with your purpose.

"Your fulfilment does not hinge on whether you stay or leave your employment, your relationship or any situation for that matter, but more specifically, it depends on you honouring yourself. Then you are aligned to what you need, you risk being true to yourself and surrender into a whole new approach to life. You let go into new possibilities, even if that means walking away from a relationship, a habit or a job."

*W*e get so attached to false identities and conditions that restrict our spirit and impede our dreams. It's easy to be controlled by logic, but the mind alone does not render us happy. Without the willingness to tap into the greater wellspring of our spirit-being, we risk getting in our own way. The story of my client, Amanda, illustrates this well. She could not pry herself from a job that she no longer valued, no matter how much the spirits told her that this was her soul's wish. They even told her that her body would not continue to comply with the pressure of going to a job that she hated: that life would force her to value her needs. Amanda needed to work fewer hours, focus on her creative projects and let go of the fear that she could no longer support herself financially. In fact, Masiandia told her that she would be looked after and not to worry; they insisted that she had to leave her job.

Amanda didn't leave her job, as she couldn't fathom how she and her husband could do without her income. The spirit's message answered her prayer, but she could not step out of her desperate need for guarantees. This issue persisted for many months with the same message repeated regularly. After a missed appointment, I didn't hear from her for a while. When she did see me again, she was in profound physical pain.

At work, an accident occurred where a moving truck struck her in the abdomen, and not long after that the Workers' Compensation Board returned her to work before she had fully healed. In fact, she would still be in a lot of physical discomfort for close to two years. About two weeks after returning to work, still in pain, Amanda finally quit. Interestingly, she received a call from her employer the following week, offering her a part-time position that required fewer hours and less physical strain, which she gladly took. She did eventually leave the company again however, and a year later they offered her an even better position with less hours and more pay. Furthermore, the time that she was off work gave her husband the opportunity to rely on his ability to provide for them both, which gave him a sense of meaningful purpose.

Masiandia: *"Your spirit can only support you as far as you let it! It is impossible to receive the input of your spirit if you 'think' that your mind is the boss. In partnership with spirit, the mind inevitably co-creates the outcomes that you truly want, which are first projected by your spirit into a myriad of possibilities. These outcomes are communicated to your mind through your intuition and through your sense of spiritual integrity and self-worth.*

"By allowing your spirit to pull the strings, so to speak, it works on your behalf by sending energy-signals to your pineal gland, the brain's higher-vibrational transmitter. The pineal gland acts as a communication device, a receiver for higher frequencies. It communicates with the hypothalamus gland, which serves as the intermediary filtering system between spirit and matter. The hypothalamus then sends messages to the pituitary gland, which communicates with your whole body. The endocrine system works in tandem with the central nervous system, which maintains overall body-awareness. Spirit and matter form a symbiotic relationship that is ingenious. This means that your body is highly intelligent and can receive inputs of vibrational frequencies from your spirit to support a healthier nervous system and cellular body.

"Your body receives these energy signals through the feeling body, therefore it is by engaging with all of your feelings, at all times, that you awaken to your intuitive wisdom. In this way, the guidance of your spirit supports your evolution in an integrated way, as opposed to the sometimes-overwhelming effect that can occur when your mind takes control. You can receive the input of your spirit gently, opening yourself to Source-energy by letting go of the mind's need to be in charge.

"Your body/mind – your human nature – cannot be everywhere at the same time, but your spirit can. Spirit is in more than one sphere of existence, more than one reality and probability, thus it functions as a connective instrument, anticipating and aligning probabilities for you. By being in more than one place at a time, your spirit can determine which life-event will best serve your purpose and alignment to your prayers. The outcome of those probabilities is then determined by your receptivity.

"Your job is to expand your body/mind's ability to receive your spirit's input by relinquishing stress and fear in your body and by encompassing an empathic relationship with yourself and others. With empathy, you open your receiving channel, which allows you to receive the guidance of your spirit. By relinquishing control, you honour your spirit, which raises your vital energy and thus nourishes every cell in your body. By trusting your spirit, dear friends, you empty yourselves into wholeness."

Infinite Power of Synchronicity

There is something beautiful that happens when we trust our spirit, when we allow it to guide us: synchronicity unfolds to support us in everything and with everyone in our lives. We stop restricting the flow of our inner-voice, we cease judging ourselves, and we let go of being defended against our own wisdom. When we trust our spirits, we flow gracefully along with the synchronous events that take place in our lives; we become curious and involved.

I would like to share one such synchronous event that took place in one of my *Authentically You* workshops. A couple of days before the event, I had a sense that it was going to be tremendously powerful. I had spoken with new participants prior to the group and saw that there were growing themes: death and grieving loss. The night before the workshop, I woke up several times with lingering dreams that gave me the impression that the workshop was going to focus on completely shifting reality, letting go of old perceptions, grief and separation. Throughout the workshop, participants were amazed by the synergistic interconnection that had brought them together.

One of the participants, Janet, had initially joined the workshop to gain insight into a new work direction. As she sat in a circle of grieving women, she realized that she had a natural ability to support people in processing loss. She noticed that she often found herself in situations where people close to her were grieving and that she was able to be an emotional support for them. Many of those people referred to her as an angel. As Janet mentioned this, someone observed that she was sitting in the middle of three career coaches. Naturally, she was given encouraging ideas and support for a new work direction.

Throughout the day, one thing after another presented itself in such a way that we couldn't help but notice the interconnection between all group members. So when Masiandia said that we each had projected our spirits beforehand and agreed to meet for the purpose of healing grief, the participants felt tremendously integrated and safe. It helped everyone cultivate an intimate relationship with one another, a relationship that answered a profound need for honesty. More than one person said, "I wasn't going to talk about this," but they felt safe and compelled by what the others shared. By surrendering to the unknown, the participants stepped into the reality that was divinely designed for their healing and well-being. When we are willing to let go of control, our spirit's anticipated probabilities make their way to our human consciousness and then become apparent in our lives.

———

Embracing Guidance

Although impulses from our higher-self carry no obligation to comply, because we don't understand these impulses we often refuse to contemplate them, let alone act upon them. Guidance can then go unnoticed or blatantly ignored, as my earlier story about Amanda demonstrates. Messages from our higher-self sometimes suggest that we make big changes, which can trigger within us the fight or flight response. But how can we listen to the beauty of our longing and follow the guidance of our spirit when we are in a reaction? It's impossible. Reactions can only manifest into more of the same reaction, not help us shift into receptive responses. To create situations that meet our longing, we must connect with our spirit and sense into what is possible. But so many of us tend to argue with our spirit; we fight against the natural unfolding of our potential because we want to know what it looks like and what to do.

This is clearly illustrated in a challenging situation that occurred in private session with Celeste. She was completely determined to have things go her way. She was very disappointed that the business venture she had invested a lot of money in had proven to be unsuccessful. Masiandia reminded her that they had strongly suggested that this particular business would fail, which only served to fuel her anger even more. Celeste defended herself and explained that she was a single mother and had to rely on herself alone, that there was no one she could turn to. She was upset that they had not given her an alternative; they had not told her what else to do.

Previously, Masiandia had strongly suggested that she needed to work in an environment that honoured her values, especially when it came to nutrition and beauty. But that didn't mean anything to her, so she proceeded to set up a business in a fast food industry that she actually disrespected. In the session, their message remained the same, even though she wanted it to be something else; they still confirmed that working in a business that undermined her health and values had no possibility of future success, because it didn't align with her longing. But she didn't want to feel her longing, because she couldn't figure out its practical outcome.

We cannot escape who we are or the situations that arise to awaken us. Superimposing our will onto reality doesn't give life a standing chance to evolve into something else; it doesn't align us to what we really want. We must listen to our spirit to become opened to greater potentials.

Yet Celeste refused to connect with her spirit or take responsibility for her choices. Instead, she blamed her despair on issues that were stacking up against her fast-food business – issues with permits, bylaws, problems with equipment and conflicts with neighbouring businesses – let alone that she didn't enjoy what she was doing.

What stood out for me in her session was that Masiandia was relentless in pushing her to take responsibility for her actions. They even went so far as to tell her that she had wasted a lot of money for nothing. This method of communication is so unlike them that I felt caught between their message and my desire to support her in discovering a direction that would serve to shift the situation. Back and forth, I tried to empathize with her feelings, while Masiandia provoked her. They concluded that she would leave the session unhappy with them, as unhappy as she was with her business. They also said that they were giving her an energy-transference, a strong elixir for change, to support her in making the necessary changes from within herself. By the time she left, however, Celeste was indeed unhappy and in judgment, declaring that I was channelling lower-vibrational beings.

After the session concluded, I too was unhappy and demanded to know what that was all about. Masiandia explained that they had had to push her in order to create an energetic jolt that was similar to a car crash, so as to prevent an actual fatal car accident from occurring in her life. They explained that Celeste's refusal to honour herself was bringing about the probability of her death in the near future, which they simulated energetically through the jolt that triggered her anger. Ultimately they were forcing her to connect with her passion to help her choose life. She had been in so much resistance that there was no opening for this information to come through in a gentler way. Instead, her anger created a strong energy frequency that propelled her into fighting for her life. As a healer, I accepted being a conduit in supporting her to break free from destructive patterns. And I wasn't surprised that I didn't hear back from her for a year, at which time I received an email letting me know that she realized she had needed the forceful guidance to reconnect with her value.

We breathe life into what we want when we are willing to cease denying the potential of what wants to unfold naturally in every moment. Celeste had an interest in holistic living, natural food and beauty, yet she insisted on building a business on fast food, which she actually had no interest in. What a dichotomy. That would be like me remaining a bartender many years ago, when witnessing people change with the influence of alcohol was so painful to watch. I had to resign, and it was frightening because I didn't know what else to do, yet obviously something different wanted to emerge in my life. I couldn't possibly be guided in a new direction while remaining caught in the grip of a secure but completely unfulfilling job. So I quit, and became very depressed. I rested and I prayed, and I created a business card for a mural-painting business, even though I had little experience. My depression quickly faded as I discovered a new path, a path that encompassed my artistic talent. In a short period of time, I learned how to do specialty wall finishes and started my own company.

We have to start somewhere, such as with being honest with ourselves, so that we can discover new possibilities. How else can we receive the unconditional support, the energy elixir, from spirit?

I personally don't fight with spirit anymore. I don't say, "No, no, no," or "But how, but why?" I remain curious whether I agree with the guidance or not. I question the guidance to get a better sense of what my part is in its unfolding, but I don't refuse its entry into my life. I say, "All right, what next, and please show me the way." That doesn't mean that I don't get scared, or feel insecure. I feel all of that intensely, and I still say, "Yes!"

Complete Surrender

Masiandia: *"Each rising of a new day deserves your absolute joy and gratitude. This requires complete surrender and commitment to the life you really want – not settling for limitations. In order to manifest the life you really want, it is important that you let go of limiting perceptions that shadow your potential. To manifest your longing, you must release insecurities, self-doubt and shame. We are not asking that you bury these difficult feelings under judgment and more control. We are talking about letting go into the new, which means releasing your painful self-doubt into the arms of Divinity and letting yourself be filled with higher purpose. To welcome the life that you truly want, you must bring every-thing to the light of spirit – allow the Divine to love all of who you are, so you can be freed."*

I want to acknowledge that it can be so difficult to surrender into the arms of Divinity. We oscillate from inspirational ideas to limited perceptions, and then we try to relinquish the old conditioning while also grasping for the future. On the one hand, we can be enlivened by our longing but then equally conflicted by the confusion that comes from be-ing defended against the unknown.

Old mindsets resist temptation, even when what tempts us is soul-purpose and happiness. The promise of love, the possibility for growth and a dream come true are sabotaged by self-defence and self-doubt. Some people are so accustomed to rejection that they remain relentlessly distrustful no matter the love and support that is given to them. So as I contemplate Masiandia's message, I am aware that memories can over-shadow the present before we even have a chance to recognize this is hap-pening. Unconsciously, we strip our dreams of vitality and bury our po-tential in past neglect and disappointment.

To free ourselves, we need to relinquish the burden of carrying these painful personal histories and remember that we are not alone. We are in-tricately woven into a larger tapestry of soulful purpose, and there is a uni-versal well of support to draw from, beyond the confines of our resistance. It is necessary to cease trying so hard to evolve, to understand, to change, and instead let ourselves flow with change, because it is inevitable.

Masiandia: *"Fighting with the force of change only causes pain, but letting go is not painful. It is refusing to let go that is painful. It is soul-damaging and destructive. You cannot force life to match your expectations just because you're afraid of facing change. Life is unpredictable, and this cannot be altered; it is part of the larger framework of the karmic relationship between your soul and human nature. The key is to relinquish control in order to open yourself to the grace of life's generosity, to ultimately receive your soul's embrace and its alighted gift. We want you to pledge your alliance to a new life that is born out of letting go of past conditioning, to a new life shaped by your creative potential."*

Letting go reminds me of pruning trees or reshaping a garden. Beautiful landscapes need to be maintained and flowerpots cared for, otherwise plants outgrow planter boxes and become unhealthy. We need to prune back our own overgrowth, our outmoded belief systems, to reshape our consciousness and renew ourselves.

Life tends to be the pruning shears, the catalyst for our own renewal. We are shown the way to release, to expand and open into the new. During a three-month journey in Southeast Asia, my travel experiences served as the pruning shears, while I recited a prayer given to me by Masiandia to help stabilize my energy. The prayer was, "Oh Great Spirit, I give my spiritual curiosity to this world and receive its blessing. For this I am grateful and pledge my full commitment to my self-value and to the value of others." These words assisted me in seeing beyond difficulties that arose travelling in a developing country.

Being in a strange land, amidst cultural differences and the challenge of language barriers, brought out the worst in me, as well as positive qualities I didn't know I had. I had not anticipated my reactions or some of my abilities to adapt; they were equally unpredictable. Each day called for me to "let go" over and over again. My expectations faltered as oftentimes accommodations, places of interest and transportation were not as posted; photographs were deceiving and services promised didn't actually materialize. Also, my sense of aesthetics was compromised when natural landscapes, waterfalls, beaches and even villages looked great from a distance, but upon closer view, debris and litter marred their pristine beauty. Yet I was able to transcend this in the experiences I had with the people. Though their language was completely foreign from my own, that didn't impinge on my appreciation of the joyful innocence of the children and the purity of laughing together at our differences.

But some differences were hard to reconcile, especially when I saw a man throw a garbage bag out of a moving bus. I remember reciting the affirmation, "I give my spiritual curiosity to this world…" But this prayer could not console me when, after climbing a long flight of stairs to a mountaintop temple, I encountered a dying dog. The dog's hair was stringy, barely covering his bony frame, and his eyes were red with mucus. He followed me wherever I walked, heaving and panting. I felt sick with regret and helplessness. "Release him," the spirits told me, "look beyond his pain."

Nothing is as it seems; our human awareness cannot fathom the bigger picture or understand its significance. Letting go is so unpredictable. It's not something that we can just "do", but we can pray for it and allow it to unfold naturally. Letting go is then about surrendering, not pushing something aside as we tend to initially believe. When I finally let go, when I accepted the dog's fate, I no longer felt helpless. Instead, I just loved it. The spirits helped me realize that the dog was looking for love. But still, my intellect, my human nature, had difficulty with this perception because I wanted to save it, feed it – just do something. By remaining curious, I let go of trying to figure out what to do, even trying to understand why it was dying, why the monastery did not look after the dogs. I came to realize that the dog and I were in the same place and time in divine order, and the sorrow I felt no longer prevented me from appreciating its presence and value.

Masiandia: *"Nothing remains the same – everything must shift to accommodate change. That is the essence of nature, of Gaia, for which resistance is futile. Only humankind tries to suppress the course of nature and define the value of life based on your comfort level, while nature follows a completely different course. Everything around you has nothing to do with sating your fear and worries and everything to do with the alignment of probabilities that best serve soul-purpose.*

"Stop measuring your quality of life based on your comfort level, because it prevents you from honouring your spiritual integrity; it overshadows you with pain, not love. No matter that change can be frightening, nothing remains the same no matter how much you ignore it or hold back the reigns, because everything is impermanent. In letting go, you allow it to transition to its next stage of evolution, unbeknown to you, undefined by you, free of your discrimination. Let go to let Divinity unfurl before you and from within you."

Relinquish Who You Think You Should Be

Masiandia: *"You have not incarnated on Earth to struggle, yet many of you do when you assume that only when you are 'successful' will your lives have meaning. Many of you believe that when you finally arrive at the finish line you will be happy; when your finances are in order then you will be secure and can finally trust the Universe. You think that you will no longer be overwhelmed when a project is complete or when you find the 'right' formula, the 'right' remedy, and so on. Most of you believe that when you receive recognition for your efforts, your self-value will be valid, all your hard work will be worth it, and only then can you rest. Many of you think that when you find the perfect relationship you will know that you're lovable, and when you are given this reward then God must indeed love you.*

"You want guarantees before you believe in the possible. But there is absolutely nothing real about this. You must let go of all these expectations and be your own person, live by your own values and honour your natural pace because if you don't, you risk ill-health, accidents, setbacks and a very empty life.

"Liberation comes from relinquishing who you think you should be, and it is the most profound work you will ever do. By relinquishing the need for guarantees and thus your false expectations, you come to recognize your covert behaviour and shift the way in which you interact with life. For instance, you cease enduring the pressure to conform and perform for the right to be accepted and loved. You also relinquish the belief that you are supposed be able to 'do' more.

"The level of pressure to succeed is especially prominent in education. Students particularly put themselves through intimidating stress to make the grade. But the pressure is not just their own; it is shaped by an educational system wherein there is an urgency to excel with high marks as well as plan for the future. The pressure is unhealthy and must be relinquished in order for the student to fully absorb what he/she is actually learning. To let go of the pressure to perform expertly on a final exam, the student must realize that he/she really does want to do well on the exam. The pressure subsides when he/she acknowledges his/her desire for excellence. By admitting what is important to him/her, when he/she studies for the exam there is no longer a fear of failure but rather inspiration. People no longer pressure themselves when they are motivated by joy. Acknowledging yourselves – recognizing your values – is encouraging, while pressure is debilitating, stressful and unnecessary.

"We want you to recognize your worthiness and then pass it on. Be the teacher who believes in your students. Be the student who is compelled to learn, and therefore let go of the need to be right and the need to know it all. And for some of you, let go of the belief that you are stupid, that you cannot learn something new because there is something wrong with you. There is nothing wrong with you; the natural way for you to learn may not coincide with the learning institution or work environment that you're in. That doesn't make you a bad person, nor does it devalue the situation that is not in alignment with your needs. Let go of trying to change the situation or persons that you are struggling with, for that is a sure way to struggle some more. Instead, inspire yourself as well as others with self-acceptance and self-acknowledgment."

*J*t can take unfamiliar circumstances and new environments to initiate the fulfilment of our self-value, and sometimes it is another person's perspective that helps us grow. I recall a counselling session with my mentor in which after a profound healing process, he acknowledged me for my courage and depth. He recognized the trust I had given him and myself. I thanked him and moved on to something else, looking away from him. Then he asked me to fully receive his praise, and I shyly said, "Yes, yes, thank you." He gently insisted that I accept his appreciation, so that I, too, could recognize the depth to which I had just shared with him. It wasn't until a week later, though, that I fully integrated his message. He had recognized one of my strengths, but because I didn't see it in myself, I couldn't accept his acknowledgment. When I finally did, I saw my value.

Being Authentically 'You'

Masiandia: *"Many people conceal their feelings because they are governed by the belief that they will not be understood, or fear that their feelings will betray a deep shame. They mask their true essence to avoid being judged, to maintain a reasonable sense of security. But soul cannot be shrouded in falseness – it requires complete disclosure to shine its true light. We would like to support you in being authentically yourself by gently asking you to 'let go' of self-protection, of the masks that impede the natural flow of your brilliance.*

"We understand that some situations are difficult to 'handle' and that you believe that you 'have to' wear a protective cloak. Family members, even couples do this for years, until something gives in: an illness, loss of employment, divorce. The soul cannot thrive under oppressive circumstances; it is meant to be alive, fully expressing itself – its essence.

"Take, for instance, a situation that may frustrate you. Perhaps it is discussion with a family member that challenges you as, no matter how clearly you express yourself, your opinion is still blatantly disregarded. Rather than smile meekly and pretend that it's OK, or fight to be heard, imagine that you embrace

how you feel. Imagine that you do not alter your behaviour to minimize conflict or reject the situation in any way. Instead, picture yourself being completely authentic with your feelings, without having to convince anyone to accept them or agree with you. In this way, you step into peaceful interactions because you stand in your own self-worth; you have nothing to prove, no expectation – only self-respect. And when you respect yourself, you naturally respect others. Hence, you relinquish the need to change them, which is freeing for everyone involved."

*W*hen we allow ourselves to experience our own feelings, we are able to differentiate from the feelings and expectations of others. We cease defending ourselves against judgment and taking responsibility for other people's reactions. In this way, no one is made wrong, thus difficult situations can easily be shifted rather than worsened. This is a tool to return to "self" – to cease losing one's power to others.

I would like to share a story about my client David that describes this process of differentiation. On the day that he moved into his new home, his neighbour demanded that the moving company park down the road. She complained that the truck was blocking her way and accused the movers of being unprofessional. The moving company then parked a little farther from David's driveway to allow for her to drive away, but that didn't satisfy her. In fact, once out of her driveway, she parked the car in the middle of the road, blocked everyone's way and proceeded to yell at David, adamant that the movers should park the truck at the other end of the road. He didn't try to explain to her that they needed to move a heavy piano, but instead introduced himself, a gesture that she ignored while continuing to be belligerent and accusatory. David remained composed and gently told her that she couldn't leave her car in the middle of the road. Interestingly, she turned around quietly, walked to her car and drove away without further quarrel.

Masiandia encourages us to maintain trustful relations with others, to hold a strong frequency of acceptance and care, no matter their actions or inactions. We cease fighting with others when we stop trying to prove that we are right or explain what we need. We stay in love, in faith, in harmony. Furthermore, we secure our need for safety by maintaining our own gentle ground. Otherwise, the moment that we join someone in his/ her conflict, we are no longer safe because we have abandoned our personal space and power, our own sense of value. David did not become a player in his neighbour's story; instead, he interacted with her in a way that identified the obvious without judgment. He chose not to parrot her condescending behaviour and was thus able to moderate the situation. Even though he felt shaken, he chose to take care of his discomfort rather than blame her for it.

Masiandia: *"We know that you all need to feel safe and accepted, and we understand that in many cases, family, friends, co-workers and strangers do not honour this need, for they themselves feel unsafe in the world. You can all create a better world by looking after your own need for safety. Be the person who greets you every moment of every day. Imagine waking up in the morning with a smile from the inside out. Imagine that you're smiling to the nature that you are, to your hands, to your bones, to your heart, to your belly. Imagine that every single day you know that you have permission to be 'you' no matter what anybody else tells you."*

*A*n interesting thing happens as we smile inwardly and see our beauty – the people around us are compelled to see their own beauty. They feel good about who they are when they are around us, drawn to the light of our inner-smile, which naturally creates a supportive environment that grows mutual trust, acceptance and peace. Therefore, the best way to create mutually supportive relationships is to cultivate an intimate relationship with ourselves. It's in choosing to believe in ourselves that adversity relents. We cease projecting our needs onto others, and as we relinquish the reality that we're accustomed to, we step into a whole new way of being.

The Gift of Trust

*I*t never ceases to amaze me that all kinds of life circumstances provide us with opportunities to see the world in a new way, a way that transcends the ordinary. I witnessed a remarkable interaction between a mother and her daughter in a grocery store that gave me insight into self-responsibility and self-worth. It also awakened in me a profound feeling of being taken care of. I was standing in line at the checkout stand when the mother, the customer ahead of me, reminded me of the power we have in making our own choices, in letting go of what other people think of us and in trusting ourselves.

The daughter was playing on a metal bar that separated the adjacent stall, making flips and stretching her legs up in the air. In a stern voice, the checkout attendant told her to be careful. The little girl looked anxiously to her mother who was standing right beside her and quietly asked if it was okay for her to continue playing. The mother told her daughter that she trusted her to know her own limits. The mother said, "You know when it's unsafe. You know what you can do and what you are uncomfortable with." It comforted me to hear her say this to her daughter, words that no one in my family had spoken to me. I drew a sense of satisfaction and reassurance from witnessing this exchange, as well as a deep feeling of being believed in. I was reminded that I, too, can trust what I am capable of.

We each have so much to give and receive from one another that even strangers can act as conduits for the Divine. This could be true for the earlier story about David and his neighbour. Perhaps his calmness shifted her reality; maybe it even lessened a conflict within her. In relinquishing the need to protect ourselves against the judgments and fears of others, we serve as luminaries for a new world, a world that is born out of trust.

Beyond Grief

Masiandia: *"We understand that it is difficult for many of you to trust the unknown, to let challenging situations evolve into peaceful encounters. We also see that for many of you, life gives you no choice; it demands that you undo old programming that does not serve your soul. Life pushes you to become conscious, to awaken to who you are gently or forcefully, through opportunities, life-changes, sometimes illness and bereavement. Therefore, we cannot talk about letting go without acknowledging grief.*

"Grief is a turning inwards into dark despair and bittersweet release. It encompasses the need to rest, heal and start over. It is like exhaling, pausing between notes, and silence – a complete emptying of your feeling body, to be refilled by your next breath. Breathing is often the centre of focus in meditation for this reason, to release holding patterns from the body. Letting go then supports you in opening to your essence, so that the breath of divinity can replenish you.

"Being renewed is like a seed that when growing roots grieves its encasement. It breaks free from its outer shell, its shelter, to risk life. The same is true for the initial conception of spirit into matter; the spark of one's spirit attunes itself to life, but in order to cede into incarnation it has to let go of the shelter of its higher-vibrational radiance, a journey of deep spiritual grief as well as joy. The spirit's initial conception into form has to surrender into the fetus's development, and that is a grieving process because developing physical nature then becomes the spirit's main focus, a process of newness but also loss. Not yet an individual personality or expression of its spirit, the fetus becomes its mother's breath, emulating her every thought and emotion. During this stage, the fetus is but another organ in the mother's body, not the full expression of its soul-consciousness.

After birth, the newborn baby grieves the loss of the womb's comfort and protection, and the mother grieves the loss of her pregnancy. She no longer holds within her the amazing, intimate relationship she previously had with the

unknown; now she must face the unknown, she must grieve the loss of control;
after all, her life will never be the same.

"Loss occurs in every single moment of your life, just as your body goes
through cell regeneration, excreting dead cells to replenish your entire physi-
ological system with new cells. The same is true for exhaling: it releases carbon
dioxide from your lungs, and each new breath fills you with oxygen. Loss is
therefore inevitable for it is part of the natural life-death-life cycle that makes all
things whole."

*I*n every moment, our body undergoes an active process of cell regeneration. According to scientists at book.bionumbers.org, "100
million new red blood cells are being formed in our body *every minute.*"
Researchers have calculated that most of our cells are replaced every few
days, while some types are believed to be on multi-month or multi-year
renewal schedules. In the process of regeneration, the cells are excreted,
exhaled and replaced by new ones. The cells give themselves up to maintain the integrity of the whole body, mind and spirit.

Masiandia: *"When you understand that every cell-death serves to revitalize*
your entire physical vitality, you come to appreciate that you are made new over
and over again by releasing the old. Death and loss are always paired with new
beginnings. It is a process of spiritual emergence that opens your heart to God.
So when it comes to death, which is the passage into the afterlife, it is a transi-
tion, not a stopping force. Death is not the end to life; it is a natural process
that returns the spirit to the soul, which continues the cycle of soul-purpose.
Remember, you are not separate – you are one with the Divine.

"It is highly important that you suspend your fear of death, and surrender
your attachment to those who have passed on, because your anguish does not help
their spirits evolve. Suffering a person's death creates an energy-frequency that
holds his/her spirit back, locked into the stronghold of your despair. You must
free the spirit to help it align with its whole soul-vibration. Your loved ones who

have passed over begin a new cycle in the afterlife, a new expression into eternal life. Their journeys continue, not separate from you but linked to your spirit. It's the human mind that doesn't see, doesn't realize that death is not the end.

"Our dear friends, there comes a point when it is necessary to allow grief to evolve and become a sanctuary for repose. You can rest in the certainty that all life and the afterlife are interconnected and that spirit is infinite and everywhere, eternally linked with you."

The author Moyra Caldecott talks about this in her book *Multidimensional Life.* She shares her initial concern for her husband after he passed away. She feared that asking for his help would interfere with his progress in the afterlife. Then she was reminded that in the other world there is no time and space. She writes, "He does not have to come to me from somewhere else to attend to me – because he has never left, just changed."

In her book, Caldecott describes the Universe as not only made of matter, subject to the laws of physics, but as infinitely more complex. She speaks of an infinity that we cannot understand by guessing at. Yet we can know that such complexity is in existence, "because we feel the effects," she writes. Caldecott also suggests that there has to be more, as our existence tells us so.

As a channeller and artist, I *feel* the effects of infinity; I create in the realm of the unexpected, the mysterious and holy. For me, there has been more, as I've connected with my mother's spirit. It is comforting to know that her death never really took her away from me. I remember as a child praying to God, asking him to tell Mom that I loved her, until one day I realized that I could talk to her directly. I didn't discover that I could receive her communication until much later. My first encounter with her spirit was in my early twenties. It was in a session with a clairvoyant that I felt an odd pressure on my left side, right before the reader told me that my mother was standing to my left with her hand on my shoulder. My mother wanted me to know that she was always with me and that she would help me heal.

I have heard many stories of people reuniting with those who have died, and in many cases I have been privileged to be the medium in this regard. I was in tears in a session when my client's deceased husband expressed his love for her through me. He urged her not to allow her pain to separate them; he needed for her to be open to him so that he could continue to take care of her. It was a karmic promise he had made to her that also served his evolution, and it was necessary for her to let go of her anguish so that she could feel his presence. The more she opened to him, the more she sensed him around her, and she felt safe again, the way she had when they were together.

We can be touched by spirit in beautiful ways, in ways that transcend our reality and remind us that we are not forsaken. A story shared by Cynthia in one of my workshops illustrates this beautifully. After her father's death, Cynthia and her family joined together for a Celebration of Life in the centre of a grove of trees. A crow circled overhead, sweeping down towards them and then onto a nearby branch. It remained there the whole time that Cynthia and her family shared stories about their dad. Cynthia was drawn to the crow, captivated by its presence, and aware of it staring at her and her family. The crow stayed with them for the entire time, and even as Cynthia and her family walked away, it remained and watched them leave. Cynthia kept looking over her shoulder as they walked away, and the crow didn't fly off; it kept staring at her until it faded out of sight.

Another participant at the workshop shared a similar story about receiving profound reassurance. After her partner's death, Janet released her beloved's ashes into the ocean. The water lapped at the ashes while a seagull circled the sky and swept lower and lower, almost touching her head. The seagull seemed to reach right into her soul, touching her in a mystical way. When she looked down at the sand, she saw a pattern that was personal to her and her beloved, a shape that spoke to her heart. She knew that her partner was communicating with her.

   We truly are not alone, and these are the miraculous moments that happen in our lives when we open our hearts, open our minds and surrender our sorrow ... into joy.

I will never forget you, my darling
I will be the brightest star in the
night sky twinkling delight,
and the moon illuminating every
corner of the world for you.

I will be the infinite companion who
comforts you in the darkest hours.
You need only listen.

Forget everything you think
you know about death.
Don't believe even your sorrow.
I am not separate.
I did not leave you.

Oh my sweet child,
let me take care of your shadow;
let me heal the past and release
the ancestors that came before me.

You have only your innocence to
shelter, and I your eternity to
embrace.

Let me guide you home
to what is sacred.
Let me show you the way
to Source.

My beloved,
your courage is my forgiveness –
your willingness my freedom.

I am forever grateful.
for you have been in my life,
part of my soul and will always
be with me, as I with you.

Renewal, A Journey into You

Weather storms never cease to amaze me.
Lightning strikes and the ground renews itself.
Life spawns the birthing of each day –
a day to forgive and unite the blessings
                    of true love.

I will not stand in the shadows of yesterday.
But instead bear witness to each moment's
newness and the gift that is shared in devotion.
I give you this blessing – the blessing of trust
and the great act of commitment
                    that trust demands.

May this blessing devour any fears that
threaten to break you, while you embrace
                    a life ready to be lived fully
and shared and enjoyed peacefully.
Let that be the strength that endures and the
                    faith that knows the meaning of love.

Spiritual Renewal

I was walking along a tree-lined street with a friend, when he looked up at one of the trees and said, "Isn't it a miracle? We exchange breath with these beloved trees. They are sustained by our exhalation and in exchange give us the kiss of life." The interconnection between the carbon dioxide we exhale into the atmosphere, which trees need to survive, and the oxygen released by the trees to sustain our existence, is in essence renewal. This exchange is part of the cycle of death and rebirth that is continuously linked to existence and occurs throughout every moment of our lives.

It is by flowing voluntarily with the currents of our lives that we cultivate harmony, for we allow the cycles of death and rebirth to be a force of renewal that supports our spiritual emergence. We let go of old patterns to be reborn into new purpose, actively surrendering our limited beliefs into awakened possibilities. Our active surrender then immerses us in the transformative gift of renewal – a shift in consciousness that ushers in the new.

Spiritual renewal is a way of being that no longer works within old frameworks; it is not an end point or even a desired outcome. Nor is it something new; it is actually a process of *making* new. It is the current of our desire propelling us forward, an activation of energy that merges intention with reality, and which manifests our purpose.

As I contemplate the significance of this creative force, I see that spiritual renewal is a state of grace that yearns to move freely in all areas of our lives. Ultimately, it is a way of being that is not one expression but many, such as feeling sad and equally joyful. Essentially there is no difference between sorrow or delight. Whether we experience pain or non-suffering, both expressions are parts of the same fabric, which is our witnessing Self. When we no longer identify with either suffering or joy, we cease evaluating one as better or worse than the other. Instead, we welcome our whole expression, which awakens us to deep love that transforms distress and physical pain into a profound sense of self-care.

We embrace the gift of renewal by no longer discriminating between good and bad, which naturally supports us in actively surrendering into the multitude of experience that makes us body and soul. This allows us to draw in the guidance of spirit, which when joined with our human nature creates the perfect synthesis for manifesting the sacred into everyday life. Just like the trees with which we co-exist in a mutually sustaining way, our mind serves to express the beauty of our soul, and in turn the soul serves to expand our sense of purpose and meaning.

Masiandia: *"Spiritual renewal is life-changing alchemy that honours all consciousness; it welcomes everything into the life-death-life cycle of evolution. Nothing is left behind, as all cycles from death to rebirth are constant and fluid, absorbing one matter into another, such as trees consuming the release of your breath to revive you with life-force energy.*

"Alchemy is the art of magic and enchantment, enticing base energy into beauty. It is all about raising the quality of perceptions: seeing and sensing beyond limitations, so that what is left is wholeness. When you know that you are not solely your mind, you are able to align to multidimensional consciousness. You are not limited to choosing between your human nature and your spirit; you are both and so much more. You are not only your mind or your emotions, or your spirit-consciousness; you are many facets, many expressions of your soul.

"Multidimensional consciousness encompasses all of these facets – it is the place in which all expressions meet. It is the point at which everything is interconnected, a source of oneness that is not singular, but vast. God is not one thing but many expressions.

"Your greatest sense of purpose is found beyond your identity and social conditioning. You are intrinsically whole and can embody expanded states of consciousness that encompass so much more than what you expect or anticipate.

Spiritual renewal is then an in-depth surrender into who you truly are and the natural evolution of your life, unfolding the old into the cycle of creation."

Since the life-death-life cycle is fundamentally a process of regeneration, not a static set goal, I puzzle over how we can surrender to its gift of renewal when we are so programmed for arrival, not the journey. Social pressures, competitive businesses, demanding jobs and health issues can instantly overtake us, tromping the popular saying, "It is the journey that matters, not the destination." Seldom does the mind yield to the journey of transformation, for it is preoccupied with the outcome, not the process. Also, the mind is programmed to overcome imperfections in the effort to be worthy enough for success; therefore, the body is in a constant state of unease, not resting in the evolving unknown.

Masiandia often says that we must bring everything with us into the rousing mystery of the present moment, our willingness and unwillingness, defiance and compliance, fear and exaltation. We must bring every thought, shame and discomfort to the door of our acceptance, to receive its guidance. Then it's not about the journey's end, nor about our purpose and intention; it's a matter of trusting in the unfolding. What is important to remember is that we don't have to be perfect. As Mary Oliver says in her poem, *Wild Geese,* we don't have to be good nor cross the desert on our knees repenting, since no matter our despair, the world goes on. I love her line, "You only have to let the soft animal of your body love what it loves."

When we let our body love what it loves, we give *fully* to life; we give who we are, not what is expected of us. We break free of constricting ideas, not by hiding away from them, not by overcoming them, but by embracing who we are. Then renewal transforms us beyond our understanding, beyond our ideas of how it should occur. Renewal becomes a magical force that expands our consciousness into new states of creation and belonging, as Oliver suggests in the last lines of her poem, "Whoever you are ... the world offers itself to your imagination, calls to you like the wild geese, harsh and exciting – over and over announcing your place in the family of things." That is the gift of renewal; it's our place in the relationship between spirit and matter, the place where our imagination, intention and focus is powered by the guidance of our soul.

Embracing the Journey

The more I contemplate what renewal means to me and how to surrender into its natural flow, the more I find that words do little to express the inner knowing that resides within its mystery. Words fall short of conveying the intensity and grace that conscious surrender embodies. It's that place within that holds the interplay of frustration and wonder, uncertainty and complete devotion. Spiritual renewal brings us into the senses, the way of the heart that is beyond the intellect and which arouses our longing. It is a state of witnessing beyond perception, beholding with the inner eye the vast beauty that is all around us.

This awakened state is a sacred marriage between the self and the Universe, which lives and gives wholly in love. My friend Paul's journey of learning to paraglide is a fine example of embracing the path of renewal, of living fully and letting the body love what it loves. Paul had yearned to fly for so long that even in his sleep he dreamt of flying. Still, he felt some trepidation when he was preparing to leave for the flight training – fear he transformed into courage as he consciously chose to believe in his dream. And he trusted in his studious attention to detail regarding the safety procedures that would allow him to surrender with care.

I heard from him soon after his first flight – he had flown on the training hill and was bursting with eagerness to fly at higher altitudes. Someone who had experienced initial apprehension, he now laughingly referred to the short training-flights as teasers and excitedly anticipated the mountain flight, which would be at an altitude of 400 metres (1400 feet) or more.

He was just two more training days away from his solo mountain flight, however, when the winds became too strong to fly at all. As a novice, he was only permitted to launch in winds less than 15 kph. So for a few more days he practiced his kiting; he learned to lift and land while still on the ground, to dance with his new wing, as he described it. He learned to feel the kite's every nuance, to respond almost in advance to keep the kite strongly positioned over his head. He said, "To the casual observer, it might appear that she (the wing) is temperamental. In truth, she is anything but. She is actually totally solid and present in every moment, responding to the sum total of the wind's many facets and my minute adjustments/inputs that signal my intentions."

Well, his training paid off, because a few days later I received the great news that he had graduated from a 30-metre elevation to a 940-metre (3,100-feet) elevation. He was elated, not only because of his mountain flight, but because all the days of practicing deepened his sense of understanding and spiritual connection.

I see Paul's intimate understanding of his wing as a metaphor for the human/soul relationship. Spirit is a faithful presence in every moment of our lives woven within life's many facets, and our human experience is the input, focus and intention. Spirit responds to the winds of change and offers us infinite possibility, and our human intention forms the perfect synthesis that serves to inspire us throughout every stage of our renewal. Spirit synchronizes events that are intended to answer our prayers, which require our active surrender to fulfil. Spiritual emergence then comes from the willingness to dissolve disbelief, shame and grief ... into the unknown, which allows our lives to flourish in meaningful ways.

Rights of Renewal

Masiandia: *"Renewal is the pivotal energy within all creation, the kernel at the centre point of all cycles in your life, all ages and life-experience. It is the heart of everything as well as the movement that follows, like the potential of a seed's life-death-life cycle that is not the germinating seed, or the blossom or death, but all stages interwoven. Therefore, renewal is all time and space, and when you realize this you don't over-identify with any cycle in your life. Instead, you flow with your life-experiences unimpeded, as a whole expression of the human/soul relationship. Then you remember that God is truly within you and that you are not alone.*

"When you remember that you are whole, you don't confuse loneliness with abandonment or struggle for love or for success and abundance, for your wholeness completes you. This is how you are transformed, not into something new but into your creative enfoldment, a journey that is divine no matter its length of time, no matter its fruition. It is the journey of creation that is renewing, which fills you with inspiration and purpose, not the destination. The destination is only a projection of your longing, not the magnetic force of your longing. Beyond the scope of expectations, your yearning has the power to enrich your life with soul."

We tend to expect so much from our lives that we don't accept that some of our rites of renewal are indeed lengthy. Some journeys are longer for reasons unbeknown to us, reasons that are beyond our best efforts and belief. Some of us experience disheartening loss and misfortunes that seem to be the ruin of our dreams or the forces of nature that dams creative continuity. But Masiandia would remind us that in every situation in our lives there is purpose: karmic order, spiritual cultivation and opportunities to stay in love.

My lengthy renewal cycle as an artist, for example, has granted me numerous opportunities to practice faith in lieu of disappointment and discouragement. My big dream of being a successful artist didn't unfold as I planned, and I encountered a few setbacks along the way. My biggest success as an artist was my biggest failure. A gallery that represented my art sold a large number of paintings equivalent to about a year's income, but they did not pay me, and they lost five paintings. After a drawn-out legal process a payment plan was agreed upon, but four months later the payments were cancelled as the gallery closed their bank account. They moved to a new location without notice and changed their gallery name. A writ of seizure was obtained followed by Sheriff Services, but there were no monies found, as the owner had no valuable assets in his name.

In retrospect, it was a costly lesson that taught me to create better systems for organizing my inventory and keeping track of gallery sales. It also taught me to exercise better boundaries and to take ownership of my value as an artist. It has been a journey of dissolving disbelief, strengthening my right to be supported and acknowledging the beauty I create. My art has stood the test of time and failure and has given me something profoundly significant; it has opened me to channelling. It has filled my life with colour and healing. And there is nothing in the world more natural to me than stepping into my studio with its faint scent of oil glazes and wax, and resting in the certainty that my lifelong commitment has blessed me with purpose.

The rites of renewal touch us in different ways throughout our lives – ways that need to be honoured, so that we can receive their inherent gifts. I'm especially mindful of this, since in my line of work as a healer, I often come across workshop promotions that promise quick ascension, offering an accelerated journey to awakening. But in truth, one might not see breakthrough for years, not because there is a lack of commitment or willingness, but because some processes follow a slower and more gradual pace. For example, in nature, some trees take years to become established.

I'm reminded of Milton Erickson, whose life and work illustrates a classic example of finding one's own voice and inner-strength through perseverance. Erickson contracted polio during his adolescence in 1918 and again at the age of 51, and near the end of his life he was confined to a wheelchair, yet he revolutionized the practice of hypnosis. Erickson saw the relevance of the therapeutic value of hypnosis and is noted for approaching the unconscious mind as creative and resourceful, though his methods were so unique that in the 1950s the American Medical Association tried to revoke his practitioner's license. What's interesting is that the evolution of his hypnotherapy theories and practices grew as a way to overcome his own physical limitations.

In *My Voice Will Go with You, The Teaching Tales of Milton H. Erickson,* Erickson recounts the story of being bedridden at the age of 17. Due to polio he was paralyzed and unable to speak, so he passed the time observing his environment. He discovered the significance of non-verbal expression, noticing the differences between verbal communication, the tone of voice and body language. He writes, "I was quarantined on the farm with seven sisters, one brother, two parents, and a practical nurse. And how could I entertain myself? I started watching people and my environment. I soon learned that my sisters could say 'no' when they meant 'yes.' And they could say 'yes' and mean 'no' at the same time." He was intrigued by the relationship between the unconscious and conscious mind, and that later inspired his work with hypnotherapy.

During this time of studying non-verbal expression, Erickson transformed his disadvantage into a learning tool that developed his powers of observation, which unbeknownst to him in his youth, would come to have an impact on countless generations of therapists and patients. During his illness Erickson also paid close attention to his baby sister learn to walk, from her crawling to balancing herself as she moved from sitting to standing positions. He focused intently so that he could learn how to walk again, laying down the building blocks for his whole life, an experience that he would later weave into his therapeutic stories to help people overcome difficulties.

No matter the length of our own renewal cycles, adversities make us stronger when we trust in their inherent gift, when we actively surrender to the learning that is intrinsically linked to all areas of our lives. Then adversity dissolves into an awakened shift in consciousness that invites deep compassion and trust in our present lives.

Masiandia: *"It is impossible for you to foretell what will transpire in the course of your life; you simply cannot observe the future in an instant. But you can develop a profound understanding of the unfaltering gift that the present has to offer you, which cannot but unwind into the future. Harness it, open your heart, your eyes, your senses and take in the gift that this world has to offer you, so that you can free yourself into grace.*

"You are here in this world to be shaped by the tides of change, to be generous with your devotion as you surrender to the process of renewal. Let yourself dissolve to be reborn over and over again. That is how love gets in."

⸺∞⸺

Honouring the Natural Cycles of Growth

Trees go to sleep in winter; it is crucial for their renewal. They rest in the cold to protect from freezing and to save energy while there is limited access to nourishment, slumbering in a state of dormancy until the resurrection of spring. We too can save energy until the next stage in our life presents itself.

As with the seasonal cycles, there are a number of stages in the creative unfolding, such as the stages of conception, embracing our desires, excitement and focus, and creative frustration. Retreating to observe the flow of our life is a wintering stage that is indeed crucial for renewal. It gives us the energy needed to resurrect into the next stage of personal insight and realization as we step into completion. Each stage is intrinsically connected to the whole journey, supporting us in the present. It is essential that we deepen our responsiveness to the natural timing of these renewal stages so that we can open our hearts to the kaleidoscope of God's love, and restore every cell in our body with life-affirming presence.

To deepen my own responsiveness and understanding, I draw on the guidance of our planet, Gaia, and endeavour to honour her gift of renewal by giving her a voice in this chapter.

Channelled Message from Gaia

> "The seasons are not separate from each other, as it appears to human perception. Seasons are each part of a collective consciousness that fuels evolution from one form of reality to another. This is like day and night that belongs to a whole system, without which day would not exist and night would have no purpose.
>
> "In the entire world, there is need of rest, which the dark provides and the seasons nourish. Without winter, nature is a desert land for which there is no renewal. Without spring, there would be no germinating crocuses bursting out of their shells; there would be no blossoming tulips. Imagine a world without summer, where nothing grew and there were no harvests. Autumn would be lonely if not for the certainty of the intimacy that winter offers."

I love to imagine the seasons as intimately connected, and to further my understanding I draw on the intelligence of the nature-essence directly aligned with the seasons.

Channelled Message from the Deva of The Seasons

> "You have forgotten us – you the man, the woman, the child offended by our uneven temperament. You have forgotten how to communicate with us, how to tell us your stories. You have forgotten that the wind is ever changing and dynamic and is a

supporting element in your lives that you long to be a part of –
you long to dance in our arms and be one fluid motion.

"You had promised to ascend, to come to us willingly and
rest in safety, not fight with our patterns and make war with
nature. We are not your enemy, nor your resource to do with as
you please; we are your arms, your body, your internal organs;
we are the sun and moon; we are the seasons that pass, the in-
separable momentum of renewal.

"Come to us as willing partners. Come to us unafraid, for
if you falter – if you are pained or die into the other side of the
veil of consciousness – you will not lose our love for you; nor
will you lose your spirit, your eternal beingness. We welcome
you over and over again even if you're in resistance or whether
you love us in return. We hear your calling – the emergence of
your prayers, and pattern cycles of renewal in support of you.
We design pathways and manifested outcomes that best align
to you in answer to your prayers. You are never alone, always
held in love. Let us love you – let the spirit world help you and
inspire you to live your dreams.

"Come to us; let us invoke your splendid nature and soul-
purpose, so that unafraid you will be fluid and perfectly aligned
to the currents of change, as though you are made from the cur-
rents of change, because indeed you are."

*A*s I take in this message, I am uplifted and equally overwhelmed
by the immensity of what it entails. *"Come to us willingly,"* is an
invitation that every cell in my body wants to give in to, and my eyes well
up in tears as I recognize how much I have resisted. I'm overwhelmed by
the intensity of humanity's refusal to work in tandem with nature and in
how that has impeded us from creating a world that is at peace. Must we
continue to struggle against our differences as well as the incongruence

between what we want and the adversities that inevitably surface along the changeable currents of the seasons?

The cycles of renewal, when honoured, provide us with the answers to our prayers – they are the impetus for change. We honour these cycles when we stop trying to avert life's journey, when we cease denying our intimate relationship with both nature and spirit. Ultimately our role is that of the non-judgmental witness, the self that observes with profound compassion and curiosity and is opened to the essence of all life along with the unseen. As the witnessing self that has free will, the guidance of the unseen world cannot take over our body and mind; it's our responsibility to *choose* to renew ourselves. We must do our part, and as the Russian proverb says, "Pray towards heaven, but row to shore."

Our part is to receive the guidance of spirit and let it give meaning to our life's creation so that we can sculpt our life into new forms through prayer and surrender. We create anew, over and over again, by honouring our part in the cycle of growth and the natural flow of things.

Roots into Infinity

A friend once said to me, "A tree doesn't grow from the sky down, it grows ring upon ring from the earth upwards." It may seem blatantly obvious, but I do believe many of us forget this. We expect God to hand over what we want without taking the time to cultivate an intimate relationship with what we want. We must start at the root of our longing to nourish what needs to grow through us and into our lives. In that way, we honour the Divine from our roots into infinity.

In a session with my client Frances, she asked me, "But why does God not want what I want?" She wanted a better home, resources, money and a clear career-direction. At the time of the session she wasn't working and didn't actually want a job, because she didn't want to be "part of the system." She didn't want to work for someone else's dream, but she also did not want to work for herself because she didn't like her set of skills; she didn't want to program computers or design websites. She wanted to learn to channel, undertake spiritual endeavours. Masiandia said that to learn to channel she had to cease rejecting life; channelling is an opening to spirit in everything. But she didn't want to see spirit in everything around her, not in the ordinary day-to-day; she wanted an exalted version of God, to hear his voice and receive concise messages, she told me.

Frances was upset with her life and with God because she didn't have what she wanted, but she was completely resistant to taking the steps towards creating it. Healing does not happen by willing it to happen. One does not discover the ultimate job while in the process of resisting. Discovery doesn't unfold while opposing day-to-day reality, but rather by accepting it.

This reminds me of something I said to my therapist many years ago. I told her that the world was going too fast for me – that the pace of society was volatile and frightening, and I just couldn't keep up. She recognized that I was rejecting life and told me that I was part of the world, not separate. I came to appreciate that aspects of the world that I didn't like were within me, and that I needed to do my part by evolving, not disengaging. I also came to understand that I could find my own pace in life and trust in who I am.

It is when we reject the things that discomforts us that we fight with life, which generates reactions within ourselves, as well as with others, and which closes us off from golden opportunities. Unless we are willing to take the first step in believing in ourselves, no one can help us, not even our spirit guides, for they cannot interfere with our free will. They remain loving witnesses, providing us with support the moment that we allow it to flower in the present moment.

Frances found her way to embrace the present moment by trusting that God is not merciless, and she followed the guidance of spirit by taking a huge leap of faith in herself. In her own natural timing she found the courage to embrace her fear and claim her natural abilities as both a programmer and intuitive, allowing guidance to emerge not as the direct result of her wishes but as a healing and unfolding journey.

Masiandia: *"There is no time like now to step onto the path of non-resistance, even if that simply means observing your resistance with deep care and acceptance. What can you do in a state of resistance – pry yourself open? No!*

"You can choose to allow yourself to open, choose to be effortlessly propelled by the force of your desire to change. Change into what, where, how? Only the natural order of your life can answer that: not the present moment, but rather its unfolding.

"People struggle with life until they choose to not struggle anymore, and that happens only when they become non-judgmental witnesses. Be the loving witness who observes everything in life through the filter of acceptance, so that you can honour every stage of your soulful development, in order to be fully present to all that life has to offer you.

"The Divine does truly want what you want, but not necessarily in the same order of time and space as you expect it. The Divine is not interested in your obstructing the natural order of things, or in your disrupting the constructive input of your higher self. Your higher self provides you with providence, with divine intervention. As we mentioned in the previous chapter, your spirit collaborates with future probabilities to co-create opportunities that best serve your soul-purpose. Your spirit is intrinsically part of God and is working on your behalf.

"It is thus important for you to realize that you cannot interfere with divine order, just as divine order cannot interfere with you. Divine order has a purpose and you in turn have free will. You cannot deny the emergence of your soul, and it cannot bypass your human nature. The two must meet in harmonious interconnection. Your part of the partnership is to digest your resistance, fear, disbelief and need for perfection, in order for perfection to be fulfilled. Digestion

is restoration into wholeness, releasing the old into the creative cycle of life. It is a continuous state of renewal that fulfils your dreams, as you surrender willingly."

Natural Order

*N*ature does not stop at the gateway of worry and concern – it continues. A rose bush doesn't suddenly cease growing because it judges life. Birds don't abandon migration for fear of not arriving at their destination, yet that is exactly what we do; we allow fear to paralyze us, to impede our own renewal. Nature doesn't stop trusting in the natural order of life, for it is intrinsically part of it. It is part of the cycles of evolution – fluid stages of development from birth to death to rebirth – and it doesn't struggle with these stages because it doesn't need to dominate reality.

We are part of nature – our mind, motor skills and biology – and this fact is a reminder of the fluidity needed for our evolution. Flowing with the momentum of shifting energy is what is needed to support our soulful emergence. The beauty of nature is that it always follows its own rhythm and can serve to help us follow ours, as we remember that we have incarnated on Earth to be part of its natural cycles, not govern them.

Our renewal then depends on integrating all aspects of human nature, all cycles of development, so that we can embrace evolution. Like a butterfly that develops through stages of metamorphosis from pupa to imago, we also go into transformational stages as we unfurl into maturation, a process that is often overlooked. Because we tend to focus predominately on the later stage, centred on achieving what we want and not on evolving consciousness, we define the journey in a linear way, which does not inspire change.

What moves us to evolve through life? It is not the outcome or the reward that inspires us in fulfilling our dreams. It is honouring our dreams in the present, cultivating a faithful relationship with them now that sets in motion the energy needed to support us in living our dreams. Unless we establish an intimate connection with what is naturally occurring in each moment of our lives, we are not motivated to evolve and may never know the beauty of our spiritual potential; we don't emerge into a more connected and expanded way of being.

Interestingly, a butterfly in its final, winged state is called the imago, and the Latin plural of imago is imagines, which is to conceptualize and create. We re-create our sense of self continuously by honouring the stages of renewal from conception to completion. It's also intriguing to know that a caterpillar is not actually transformed into a butterfly; it is dissolved into liquid within the chrysalis. In the cocoon the caterpillar releases enzymes that digest nearly all of its body. What's left inside the chrysalis is a nutrient-rich liquid from which the butterfly is formed. By recreating ourselves, we dissolve our perceived notions about life and who we think we are; we release the influence of our ancestral blueprint and the projections of other people's impressions, and this serves to redefine our own sense of what is essential to us.

My close friend Sofia redefines what's important to her continuously, as new situations arise in her life. However, there was a time when she was so afraid of shifting reality that she almost sabotaged the very change she wanted. Sofia practically talked herself and her partner out of moving to a better home that was about 40 minutes from Vancouver's city centre. She was concerned about the commute into the city for her work and that she would be further from her friends. She had hoped to first get a full-time position in a North Vancouver branch of the credit union she worked for, but the prospects did not look good, so she wasn't sure if they should move. But her dream was to live closer to nature.

Masiandia told her that her friends would visit and that she would pick up shifts closer to her new home. And that in a short period of time she would gain full-time employment in the North Shore area. They recommended that she take the first step into the new life that she yearned for, and honour the opportunity to reside in a much better apartment with a fabulous view.

Sofia and her partner did move, and less than two months later she called to tell me she got a full-time position. She hadn't just waited for a possibility to come to her, though. Instead, she worked a number of extra shifts at various branches, and also marketed herself to those branches with supporting recommendations from other managers. She later told me that there were moments when she panicked, afraid that she wouldn't be able to find a full-time position. But even though she was afraid, she focused on being positive and assertive, invested in not going into debilitating anxiety. "When I fall into panic, things fall apart. In trust, things flow smoothly," she told me.

I remember how much Sofia had wanted to work in a credit union and that she was initially hired for a transitory posting in Vancouver over two years prior to this position. Her desire had been stronger than her doubt, since the fact that she lacked credentials didn't stop her. She persisted with the exploration of her longing, pushed by a force stronger than her own. When she had her first interview, she sat with growing anxiety across from three managers. She chose to express her fear to lessen it and to be authentic, which the interviewers admired. She was initially hired for an on-call position and the first few months were challenging, as she felt profoundly insecure, but she nevertheless grew her confidence and abilities. Things fell into place for Sofia because she took the first step; she let herself be more than her fear, more than her past, more than her insecurities. She trusted in something bigger than herself.

As Masiandia says, *"Take the first step so that divine order can support you."* Providence moves in the moment that we are fully present and allowing – when we are dedicated.

Renewal Is Evolution

Masiandia: *"You are multidimensional beings that are part of a continual move-ment of metamorphic interdependency, infinitely engaged in perpetuity. There is no beginning or end – no outcome that does not consist of its initial origin. Renewal, in essence, is meaningful eternity. It has meaning by virtue of its evo-lution – an evolution that is not linear but whole.*

"Your body, all nature and planet Earth are intrinsically part of an inter-dimensional co-existing partnership with God. This means that all of the Earth's life cycles – which you reflect at every stage of your life from birth into adulthood, through sickness and in health, in love and eternal devotion – are immanently part of the multidimensional Universe."

I find it so reassuring to realize that I am more than this time and space – I am all time, and my spirit is not only here and now but also in eternity – it goes on forever. The concept that renewal is not a des-tination but a way of life that encompasses all time provides me with a tremendous sense of trust. I am not only making my way towards some-thing – I am at the point of departure as well as completion; I have arrived at the beginning, and I am whole. As T.S. Eliot wrote in his poem, *The Little Gidding*, "We shall not cease from exploration. And the end of all our exploring will be to arrive where we started, and know the place for the first time."

When we do not cease from exploring, every moment of our lives is filled with the potential to awaken us to what's real. Then we do arrive where we started, like the caterpillar that is destined to become a butter-fly – the butterfly is not its destiny, but the journey is. At the end of our exploration we arrive where we started, because there is no end. We ar-rive in the present for the first time. This is where every moment is full of potential – right now!

The present moment is the journey, the unfolding exploration of our dreams, the quest for fulfilment. It is never ending, eternal and complete. At the end of all our exploration, we arrive in the present and connect with our dreams. That is the power of renewal, letting what wants to unfold in each moment disentangle and expand intuitively. And what wants to unfold has always wanted to unfold; flowering is essentially part of its design – its existence.

Activating the Body's Spiritual-Intelligence

Masiandia: *"Spiritual renewal is a way of living with intention, providing new, life-affirming messages to the cells of your body. It activates the spiritual intelligence within your body – within your DNA. Your DNA is the foundation, the sacred blueprint in which your spirit and body meet. By activating your DNA, you build an alliance between physical nature and divinity, which magnetizes your energy field. This strengthens your point of attraction, which draws to you what you need for support and sustenance. Activating your DNA, the nucleus within each cell of your body, also generates restorative energy. When your body is restored to its rightful higher-frequency, your soul nourishes you and is nourished by you. This creates a strong interconnection with your spirit that supports deep healing and awakening. Ultimately, spiritual renewal is a state of surrendering to your soul, allowing your physical nature to be filled from within with multidimensional energy.*

"Physical energy alone does not nourish you – you cannot separate Spirit from matter without contributing to an imbalance of energy and resources in your life. Operating within three-dimensional reality alone robs you of spirit; it deprives you of the guidance and wisdom of your higher-consciousness. This compromises your health and vital energy; it weakens your magnetic field, therefore, your needs and your longing cannot be met.

"You must remember that you are not only your body and this lifetime; your soul is multidimensional. Ultimately, your soul is comprised of more than one lifetime, more than one spirit and more than one body, as described in Chapter

One. Therefore, activating your DNA unites you with your spirit and cultivates
in-depth unity with God, which provides you with the sustenance you need to be
balanced and whole.

"To activate your DNA, fill yourself with a deep sense of purpose by asking
yourself, 'what fills me with vitality and meaning now?' ... 'What makes me feel
alive, whole and nourished?' "

*I*t's fascinating to think that we activate our DNA through spiritual renewal, an activation that interconnects us with our spirit and ultimately with our soul's purpose. In this way every cell in our body is replenished with the sacred imprint of our soul, not depleted by limited thoughts and social conditioning. The cell nucleus, the DNA, is meant to hold and evolve the encoded imprint of our soul, so that the cell can be renewed with higher vibrational energy. Spiritual renewal then aligns us with our multidimensional existence, which awakens in us a deeper sense of who we are, and it allows us to draw immeasurable guidance from our soul.

All our multidimensional lifetimes overlap with the present and hold key-knowledge that can aid us in better understanding who we are. This not only renews our sense of self in the here and now but also supports these parallel lifetimes. Our DNA then serves as a relay system between lifetimes that nourishes our whole soul, not only this body. Thus, we are not limited to this time and space; we can communicate with the unseen, parallel lifetimes, spirit guides, our higher self and those who have passed on. We can also communicate with the spirits of the people we know who are still living.

We are so interconnected and inseparable. A friend once told me of a time when he was going through profound discouragement and all of a sudden something intervened and tapped on his consciousness. He recognized the energy as being sent by his friend, as if she was there in the same room with him, totally interrupting his train of thought with a new point of view. While he could have rejected it, he opened instead; his free will accepted the new energy message. When he mentioned this to her, she told him that she had been praying for him. He had felt her spirit reaching out to him.

Embracing Your Multidimensional Existence

*I*t's freeing to realize that within us is a consciousness that can see and sense so much more than our Earthly experience. It is truly remarkable and awe-inspiring to be given immeasurable insight from both the past and the future – from past-life memories and age regression to communicating with our future.

A few years ago, Masiandia encouraged me to channel my future in a journal entry to help me understand their teaching. Through channelled writing and inner visioning, my future-self appeared to be around 65, with a profound quality of calmness and stillness. In communicating with her, I felt safe and reassured. Her message gave me a distinct sense of being on purpose and helped me feel deeply loved.

She told me that I have my own future to fulfil and supported me in making better choices for my health, since she herself had gone through serious issues that I can prevent. I came to understand that her experiences serve to clear the passage for me and that I play an important part, not in following her but in learning from her. This has helped me understand that the future is not predestined; it is not a goal that has to be reached, nor is it proof of failure if we don't achieve it. Instead, the future is our past, for it has already occurred in a way that we can call on for support.

In preparing me for channelling my future, Masiandia asked me to suspend linear thought. They said that the linear mind couldn't understand how a future-self would have experiences that my present-self may never have, because it perceives reality as cause and effect, not as probabilities. They reminded me that my spirit-consciousness operates beyond linear thinking. It is not bound by time and space; therefore it has more than one past, more than one present and more than one future. Masiandia said, *"Your future exists as clearly as the present and the past. This is possible because all time is now. So you see, you can communicate with the past and the future because they co-exist in the present, just as parallel lifetimes co-exist."*

In my continued communication with my future-self, I receive so much support and reassurance. I'm given guidance from her experience, not told what to do, because I have my own choices to make. My intent is to always embrace what wants to unfold naturally in each moment, and I have come to appreciate that each moment is part of something much larger than my linear perspective. Whether we communicate with the future directly or receive intuitive impulses, we are always interconnected with all time, which serves to provide us with guidance and insight.

In one particular journal communication with my future-self, she helped me restore harmony in my relationship when I was thinking of leaving. My partner Vern and I were struggling with an old pattern that I desperately wanted to be free of, when she told me, *"Oh my dear, I have experienced your struggle many times; I have been witness to Vern falling behind a curtain of disassociation, which triggered passed issues of abandonment for me. It has been hard and very lonely at times, and I understand your discourage-ment. However, I did not leave him, and for that I have no regrets – I love him so much. I would not want to journey through life ... without him. I would miss him terribly.*

"You must maintain your own vitality, your own strength ... Awaken to who you are. That is your work: you must remember who you are, remember that you hold the key to transformation – you hold the key inside your need for more. Demand it, expect it, and don't ever let yourself live without it. You deserve more love, more belonging, more joy, more freedom, more play ... because it is the path before you, calling your name."

Her message opened my heart and affirmed my self-value, and the value of my relationship. Through her courage, I learned how to stand up for myself in a way that served both my partner and me, and through mutual support Vern and I created the balance we needed.

Masiandia: *"Our dear friends, the future is part of the present; it is another thread in the tapestry of your life. You are so not alone!*

"You can indeed communicate with your future-self, a year from now, five to twenty years from now. Start by listening to your deepest longing, and don't let discouragement prevent you from trusting in what's possible. Sit down with pen and paper and a tall glass of water. Hydrate yourself, breathe and write the words: 'My Future Self.' Ask to be connected to the future self that best serves your purpose now. Then allow yourself to be filled with a feeling or a deep sensory knowing, and let thoughts flow onto the paper.

"It doesn't have to make sense, and it may take some time to get comfortable with this idea. You may only receive one or two words initially, so let those words count; observe what they mean to you before you grapple with interpretation. Your future self may say something like, 'I miss you.' If you don't initially know what that means, you can let your future-self miss you until you fully arrive in the moment. Then your future-self will no longer miss you, and in this way its message will come to you easily.

"You can do the same practice with the past. Sit down with pen and paper and a tall glass of water. Hydrate yourself, breathe and write the words: 'My Past Self.' Wait to sense what age you are remembering, and write that down. Then allow yourself to be filled with a quality, a nuance, maybe a sense of purpose in recalling a specific age and feeling. This is a good way to recognize your core-beliefs. For instance, your past-self may say, 'What's the point of doing this, it will make no difference, and it's meaningless.' Then you can feel into that indifference, and notice how it overlaps with your present life. The more you listen to your past-self, the more you will connect with your current attitudes about life, and the same applies to connecting with your future. For instance, if your future-self says, 'Well, things have really gone astray: I failed to find happiness in relationship, I never created the family I wanted and I'm struggling with my

health,' then you know that your core-beliefs are not aligned with what you truly want and that changes are in order.

"This may sound like a crazy practice to you, and may even seem completely impossible since you may not be a channeller. But then, so what? Try it anyway. In fact, try communicating with your body. Sit down with pen and paper and a tall glass of water, hydrate yourself, breathe and write the words: 'My Hands,' or Liver, or Physical Discomfort, or Illness. Then connect with the felt-senses that reside within your body-intelligence. Perhaps you will feel frustration; that's good. This lets you know that your body is holding the frequency of frustration. Now, let the frustration communicate on paper. It may say something like, 'Stop pushing me around, stop controlling me, stop under-nourishing me – I need love!' Great! Maybe it can give you exact guidance on what is needed, such as, 'I'm low in vitamin D, or the stress level is depleting my immune system.'

"Ultimately, we are encouraging you to cultivate an intimate relationship with your whole self, in order to encompass countless possibilities for spiritual renewal. There is nothing that stops you from being whole, other than yourself. Get out of the way; let the stream of soulful wisdom and your body-intelligence guide you. That is your birthright – it is your joy – your eternity."

I open my lips to sing God's name …
a bird trills pure sweetness inside my mouth.
Moons and planets and stars play hide and seek,
rolling around and tickling universes inside me.
I look again within, and see kaleidoscopes of God
laughing in every cell of this body.

~ Sheila Geraghty

Spiritual Commitment

*The seasons pass
one into the other.
Daylight changes
with all the moments
in between.*

*I am winter,
cold and in need of fire.
Bring me to your hearth –
cook for me a pleasant meal
of spices and warmth.*

*I am spring,
sprung alive
and risking everything
for love.
Give me your trust
and revelation.*

*I am summer
full of fun
and the harvest
of plenty.
Receive my abundance.*

*I am autumn
the land of falling
into you,
unrelenting and real.
Here is my trust –
the eternal certainty
of change.*

Engaging the Sacred

*M*y father once told me that the mystical journey cannot be cast aside, that once we have sought the Divine and walked the path of spiritual exploration, we cannot turn back.

When we are awakened to our soul, we cultivate a deeper sense of devotion to what is precious and meaningful to us. When we are devoted to what we love, our sense of belonging and inner peace grows stronger, and what had previously affected us negatively is now transformed by our growing compassion and acceptance.

Engaging the sacred is a way of living in harmony, rather than projecting worry, shame and strife onto our environments. Because whatever we concentrate on is what we grow, it is far more enriching to focus on what inspires us than on what depletes our energy. Thus, if we're committed to finding the most growth-oriented perspective on life circumstances, if something frustrates us, for instance, the frustration quickly evolves into in-depth awareness rather than anger and separation. It's really about making a choice, a shift in perspective, which requires keeping our focus on what truly matters to us. If fighting with others and ourselves is what consumes us, then that is what we're going to experience. But if harmony, communication and passion are what matters, then we won't waste any more time and energy on struggling.

The smoothest way to arrive at any desired outcome is by ceasing to fight with the way things are. This requires a quantum leap: stepping into the reality we yearn for by building a bridge toward it from our current experience and perception. This bridge is our willingness to engage with the sacred in everything, in the mundane as well as the spectacular, in life-crises or moments of wonder. The mystical journey honours the sacred mystery that resides within everything; it is a profoundly nurturing way of life that releases the old without us having to wrestle it to the ground, without us having to work so hard at shutting out the past to make way for the new. When we focus on the new – it arrives!

In my experience, calling in the grace of God and living from the heart is a long-term commitment that requires constant rededication to the things that we love and take care of. Musicians have to retune their instruments regularly, and so do we have to retune our own instruments: our body and mind, focus and intent, and our willingness to be guided.

Our whole spiritual life is in a state of constant refinement, yet so many of us expect perfection. Somehow we believe that our instruments should always be in-tune and working optimally, to the point that as a collective we have become disconnected from nature – our own nature. We live in an artificial world dominated by the pressure to manifest exactly what we want when we want it. We have forgotten that we are infinite beings that are intrinsically part of Divinity and that what we yearn for is made manifest out of our union with spirit, not out of our expectations.

So it is not surprising that moments of spiritual fine-tuning, deep compassion and connection are not a constant in our lives. The experience of a weekend retreat, a prayerful evening of chanting or magical connections can fade as we busy ourselves with our daily lives. Our sense of the spiritual can be quickly absorbed by duty and responsibility, pulling us back into unease. To this Masiandia says, *"Become bewildered, closed off, offended, disconnected from your inner vision – to be pulled back into your need for balance. Let the discomfort return you to your essence so that you can give it your utmost presence."*

Like any fine instrument, we go out of tune and need to readjust our frequency; we cannot expect to remain in complete harmony at all times. Ultimately, the process of fine-tuning is an exquisite interaction with self, a state of observing the self spaciously.

Masiandia: *"You are each holy and magnificent instruments of the Divine, designed to express your highest purpose in both order and chaos, familiarity and utter unknown. And like an instrument, you are affected by change and need to realign constantly.*

"Spiritual commitment is the willingness to return to harmony. It is a path of being-ness that accepts and honours reality as it is and simultaneously changes reality with the presence of your devotion. Your spiritual commitment is powerful medicine that has the potential to completely change reality because it is not interested in repeating the old story. Because the need for change is vital, any level of readjustment is welcomed, even a small one. And there is no need to overhaul your entire life — just as there is no need to throw away a perfectly good instrument — unless you are set on rejecting everything about yourself. You are beautiful beyond words. To us, you are God, therefore there is nothing to reject. You are a sacred part of the whole of divinity.

"You can be like a conductor who brings out the best in all the musicians in an orchestra, by bringing out the best of your own body, mind and feelings. You can listen to your body like a conductor who is aware of each musician playing in an ensemble. Every moment within the orchestra's musical performance is a state of being, an all-encompassing space that is ready to be shaped by the conductor and each musician. Every moment in your life, within your own inner symphony, is a field of potential awaiting your presence. You must give yourself to it entirely to activate its full potential, to conduct an incredible piece of music, a masterpiece!"

Masiandia first introduced this metaphor of the maestro in a series of workshops. Each person was asked to listen, like a conductor, to the playing of his/her inner body. Listening to the sensations and feeling-quality of the body allows us to know what message we're sending to our cells. Just like a maestro who has the ability to guide the interplay of all musicians, we can interact with our bodies in a harmonious way that encompasses both introspection and inner guidance.

In one of the workshops, Masiandia asked one of the participants,

Joan, to tune into the message she was sending to her body by observing the quality of her felt-experience.

Joan said, "I'm giving my body the message that I'm tired."

"Is that a sad note or jubilation?" Masiandia asked her.

She replied, "It's sad."

Then they asked her, *"Are you communicating to the cells of your body that you* shouldn't *be tired?"*

Joan was surprised to realize that that was exactly what she was doing.

Masiandia suggested that she change the tone of her message. They repeated her same words with a slightly upbeat pitch, relinquishing the intonation of judgment.

When asked how this new intonation felt, Joan was even more surprised at the calmness she was experiencing. She said, "It's alright to be tired. It feels restful and peaceful, quietly joyful, like gazing at a calm lake."

"The body doesn't trust the conductor when the maestro is disapproving, nor does the conductor trust the body," Masiandia said to the whole group. *"Imagine being the conductor who scolds the musicians."*

Everyone laughed.

This reminds me of the maestra Edette Gagné I saw conducting the Coast Symphony Orchestra in Sechelt, BC. She was anything but disapproving. She was enigmatic, passionate and on fire – a beautiful diva dancing with her baton, which moved me as much as the music. One of the musicians told me that he loves working with her; he respects the way she brings together the various levels of mastery and amateur talent within the ensemble. She is caring and mindful with the musicians, ultimately bringing out the best in them. When the cells of our body receive this same kind of respectful and passionate message, we naturally return to a whole state of balance, which is the inspiration that our body, mind and soul needs to thrive.

Vision and Fluidity –
Trust Where You're Going Without a Map

Spiritual commitment is a state of trust-in-action: taking charge while simultaneously yielding to the guidance found in every life-experience. It is like two dancers that cascade into one another's arms while synchronously remaining completely alert, agile and in command of their own bodies.

That is the complexity of the dance of life: we must let each moment be our guide without projecting our will, yet remain wilful enough to say "yes" to life's changing currents. As Alan Watts writes in *The Way of Zen*, "The only way to make sense out of change is to plunge into it, move with it, and join the dance."

Masiandia: *"Spiritual commitment is a way of life that necessitates the willingness to not know and at the same time trust in your awareness and passion. It's a dance of yielding to the path right before you by ceasing to project your expectations and dissatisfaction, while simultaneously believing in your vision. It's about being assertive and equally letting go, remaining both on purpose and relinquishing authority over your life. You have free will, but your soul knows the way home. You are the body, the personality that has the courage to feel, and your soul imbues that courage with meaning, energy and life-direction.*

"It is by relinquishing attachment to any particular outcome that you cease telling your body and mind what to do, where to go and who to be. You surrender to the guidance of your soul and step into the unknown willingly.

"We understand that for many of you this is frightening, for you are not committed to the unfolding mystery of your soul-journey but rather are busy resisting it. The role of the ego-mind is to protect you from loss and failure, and because it is over-identified with survival it prevents you from knowing the mystery of your soul. Your resistance to the soul's powerful presence prevents you from actualizing your dreams. Because every dream and desire you have is

born of your soul, how can you manifest your dreams if not by welcoming your soul? Your soul 'is your dream' – it is your greatest ally – it is your greatest joy.

"Your ego-mind wants to be in charge of your life to safeguard you from the unknown, due to believing that it alone is responsible for manifesting what you want. But in truth, the ego must unite with your soul to receive the guidance needed in order to manifest what your whole self wants.

"In order to fulfil your desires, you actually need to trust where you are going without a map. You need to accept the map-less-ness of the wisdom of your soul, a source that is destined to fulfil your desires. What many of you don't realize is that when you let yourselves not know, you become supportive agents that permit the unknown to guide you. To receive the guidance of your soul you also must relinquish resistance, for the unknowable mystery of your soul cannot guide you unless it is welcomed."

*B*ut many of us treat the unknown as a force to reckon with, like a feared mythological creature, a shape-changing monster. How do we welcome the guidance of our soul when we fear where the unknown will lead us, when the way in which we perceive the unknown is through past-disappointment? We need to remember that the unknown is the magical realm of possibilities that we yearn for; it is the heart of divinity that in turn yearns to give itself to us.

A friend once recounted a tale of a princess who hid in an abandoned castle to escape a hideous creature that was chasing her. The creature threw itself at the fortified walls, it screamed and moaned, and the girl was terrified. She waited and waited, secure in her inner enclosure, until the monster was silent. When she heard it no more she risked leaving the confines of the castle to find that outside its borders, the monster lay dead. It had exhausted itself trying to reach her and awaken her to its beauty. When she approached it she discovered that the monster was her; it was her heart. The great unknown had frightened her so much that she didn't see it for what it was.

What we long for: love, purpose, openness … flings itself at the walls of our resistance. Love wants in; the soul wants in; the unknown wants to give us what we need.

This concept of good things flinging themselves against our walls while we mistakenly fear them, reminds me of a description related to me by a man who has the ability to travel within the Earth's grid patterns. He sees, caught there in the lower planes, the most horrible dark beings which he is frighten of and feels powerless to change. What stood out for me is the message Masiandia gave him.

They told him the reason the beings are horrifying is because that is how he sees them. *"Shift the way you perceive them,"* they told him. *"See them with love so you can see their true shape."*

When we see the true shape of things, we no longer try to change the way things are; we don't fight with reality or flee from it. We embrace it completely, even though it may feel like the familiar fabric of our existence is coming apart: our relationships, work, family and sense of personal identity. Everything we know is turned upside down and inside out; all our judgments scatter to the winds, and we're left empty and finally willing to be filled by something bigger than our personalities. We're finally opened to the Divine because we're not resisting it.

Open the Castle Gate to Transform Resistance

Masiandia: *"The question you may be asking yourself now is how can you surrender to God, which is to trust the natural flow of the unknown mystery, and also make plans to set up your life in a way that supports what you want? By replacing the have-to out of your reality with the willingness to transform and therefore relinquish resistance.*

"The river of life is flowing whether you try to manage it or not, so it's not a matter of what you have to do, it's a matter of not resisting it. The question then shifts to, how can you not resist change? How can you cease holding back the

unknown – the power of your purpose – that propels the river of your life? By
accepting your resistance.

"By accepting resistance, you understand what it means to fully commit, for
you no longer make the resistance wrong. When you no longer reject your resis-
tance, it dissolves into peace, for you are at peace with it. This is how you yield
to the natural evolution of your soul-wisdom and simultaneously take charge
of your life. You commit fully without knowing where you are going, trusting
that your soul is a constant guiding force. Ultimately, when we speak of full
commitment, we are speaking about what sustains you, not what drives you.
The mind is focused on planning and securing your life; the soul is focused on
supporting your life. The two are needed to balance your whole self, to fine-tune
your soul-embodiment."

*I*nterestingly, in this way, what initially feels like resistance – like
being caught in between moving forward and waiting – is actually
commitment. It's a state of relinquishing expectation and instead stepping into soulful anticipation, which entices, encourages and reassures
us. Anticipation is an act of foretasting, like salivating at the thought of a
scrumptious meal.

In my work as a healer, I am continuously touched by the trust I am
given and the spontaneous healing that takes place. Obstacles are transformed, not because people work hard at shifting their reality but because
they become willing observers. In a session with Nanda, she opened to
her deep feelings and her soul-longing so quickly it surprised both of
us. Initially she was disassociated, completely disbelieving in what she
longed for. She was so disconnected from her dream of being in a loving
relationship that she was certain she would be alone for the rest of her life.
Her hurt, grief and loneliness were palpable to the point of being immobi-
lizing. I couldn't see an opening; I couldn't feel her spirit. But her soul was
equally strong, helping Nanda access it effortlessly.

I guided Nanda to the place in her body where she held the desire to be in a relationship, and within minutes her heart opened. She was confused and wanted to know what was happening.

"What are you experiencing?" I asked her.

She replied slowly, in a soft and hesitant voice, "I feel so spacious ... and calm."

When I supported her to feel this openness even more, I could sense her growing belief and connection to her longing.

We need not strive to break free from what appears to be an obstacle or setback when we can rest in anticipation, which is ultimately receptivity and willingness. We don't have to wrestle with our insecurities, doubts and pain. We don't have to get rid of anything when we can instead transform it into something beautiful by "seeing" its beauty. Then our demons become our allies, our fears become a reminder to believe, and our hurt arrives at the place within us that we go to for comfort.

In this way, we cultivate an intimate relationship with our desires, which aligns us to the manifestation of what we truly want. Then it no longer seems like our longing is outside of us, unattainable or forbidden, for we embody it completely. We take charge of our dream while simultaneously yielding to its natural gestation and birthing. Anticipation is born in the rubble of the old; it takes root when we give it our presence: when we make room for the unknown.

Aim True

Masiandia: *"Fully committing to who you truly are connects you with a profound sense of resonance, and it gives you permission to risk change. It is empowering to be open and curious – to trust your life, your thoughts and feelings. Risk feeling let down, hurt and disappointed, for the path before you is surely perilous at times; it beholds many adventures, great joys, love and heartache. Please don't protect yourself from living – live!*

"No matter what you aim for or the strength of your conviction, you will

falter, not because you are not aiming true but because you are still searching, you are learning and evolving. You don't have to know where you are going in life or where the journey will lead, in order to know where to aim. Because the only thing to aim for is what is right before you, which is yourself! Aim for your heart, your breath, your willingness to evolve, and let this aiming be filled with the presence of spirit, which always guides you."

When we aim towards our heart, we become unguarded and indeed willing to let life's mystery guide us. It is by turning inwards toward the depth of our longing that we strengthen our willingness and trust, and dissolve any holding pattern that keeps us from actualizing our dreams. Ultimately, it is our own surrendered willingness that shows us the way – that provides us with a sense of direction, which we wouldn't consider on our own. It never ceases to amaze me just how profound the guidance of spirit really is. It brings into our lives the elements of surprise and synchronicity, and purpose.

Many years ago I was commissioned to paint a portrait of a wolf for a client who wanted to give something special to her spiritual mentor. However, no matter how much I tried to paint the wolf's face, it just wouldn't come. I had to let go and in the process created a work of art that surprised both my client and me. The image actually turned out to be a profile of a wolf, a drawing that I collaged into a larger painting. I was also drawn to paint a woman's face and a deer in the background, which wasn't what my client had asked for, but nonetheless, I trusted my creative process because no matter how much I tried to direct the painting, it had a different agenda.

The images eventually looked like a mystical landscape, which I completed with a sleeping wolf in the foreground. When I presented the painting to my client, I explained my predicament and told her she didn't have to take it and that I would give her back the deposit. The painting turned out to be perfect. She loved it and thought that it was completely synchronous, as her spiritual teacher's name was Hidden Wolf. Over 15 years later, I received a letter from Hidden Wolf's wife who wanted to tell me that her husband was in the hospice where the painting was hung on the wall for him to see, and to let me know how much the artwork had brought him pleasure during the course of his life.

Our spirits know how to guide us to perfection, as we step out of the way and let it happen. With devotion, the divine mystery becomes clear. Once we suspend critical thought, our fear is reassured; we surrender to the unknown, which reveals to us what is needed in order to sustain our commitment. If a particular direction cannot be sustained, our commitment draws us in another direction that provides us with different possibilities. It's only when we struggle with indecision and insecurity that our aim falters.

Many of us don't take aim unless we know where we're going. But most of the time we don't know where we're going unless we commit fully to the moment before us, even if what we commit to is "not knowing." I am constantly reassured by how much the unknown looks after me and how "not knowing" is actually a blessing.

The story of my wolf painting is small in comparison to the countless miracles that occur in our lives without us noticing. Seamless interactions with people happen all the time and provide us with direction, connection and support. Our job is to embrace it! And it's only when we embrace reality that we discover what we truly want, what to do and where to go in life, for we let the grace of divinity surprise us, uplift us and show us to ourselves.

As an example of embracing reality, I'd like to share a healing process that my client Marra explored in session. She struggled with self-doubt because her feelings and her desires didn't make sense to her. She began by telling me she didn't want to hurt the man she was dating, afraid of what would come of her uncertainty in committing to the relationship. She felt confused, insecure and lost. Their long-distance romance didn't inspire her, so she wasn't sure if she wanted to commit to a long-term relationship with him. She liked the attention of other men and wanted to explore, but felt bad about herself and thought there was something wrong with her. She was caught in an old script of trying to be what her boyfriend wanted her to be, afraid of not being able to support herself and terrified of making a mistake, to the point of frantically struggling in the net of her own oppression.

The more Marra tried to find the answers, the more she was trapped in insecurity, until she stopped fighting with her experience. She let herself feel dissatisfied and simultaneously connect with the depth of her longing, to recognize that her relationship was a stark contrast to what she really wanted. She discovered that travel was eminent, as was her desire to be with a man who inspired her and awakened her to herself. Marra yearned to be in a relationship that was mutually devoted to a spiritual life, not continue to settle into an identity that was founded on security and fitting in. When she admitted this to herself, she felt strong. With self-respect and care, she lifted her aim in the direction she most feared – her freedom.

Although we tend to be afraid of our longing because it calls for us to let go of something that is not in alignment with the longing, life necessitates we take this risk on our own behalf; it demands our full commitment to honouring who we are. There is something magical that happens when we let go into the unknown, when we engage fully with the mystical realm of our deeper wisdom – we discover so much more about ourselves. We suspend the ego-mind and delve deeper into our unconscious, into the depth of our subconscious awareness. We swim in currents of complete surrender until we find something about ourselves that is new but has always been there.

One Hundred Percent Commitment

*M*asiandia says that when we only commit partially to the path before us, for instance 75 percent of the time, then we don't manifest 75 percent of what we want, but rather the remaining 25 percent that stands in the way of our full commitment. We don't bring about 75 percent fulfilments, but instead manifest the outstanding 25 percent setback, because we're focused on the setback. Imagine getting a stain on your favourite garment; it doesn't matter how lovely the rest of the piece is, the stain stands out. The clothing is no longer 100 percent perfect; it's stained.

When it comes to manifesting what we want in life, we need to commit one hundred percent to what we want, thus shifting into willingness the percentage we habitually give to limited perceptions such as disbelief, fear and self-protection. Interestingly, this means no longer trying to get rid of limited perceptions – for whatever we focus on is amplified. Whatever we centre on is what we manifest. Therefore, trying to get rid of insecurity, for instance, makes the insecurity hang on for dear life because it too needs to evolve. It requires our presence to transcend, not our disapproval and control.

Nothing can be cast aside; everything about us must be brought into all of our endeavours. Therefore, it is only when we engage fully that we manifest 100 percent of what we want, for all of us – every aspect of our experience – fully arrives to receive it. Whatever we want, we have to give ourselves entirely to it, whether that is health, financial sustenance, rewarding experiences, peace of mind or creative expression.

Masiandia: *"Your world is limited to your limited ideas, and equally abundant in relation to your expansive and heartful presence. That is the law of the Universe, comprised of a higher intelligence intricately woven within quantum energy. Everything is made of quantum energy and is part of the whole*

Universe. You are the centre of the Universe – the one who knows who you are the most intimately. Thus, if you reject any aspect of yourself, the Universe will always reflect that back to you to awaken you to yourself. The multidimensional Universe is your breath, your mind, your desires, your purpose and your creation. So it is only natural that if you reject any part of yourself, you reject the Universe because you are intrinsically linked.

Universally, rejection depletes the magnetic frequency of potentiality in your life and the life of others. Focusing on limitations only brings about limitations. Focusing on possibilities yet holding a limited thought about those possibilities, is no different. Making your disbeliefs, insecurities and fears wrong only brings about more insecurities and fears, not the expression of your faith and joy. But enjoyment of your insecurities and fears transforms them into the expression of joy.

The question then is, 'How do you enjoy your fears?' By welcoming them with open arms, without judgment. And if you do judge your insecurities, then welcome your judgment. The more you embrace these fragmented aspects of you – your albeit limited perceptions – the more you will embody deep compassion and trust, which will manifest tenfold.

"That is 100 percent commitment, dear friends. Take pleasure in who you are – all of you!"

When we commit 100 percent, we honour our value and the value of others, which inevitably promotes mutual support and sustains our energy. Ultimately it's only by devoting ourselves *fully* to all our endeavours that our commitment is sustainable.

Our employment provides an opportunity to practice and experience sustainable commitment. By giving fully of ourselves to our work, we're in a much better place to discern what we need in order to maintain that commitment. By giving fully, we know our worth, which is sustained by either financial gain or from being part of something meaningful, or both. Then our well-being and greater sense of purpose is met. Without being fully engaged, we tend to undermine our effectiveness and the joy we can experience in the work.

Retired Vancouver bus driver Tommy Tompkins extolls the benefits of committing fully in alignment with one's values in his book: *Tommy Transit's Bus Tales, How to Change the World from 9 to 5*. After attending monthly *Porridge for the Soul* breakfast meetings hosted by Brock Tully and hearing Gandi's words, "Be the change you want to see in the world," Tompkins was inspired to promote the message of peace and kindness in his work environment. Realizing he was in a line of work where he was in contact with thousands of people every week, he committed to making a positive, uplifting impression on all his passengers.

In those days before automated announcements, it was the bus driver's duty to call out the names of major streets. So what better way to inspire people than to tag on a positive quote of the day? He began to address people personally, making it a point to acknowledge them, such as, "Wow, very cool glasses, they really suit you." ... "Nice earrings!"... "Great to see you." But Tompkins didn't just compliment people, he informed them, made them laugh, was personable, always greeting them with kindness.

Having previously struggled with depression and ill-health, Tompkins had discovered the secret to transforming what had once seemed an exhausting, stressful way of making a living, into joy and fun. He surprised himself at how an eight- to ten-hour shift could just fly by while he was still full of energy.

I often ask myself, "What do I want to give to my work, to relationships and to mundane moments? Is it judgment, fear, uncertainty... or my 100 percent willingness, love and curiosity?" It is by engaging with life fully that I am able to see and sense more, and realize the potential that is trying to unfold in all areas of my life. Only then can I be generous with my heart and soul.

Stepping into The Flow of Your Life

We discover what sustains our commitments by letting the unknown guide us, which is like planning for a trip as carefully as possible, all the while knowing we will encounter situations that we are not prepared for, yet trusting that we will be taken care of. We cannot know what to expect until we are there, which requires stepping into the flow of our lives, honouring our fundamental needs now in the present while pursuing our dreams. In this way we manifest the support that our dreams require to flourish, for we are receptive to what we need, not defended against the unknown.

We cannot manifest our dreams while *fending off* the unknown. Defended, we repeat the familiar and neglect our needs – needs that are born of our soul. By neglecting our spiritual needs we only partially believe in ourselves and therefore manifest self-neglect, not abundance.

To aim true, to commit fully to the resonance of our longing, we must honour our longing now.

Masiandia often says to people, *"Live your dream now, what are you waiting for?"* But a belief in scarcity around money is often the reason for people's hesitancy. This is evident in Todd's story, a man who put off his desire to start a business because he didn't believe he had enough resources to support himself in the initial stages of development. He wanted to quit his day job so that he could start a consultation practice, and to ensure his future success in the career change he gambled all his savings, even borrowing money to gamble with. Initially, he did well with his investment and had enough money to start the business – close to one hundred thousand dollars – but it didn't satisfy his need for security. He reinvested it and unfortunately lost it all. The issue was never about the money or security, but rather his lack of confidence and the underlying belief that he wouldn't be able to succeed in what he wanted to do.

I see this lack of trust in the unknown, this attempt to control the future, when we yearn for help and support but deny when it arrives because it doesn't fit into our perfect picture. Doors open, but we don't walk through them, because we're looking for guarantees. We must cease saying "no" to life's resources, cease stopping the flow of abundance and open our eyes – our senses – to not miss out on life's generosity.

> *"Rest your brains and do not worry about the wall,"* replied
> the Tin Woodman. *"When we have climbed over it,*
> *we shall know what is on the other side."*
>
> ~ L. Frank Baum, in *The Wonderful Wizard of Oz*

Commitment Is Freedom

Masiandia: *"Many of you work hard at tilling, replanting, rebuilding the soil of your life, yet the seed of your soul lies dormant. Like a gardener who fertilizes the soil with no consideration for what it actually needs or for what the seed requires for its optimal growth, you force your will upon life, negating your truth. To connect with what your soul actually needs, you must give it the life-experience that best serves its purpose and its value, by relinquishing control and most of all by letting go of the need to know when and how your life should unfold. Of course, this calls for utmost commitment to the path before you – the path that no matter how much you try to avoid, continues to reflect your innermost needs. Your soul-seed is your purpose. It is imperative that you endeavour to provide it with what it needs to flourish, which does require spiritual commitment, or in other words, living wholeheartedly.*

"Spiritual commitment is not the same as responsibility or obligation; it isn't a law that you have to abide by. It is about being open to receiving divine guidance, which is intricately woven into all of your life experiences. Commitment then is about being open to divine inspiration, being willing to step off the edge of your fear into the vastness of what is possible at all times, without knowing

the totality of what is possible. In fact, how can you? You're not there yet! But you only lack that knowledge at an intellectual level. Remember, your spirit has already been projected into the future and brought back a number of possibilities for you to choose from: possibilities that best serve your purpose.

"Ultimately, the issue is whether you choose to honour your purpose or cater to your personality. When you honour your purpose, things do fall into place much more smoothly. When you cater to your personality, life tends to mirror your personality's fears, insecurities and underlying core-beliefs. Step off the edge; let your spirit show you the way to a life that is in alignment with your needs. Step off the edge into everything you consciously know nothing about — until it becomes known to you."

When I hear Masiandia's message, I stand on the brim of the abyss and fling myself into nothing, shouting out at the whole Universe, "Show me the way!" And the way reminds me that I do know what is in the deep end before I dive in. We all do; we sense it on subconscious levels. We don't dive into nothing, as though pushing down on the gas pedal into oncoming traffic. There are no surprises. We really do know when we're going to find a new job for instance or meet someone. We know when it is necessary to wait or when it is time to take action.

Masiandia: *"You actually do know the way before you and what it requires of you, be it courage, expansion, surrender, faith, tenderness. The framework of your life is never out of your hands; you don't experience disappointment and loss at any point without being in soulful agreement, nor do you receive recognition and support without first having raised your vibration. Your soul is intricately woven into all of your life experiences, expansive beyond the reasoning mind and supported by the sacred trinity of spirit, Earth and creation so that you can gift your divinity to everything that you are part of."*

*T*he trinity between spirit, Earth and creation is our intuition – our sense of wonderment and purpose. It is like the essence of a seed taking sustenance from the cycle of creation and spawning life. Intuition guides us from within and enriches our lives with deeper assurance and spiritual integrity.

Over the years, this instinctual nature has presented me with opportunities to broaden my understanding and empathy and most of all let right-action flow through me. There is nothing more precious than to become sensitive to the influence of our innate wisdom and open to possibilities. Years ago, I had an inspiring experience that convinced me of the power of intuition. It was in my healing practice with a client, and upon hearing her health concerns, I initially could not connect with her. In fact, I drew a complete blank. She had come to see me for integrative healing, but I couldn't read her energy-body. I had a moment of panic, until I calmed myself with the affirmation that while I didn't know what to do, the knowing would come to me.

I just accepted the numbness that I was feeling while my client lay on the massage table; I quietly scanned her body and continued to feel nothing. I let my hands move on their own, my right hand hovering over her brow, my left hand resting on her abdomen, and I asked her to gently follow her breathing. I then guided her to breathe in the colour that surrounded her. She blurted out, "It's purple, how did you know?"

I didn't! I hadn't actually seen any colour; I don't even know why I thought to ask her to breathe in the colour, except that it completely opened her energy-body, and I could finally connect with her. She became an open book, ready to be seen and supported as she expressed her feelings, as she released the emotional holding patterns that were the root cause of the health issues.

It is amazing to discover what wants to happen naturally in every moment, as we engage the unknown in a gentle and trusting way. Then the marriage between spirit and matter guides us into creation, igniting our intuitive knowledge. It happens naturally, beyond the bounds of our recognition. Instinctual knowledge is most often born when the mind is disengaged.

I heard a story told by a colleague about a time in his practice when his rational thinking faltered. For a lengthy period, he could not remember his clients' histories, stories, issues or therapeutic processes. He had no other recourse than to remain fluid with each passing moment. When he spoke to his supervisor, he was advised to trust what was occurring and discover what the present moment in each session had to offer, to look for what was being revealed. I always remember this story so that when I need to identify what to do in moments of not-knowing, I draw comfort in trusting that the unfolding mystery will show me. The sense of not knowing what to do is transformed when we cease struggling with it, when we become curious, open and resilient. We learn, grow and step onto a new path.

The Art of Forgetting

*W*e don't usually think of *forgetting* as a way of being in the natural flow of life, as a way of connecting with more insightful possibilities or magical surprises. The thought of being unprepared or caught off guard tends to leave us feeling unsure, rather than excited about what there is yet to come.

I know an inspirational speaker who was invited to present a TEDx talk. She had to create a short 12-minute speech, which was unusual for her, as she was accustomed to longer talks, and she had little time to prepare. She engaged in her standard pre-performance grounding meditation but nonetheless found herself tremendously anxious moments before she was about to go on stage. Right before the curtain call she breathed deeply, centred herself and prayed for guidance. Intuitively, she had a sense to abandon her whole speech, to forget all about the time allotted to her, clear her slate and start from scratch. She trusted this completely and stepped onto the stage with renewed confidence. Engaged and inspired, she delivered her speech, and as the audience applauded she saw the timer read: 12:02 minutes. Not only had she completed her speech in the appointed time, but it was also well received.

Whether we choose to dismiss cognitive information from our minds, as with the inspirational speaker, or fail to remember, as in the case of my colleague with his counselling clients, escaping our mental focus surrenders us toward mystical resources and support. Forgetting is the art of allowing, resting, rejuvenating, being empty so that spirit can fill us from within.

Masiandia says that forgetting ultimately returns us to our innate wisdom, because in a state of forgetting we instinctively seek to remember, not what we think we should remember but rather what we intuitively know. The moments of forgetting help us move out of the stronghold of our mental processes and learn about our intuitive selves.

"Each period of disconnection helps us discover our resilience, and learn more about how we reconnect," writes Christina Baldwin in *Calling the Circle*. She also writes, "Instead of assuming that we have to figure out what to do, we may slow down internally and ask: *'What is trying to happen here? How might I support the spiritual possibility? Where do I put my energy? What action, or refraining from action, would help the spiritual forces that are at work?'* When we pause to ask these questions, everything that happens becomes an opportunity to stay connected to Spirit."

Masiandia: *"You stay connected to spirit by remaining open and willing. In this way, when you ask yourself, 'What is trying to emerge here and how may I support the possibility?' you might well discover that love is trying to happen, and the way to support love is by forgiving yourself and others. How may you support the spiritual forces at work in your life? By loving everything about your life – everything!*

"Ultimately, spirit guides you into soulful emergence and you in turn

support the emergence by 'forgetting' what you think you know – the familiar perception of reality that you have grown accustomed to. The question you may ask yourself is, 'what do I really want in life – to struggle with reality, fight to prove myself so I can get what I want, or dissolve my disbelief into the arms of spiritual fulfilment?'

"Forgetting has the potential of drawing you into divine resonance, self-empowerment, joy and deep love. So to ignite the fire of your inner wisdom, let yourself forget. The burning coals of your spirit will then come alive, your passion will burn bright, and your life will mirror your sacred flame. Forget everything and dissolve into nothingness so that spirit can fill you with greater meaning. That is the life you long for, the spiritual fulfilment you seek.

"Forget just how magnificent you are ... go ahead, forget that you are worthy of God's love ... forget that you're loved ... because your journey of forgetting will surely lead you back to your whole self, for that is its purpose. Go on, forget your accomplishments – forget that you have the ability to change your life – forget everything that you have read in this book or explored along your journey, so that you can remember something more encompassing than what you think you know. Forget all our teaching so that you can discover it for yourself because it already exists within you."

The mystery eludes me
I walk in circles following
familiar footprints.
It's the only way to ensure
I won't get lost.

But the landscape never
changes – it's sameness
oppressive.

I can't breathe
The world around me is
unchanged.
The world inside of me
full of imaginings.

I wake from a dream
completely forgotten,
except for a sense of
something missing that
needs to be remembered.

I must recall my dream
and let every detail
emerge.
I wonder what it holds
for me – this illusive
unknown.

CHAPTER TWELVE

Love, Full to Overflowing

My love for you has eyes of fire that
pierce through the dark, reaching from
the heavens to illuminate the way.
My love is inexhaustible, a blessing
from the night to appease the storm
and shelter you from the wind and cold.

My love, you are beautiful even as you
pull away from me, afraid of the light,
afraid of me seeing through you.

My love, my love, there is no armour
that can hold me afar; I come to you
bearing gifts and the certainty that you
are my joy no matter how ashamed you
feel. Oh my sweet darling, there is no
darkness in you I cannot imagine whole
and healed.

Welcoming the Gift of Love

My grandmother once told me that as babies, when my sisters and I were agitated and upset, she would hold us in her arms until we calmed right down. We squirmed, screamed and cried, until we completely dissolved into just being. There is nothing like being held until one is completely still, such as in a beloved's embrace or in meditation, breathing, relaxing quietly. It is here in deep rest that we are opened to love and find the still point of connection that merges our conscious and subconscious minds, where our spirit and matter meet.

Love is a gift that guides us; it doesn't calculate our value. It is the spirit in all life that reaches in towards our most profound vulnerabilities and releases our barriers. The gift of love endeavours to remind us that we are sacred, and it compels us into complete trust because that is what is needed to be whole, body and soul. However, the depth of care that most of us give to ourselves, as well as the nurturing we receive from others, is limited by distrust and spurred by the belief that we are undeserving. People can become quite convinced that they are unworthy or conversely, defend their right to be loved. Support and affection then becomes something that one tries to measure up to, fight for and work harder towards, to prove oneself.

This brings me to something Masiandia shared in a group-channelling session. The spirits looked at everyone through my eyes, and after a long pause they said, *"You don't deserve love!"* After another pause, they continued, *"You simply need it ... it is natural. You need to be in love, to give and receive it ... like you depend on water and sleep."*

Do we judge a flower or tree for its need for water? Do we make a baby wrong for wanting the breast's milk? Our need for love is fulfilled when we cease trying to justify its worth, when we rest in the certainty that it is as essential as oxygen to our lungs. When we no longer struggle with the enormous task of reckoning with our sense of value, we finally stop, rest and draw nourishment into our lives. In a restful state, we receive support and sustenance. Physically, the cells of our body draw in optimal energy to balance our whole physiological system, helping us maintain vitality. Emotionally and mentally, we exude the radiant expression of our soul. And spiritually, we are opened to greater ease and fluidity.

Masiandia says that to give and receive freely is a state of "being" in love. It's a state of allowing the Divine to guide and embrace us, breathe through us and dissolve our holding patterns. Then it doesn't matter who nurtures us in return and how, because our self-honour becomes a magnetic frequency that draws in what we need. We cease struggling for respect and affection and rather are opened to it, filled from within. "Being" in love welcomes God into all aspects of our lives, as we welcome the Divine and are filled to overflowing.

Masiandia: *"It is true that to give and receive the beauty of love is not something you measure up to, because it is not a reward. You needn't compete or strive for it, for it cannot be attained. Love simply 'exists'. It is not something you accomplish, consume, have or have not. It is your birthright; not something you have a right to, as it is already yours.*

"You give and receive fully by 'being' devoted to yourself and the world as it is, without trying to change it. If everything around and within you had to change in order for you to give yourself fully, you would wait a very long time. The world does not have to be a secure, safe and reassuring place for you to welcome your divinity and be whole, nor do you have to be perfect. You can connect with your yearning now, fully, by not making yourself wrong for needing to be cherished. And you can be opened to God's love as it streams through you by feeling the immensity of your desire. You exist in this world and in multidimensional realms to 'be' heartful, to be the expression of divine grace, not only when it feels good but in all areas of your life.

"It is highly necessary that you love yourself, which is not a task to accomplish, but a way of being. As we mentioned in chapter eight, fall in love with

yourself as though you are a newborn child. Since you are reborn in each and
every moment then fall in love with yourself over and over again, starting now."

Love Doesn't Hold Back

The true power of love is that it doesn't discriminate between good or bad, worthy or unworthy. It is not a force of punishment, regret or blame, but rather a tremendous source of empowerment that sheds light onto all aspects of our lives. Love doesn't stop at the door and say, "I will not enter unless you are purified." Instead, it steps across the threshold; it holds nothing back, even if we don't believe in it.

But many of us refuse love's entry when it doesn't appear the way we want it to, when it isn't comfortable. Perhaps our spouse lacks self-confidence and does not take into consideration our wants and needs, which may trigger distrust and uncertainty. Maybe a close friend demands accountability, and it challenges our pride. But it doesn't mean that we are not loved. Still, the slightest unintended provocation can trigger old frameworks, inhibiting us from seeing that when another person either withholds or grants their affection, it doesn't signify the measure of our worth.

Masiandia: *"Anything that triggers you is a catalyst, a guiding force meant to elicit your full attention, so that you can open your senses and awaken. Ultimately, it doesn't matter what other people think of you, how big your house is, how shiny your new car, the degrees and certificates that you've accumulated or the power you wield. It doesn't matter what provokes you, who agrees with you, praises you, or conversely rejects and dismisses you. What matters is the depth to which you cherish life completely and are opened to love.*

"Love is comprised of energy, fluid and constantly moving, and does not stop at obstacles. It continues and sheds light into the darkest corners, because everything, everything, everything ... needs love. We are overjoyed in saying

this and will happily say it again and again, for it is the truth of all truths. Everything needs to be welcomed!

"Loneliness needs to be cherished. Fear of death needs to be accepted. The current of shame and the way it sabotages your happiness also needs to be cared for… so that it can be returned to balance. Also, your dreams, aspirations, wonderment, thoughts and ideas need your devotion to be brought into life, to be manifested into reality. Essentially, the gift of love is nourishment, sustenance and peace and does not evaluate whether something deserves it or not. It is only fear that discriminates, that makes the need for love wrong."

Eternal Now

Masiandia: *"Your soul cannot but yearn to love fully, to fulfil itself through you. It seeks its own freedom through human experience. And your human consciousness cannot but desire fulfilment, for it is continuously being awakened by the soul – an alarm clock ticking away at your awareness, interfering with your commonplace reality. This doesn't mean that your spirit is forcing you to evolve. Its free-flowing energy is an eminent gift of vitality that your body needs. Your well-being depends on it.*

"Being in love with everything is richly fulfilling, as it raises you to higher levels of consciousness, lifts the veil of suffering and nurtures unmet needs. This does not mean that you no longer weather pain and loss, but rather you cease clinging to the past or blaming yourself or others. Instead, you nurture profound trust in divine order by embracing the way things are without trying to change them.

"Trying to change anything doesn't actually change anything; it perpetuates the struggle for change. Let go, let love flow into your life and receive the otherworldly mystery of your soul – your eternal now. As we have said, you have not incarnated on this Earth to repeat the past, your soul's lifetimes, your ancestors' or the world's history. Remember, the past is the future, the future the past, co-existing in the present, therefore you can move beyond time and space and let

miracles happen. Let love flow in and out of you freely so that its divine gift can bless you and fill you to overflowing. By being in love, you become an open channel that allows your soul to treasure this world through you."

See with the Naked Eye –
Divinity is Everywhere and in Everything

Masiandia: *"Love is the interlinking dynamic between form and consciousness, physical matter and spiritual law. It is the centre point from which your body and soul emerges. In love, your body and soul are united as one, whole and vital, naturally supporting the balance between nature and consciousness.*

"All form – the body, trees, wildlife, even buildings, boats and cars – are intrinsically interconnected with essence, and everything has an essence. Nothing is devoid of spirit, so as we have said in earlier chapters, nothing is separate; everything is part of the whole. This means that you can access divinity at all times, because it is all around you and within you.

"The reason that many indigenous people draw guidance from nature is because they have developed an understanding that the Great Spirit speaks to all people through all things. Those that are opened to the guidance of nature, people, and even inanimate objects, know that everything is imbued with spirit. It's all around you and within you.

"Imagine looking at your life with the understanding that God speaks to you through all things. Look around you and within you and tell us what you see. See with the naked eye, not the one that discriminates, evaluates and names a changing reality that is far more intelligent than your judgments. Open your senses so that you can experience so much joy. In love, the world is a better place."

J had such an experience of seeing more as I stood on a cliff overlooking the sea, in the south of Bali, and heard the water's message spoken in tireless waves. Large swells of water crashed onto the edge of the cliff, giving me the impression that the ocean took no notice of the tourist attraction surrounding me, which I thought of as a hideous succession of decaying terraces. The sea was indifferent to the garbage strewn on the bluffs, which I had been so upset about. It also didn't matter to the incessant pulse of the sea if I felt perturbed or happy. In that moment, it became clear to me that to Gaia we can be suffering or in joy, abundant or in poverty, dying or alive, she is always home – our home. To her all life is the same, whether we are thriving or starving, rich or poor, whether species become extinct or flourish – it is all part of the life/death cycle.

As I stood along the edge receiving this message, interestingly, I felt enlivened. Overlooking the seascape with the waves undulating made me wonder at the largeness of the ocean and how it was telling me to be larger, to let my inner-ocean transcend judgment and self-protection. The sea wanted more from me, and I wanted to give it more. Love always wants more, and in love we want to give more. It fills us up, impels us from containment into release, implores us to give generously and receive fully. Like the ocean, it is relentlessly intense, engaging and mystifying. We swim gracefully in its depth when we relent, when we let love guide us home. The way of the heart is a way back home, a way of opening to Source-energy and remembering our true value. Our power and insight come from this opening, this heartbreaking embrace of life. Our wholeness and life-fulfilment come from this vulnerable receptivity that stands without defences.

Masiandia: *"To witness life without defences is to be more vulnerable than most of you allow yourselves to be, though it is what you long for. You naturally long to give and receive love freely, to be unfettered, opened and whole. You are here in this world to love and be loved completely, not restrict its flow. This longing for wholeness originates from your soul; it is a call from within to complete yourself, to be an open channel filled to overflowing with love."*

Even when love is kind,
as water is to earth –
the scorched and lifeless soil
resists.
Water pools along its surface
until it is ready to be received.
and waits to be absorbed.

It is a talisman
that grows ring upon ring
like the old grandfather tree,
until it is taken in.
The body is made whole
and replenished –
love welcomed and sublime.

Energy Cannot Be Contained

Masiandia: *"Your soul-in-body is powerful beyond measure, an energy frequency that cannot be doused, a fire in your belly that burns brightly. All energy is pure movement; it refuses to be obstructed and is unstoppable. Therefore, clenching onto energy as when holding a grudge only makes it intensify, not ease or flow freely, because it has to push beyond your discrimination to evolve. When energy pushes past restrictions it can be very uncomfortable because your holding patterns amplify, manifesting more holding patterns. You cannot contain energy without it swelling and forcing its way through you. No matter how much you try to thwart it, energy counters your resistance; it moves you, ready or not.*

"Energy cannot be impeded, controlled, coerced or cajoled without consequence, without manifesting dis-ease and suffering. Just as when the natural flow of a river is obstructed, eco-systems are damaged. Trying to control the energy movement within your life and body is no different; it impairs the vitality of your whole body, mind and spirit.

It is important to also note that when you hold onto limiting frequencies such as doubt, shame or blame, it affects not only your physiology but also the space in which your body resides: your home, office, public transport, as well as other people's energy fields. Your thoughts, emotions and attitudes are in essence moving energy; therefore, they have an effect on everything around you, because they are not isolated within your own experience.

"Have you ever walked into a room and felt instant discomfort? Perhaps the person who was there before you received disheartening news, and the energy vibration of his/her feeling of loss overwhelmed you with grief. Energy cannot remain isolated to one person alone, as there is absolutely nothing in the world that is self-contained. And since everything is interconnected energetically, nothing happens just to you. You encounter energy to feel the grief and release it. It serves you in ways that are unbeknownst to you, ways that play a larger role in the evolution of your soul.

"You can walk by someone on the street and without knowing that person

walk away depressed, not because you are susceptible to depression but rather because that energy needs your empathy. The point here is not to protect yourself from the person's suffering nor to collapse into despair, but to aid the energy in its transformation. You do this by loving the energy with profound acceptance and trust, knowing that your love is more powerful than the suffering. When you are in love, the energy moves through you freely without getting snagged by self-protection, disbelief and powerlessness. Then nothing can interfere with your well-being because you are passionate about life, present and awake.

"You may wonder, 'What energies are you encountering and yet not attending to: desperation, criticism, defensiveness?' 'What messages are you emitting from your field of energy: resentment, withdrawal and disbelief ... or devotion and inspiration?' Your every belief radiates out into the world like seeds floating on currents of air, deposited here and there. Imagine that your beliefs are seeds in the palm of your hand, and you are the gardener. What are you planting in the earth of your life? Look at what is growing and unfolding to see what your energy field is transmitting and how it affects everything around you."

It's quite fascinating the way in which we are all interconnected: the way energy moves within our spaces and our thoughts and can alter our quality of life. I read an article by Machaelle Small Wright in her second *Perelandra Garden Workbook* that relates to the influences of other people's energy. For eight years, Wright never had a problem with deer disturbing her garden. They would meander through the yard but only nibble the plants that flowed over her garden beds. They never showed signs of damaging her plants, so she hadn't developed apprehension.

One day, a reporter came for an interview for an article about Wright's co-creative garden work and noticed that the garden was not fenced in. The reporter couldn't believe that Wright had never had any issues with deer eating the garden's vegetation and kept asking her when was she going to deal with the problem. It didn't matter how clearly Wright said that she enjoyed the deer's peaceful movement through her garden, the reporter adamantly believed that everyone had a deer problem. That same night, the deer created a mess in the garden, damaging most of the plants. It took Wright a long time to figure out what the issue was and to restore harmony, because she hadn't considered that one person's influence could have such a disruptive impact.

This incident demonstrates just how intrinsically connected we are and how we affect one another. Thus, staying in a constant state of harmony is pretty much impossible, but we can remain honest observers, willing to see the bigger picture. In this way, we develop a loving relationship with our life that helps us return to balance.

Masiandia: *"Energy always seeks to fulfil itself; that is its purpose. You cannot help but desire balance, for that is the nature of who you are. Yet, like the reporter, many of you believe so strongly in what is out of balance that you don't see what's possible. Harmony is what is truly possible, what you long for and what you need. All that you want stems from the need for harmony – the need for love. The body seeks homeostatic balance and nourishment, the mind needs to learn and expand consciousness, the spirit, like all sentience, grows towards the light to be illuminated. Everything needs something; this is the synergistic quality of creation, drawing together polarities into a unified whole.*

"When you know this, when you honour the fundamental principles of your need for love, you are filled to overflowing with divine sustenance, which raises the vibration of your magnetic field. Your health and the well-being of others and the Earth impels you to fall in love with all life-experience. In this way, you can step into any room, feel the discomfort, and shower it with devotion. You can experience any person's dissonance and bathe him/her with love."

Masiandia's message of bathing others with our love reminds me of the Tonglen Buddhist meditation. It is a practice of breathing in unpleasant and painful energy and then exhaling joy to all sentient beings. The practice focuses on taking in the dissonance and pain through the in-breath and then sending out spaciousness and relief through the out-breath.

The meditation dissolves the armour of self-protection, explains Pema Chödrön in *The Practice of Tonglen*, as it softens us to what is around us. She says that the practice is a method for overcoming fear of suffering and awakening compassion "by embracing, rather than rejecting, the unwanted and painful aspects of experience." Instead of fending off pain and hiding from it, we can open our hearts and allow ourselves to feel the pain. "Feel it as something that will soften and purify us and make us far more loving and kind," writes Chödrön. She also says, "The Tonglen practice is a method for connecting with suffering – ours and that which is all around us – everywhere we go. It is a method for overcoming fear of suffering and for dissolving the tightness of our heart."

Something amazing happens when our compassion is awakened; we are opened to a larger view of reality and see others in a completely new way, a way that transcends habitual reactions.

Masiandia: *"The joy that emanates through your practice, however you choose to cultivate love, is tremendously powerful. Never believe that your empathy is unrequited, for spirit always hears your prayers.*

"Whether you practice the Tonglen meditation or are attentive to your job and passionate towards your dreams, or you listen to a friend with compassionate understanding and set clear and loving boundaries by saying no without judgment … you emit a higher frequency of devotion that the whole multidimensional Universe needs. As we have said, everything, everything, everything … needs love."

—⚬⚬⚬—

Everything Is Interconnected and On-purpose

Masiandia: *"You are exactly where you need to be in perfect time, standing beside the person, child, spouse, co-worker and friend that is imminently linked to you in a sacred way. Nothing is by chance, as all energy is interconnected and on-purpose. Therefore, every situation is an opportunity for you to return to love. When you recognize this, there is no separation, for you come to accept each other's differences, not as polarities but as two sides of the same purpose.*

"Returning to love is imminent; it is always what is wanting to unfold, even though it may not seem like it: even though countless forms of adversity threaten to overcome you. Every situation that arises in your life is designed to awaken you, not defeat you. Therefore, all your relationships, personal and professional, are a reflection of something emerging in you, whether it is a challenging relationship forcing you to grow or a friendship where you observe strength in another that you wish to cultivate in yourself. Also, everything occurs in complete tandem with your belief system, concerns and attitudes towards life and is part of the interpersonal growth of everyone involved. By being a willing participant, you allow one another's differences to serve as avenues for self-awareness. In this way, you become a guiding force in each other's lives instead of an adversary.

"Here we would add, while all your relationships are reflections of mutual evolution, this does not signify that other people's attitudes and behaviours mirror you directly. Take for instance a situation where someone is angry with you. This doesn't mean that you are angry; it signifies that your relationship to the anger, which is being expressed toward you, needs attending to. The situation may represent your general need to hold your ground when addressing issues of anger. It may signify your need to feel the fear you may experience when faced with another person's displeasure. Perhaps the other person's reaction is a catalyst to help shift your resistance, forcing you to open your senses to what's right in front of you, such as your own power.

"Personal power is founded on the release of judgment, on holding a higher

frequency of empathy and vision. It serves a broader spectrum of realization, bringing into manifestation the fulfilment of your dreams, and it also brings to the foreground the vision of others, thus galvanizing the essence of your shared purpose into reality."

I t is healing to see one another's differences as belonging to a shared purpose that supports mutual growth. It provides us with insight into each other's behaviour, helping us create harmony. In this way, we tap into resources we didn't know we had, intuitive resources that inherently come from the gift of mutual support.

This was apparent in an incident that occurred in my early twenties when I worked at a pizza restaurant. I recall making the same mistake repeatedly while taking phone orders, which upset my boss considerably. His anger especially stressed me, yet at some point I calmly asked him to please not yell at me, as it worsened the problem. I told him that by being patient with me, I would get through this and cease making the mistake. I had never spoken to anyone like this before, and to my surprise he heard me; he lowered his voice, stopped criticizing me, and I stopped making the mistake. It fascinates me that I intuitively knew to ask for his support and that he gave it to me. Our working relationship improved remarkably afterwards; he got the reliable employee he wanted and I the respectful boss.

The needs of another person are not separate from our own, and these needs correlate directly with our growth. For instance, a spouse's inability to work can reflect the other spouse's need to trust in his/her own ability to provide for them both, which can grow self-confidence, resilience and a sense of purpose. Someone's need to communicate his feelings is the other person's need to learn to listen. A child's troubled reactions are the parent's lesson in evolving their parenting skills.

Our needs are not isolated from one another's, but part of the larger picture. However, we often feel that our needs are running up against the needs of another and that need-fulfilment is a win-lose situation. It can become like a contest where contestants appear to compete against each other, when really they are supporting one another. Without each other's participation, there would be no competition. Vying for the prize allows them to play off one another, serving to expand their abilities, which they would otherwise not excel on their own. The person who wins the prize is not necessarily the best contestant but most likely the one that "needs" to win, in order to sustain his/her life-experience and purpose. That's the interesting thing: win or lose, the contestants are in the position to make new choices that support their growth.

It only appears that the contestants who have lost the competition have not succeeded, but we can't really know that. The courage to be in the competition may be their prize; they may have triumphed over a personal challenge, gained experience, acknowledgment and inner strength by being part of the event. Just as it only seems like the winner gets it all or, for instance, that when a man meets his soul-mate he is lucky, or that the kid with rich parents has all the fortune and possibilities that a poor kid lacks. I don't think it's this cut-and-dry. A monetarily fortunate child is not necessarily better off than a child in poverty, for he may not learn bravery; he may not face his fear of death and discover his soul. He may never know what it is to be part of a large movement in social change. The less fortunate child, on the other hand, may never know what it feels like to be secure and certain of his future. Certainty could be what the fortunate child needs to grow to serve his soul-purpose, while the other child's soul is growing courage. These things are out of our hands but not out of our hearts. We can return to love and trust that there is nothing that is "not" in divine order.

Returning to Love ... To Thy Whole Self

*T*here is no danger in surrendering to love, in letting our soul fulfil us. It is the degree to which we hold back that pains us and prevents us from knowing our true freedom. Many years ago, I experienced a personal healing-process at a transformational workshop that was filmed on video. In the process, I remember struggling to break free from constricting body sensations, but interestingly when I saw myself in the video afterwards, I was startled to see how little my facial features expressed what I had actually been feeling. I had been holding back, not letting others see me in fear that they would let me down. I was so used to doing things for myself, not leaning on others for help, that I didn't show anyone my vulnerability.

Over ten years later I saw myself on video again, after a filming of one of my group-channelling events. I was filmed in a circle of group participants, gazing upon each person with so much affection in my eyes, expressing silently a deep love for everyone. Interestingly, as I looked at that video, I felt tremendously frightened. I saw a vulnerable, open and transparent woman with no defences. Conversely, I was also inspired, as I noticed the level of calm and inner strength that this stranger, who was I, embodied. Still, after seeing the video I struggled with my vulnerability for close to a week. In fact, I fell into a deep depression, convinced that to love to such an extent would lead to certain failure. I wanted to hide, run away. I wanted to die. I was a helpless child all over again, feeling utterly defeated, whose love did not save my mother; it didn't help my grandmother find joy; it didn't safeguard my sisters or my father from pain. But my spirit would go on loving, and in that moment it loved that frightened little girl.

What astonished me the most in the video is that the love I saw in my eyes was completely detached from how people chose to receive it. I just loved them. In a way, it wasn't about them. I allowed myself the freedom to "see" them, to hold a high frequency of spaciousness and trust. Honestly, it is so much easier this way: to let our love eclipse the beliefs that keep us separate.

Masiandia: *"Surrendering to love is returning to wholeness – it is the embodiment of your true sense of self and ultimately remembering who you are. This is a devotional act of coming back home to you – to your sacredness. Embodying your soul-consciousness is a journey of recognizing that you have never fallen out of grace, never disappointed the Divine, for you are the Sacred in all that you breathe and exhale and live.*

"As you remember that you are sacred, still you will at times forget and become afraid and discomforted by other people's differences as well as your own uncertainties. Observe and breathe through this, fill your lungs, chest, ribs and belly with your prayer to return to love. This journey, this commitment and honouring of yourself and the world, brings you in contact with what you need in each moment of your life. Not what you need from life, not what you need from others, but what you just need. There is nothing in the world more freeing than to stop the incessant cacophony of your history and become present to your need. Then everything returns to harmony, and without effort the need is met. Remember, you need to be in love, to give and receive it fully … like you need water and sleep.

"Our dear beloved friends, we cherish you; please cherish yourselves. Come home to your innermost need for love, and celebrate yourself until the need is appeased and held in the sanctuary of your soul's embrace. Be the eyes that pierce through the dark, the fire that warms you, the shelter from the storm. Be the one who welcomes you and loves you into eternity."

When you think of me by that grand old tree,

oh darling, darling, darling there I'll be.

When you come to me wanting to be free,

darling, darling, darling there I'll be.

Time goes by and you wonder why,

You try and try, but from love you just can't hide.

~ Richard Nardelli (Dad)
Song Lyrics from *Darling, There I'll Be*

In Gratitude

This book has been a long time in the making, and many people have supported me along the way. I am grateful to Rocky Krogfoss and Kathy Irwin for being part of my initial book-study team, for Rocky's incredible belief in me, and Kathy's insightful questions and immeasurable help transcribing the recorded messages. A special thanks to Beatrice Winsburrow for her encouraging feedback with the first rough draft, and for helping me break through my fear of disclosing personal details in chapter two.

I am honoured by the support of my dear friend Brian Arnold, whose spiritual wisdom and sensitivity helped me redefine the direction of the book, as well as challenge me to ask tough questions and look deeper for answers. I have deep gratitude for Marni Norwich, the toughest editor possible, whose attention to detail taught me to set my ideas down clearly and who with heart-full commitment helped me bring the book to life.

Thank you to my friend Paul Hood, whose feedback, antidotes and enthusiasm helped me better understand the importance of the book's messages. Many thanks go to Agio Publishing for making this book available for you the reader. To Bruce Batchelor for his caring attention to copy editing and proof-reading the final manuscript, and Marsha Batchelor for the evocative book cover and creative layout design. I want to acknowledge the love and support that I have received from my partner Vern, whose confidence in me is a gift that I cherish, and whose photography inspires in me a deep sense of magic and stillness.

Printed in Canada at
IslandBlue Printorium Bookworks
Victoria, BC

49294512R00177

Made in the USA
San Bernardino, CA
19 May 2017